The Age of Instability

DAVID SMITH has been economics editor of the *Sunday Times* since 1989. He is also an assistant editor, policy adviser and chief leader-writer. He is a regular contributor to the CBI's *Business Voice* and other publications, and speaks and broadcasts regularly to a wide variety of audiences. He also runs his own website www.economicsuk.com. Prior to joining the *Sunday Times*, he worked for *The Times* and *Financial Weekly* also the Henley Centre for Forecasting and Lloyds Bank.

David Smith is the author of several books, including the bestselling *Free Lunch: Easily Digestible Economics* and *The Dragon and the Elephant: China, India and the New World Order*, both published by Profile Books. He is a visiting pr   London.

ALSO BY DAVID SMITH

The Dragon and the Elephant
Free Lunch

The Age of Instability

The Global Financial Crisis and What Comes Next

David Smith

PROFILE BOOKS

First published in Great Britain in 2010 by
Profile Books Ltd
3A Exmouth House
Pine Street
Exmouth Market
London EC1R 0JH
www.profilebooks.com

1 3 5 7 9 10 8 6 4 2

Designed and typeset in Granjon by MacGuru Ltd
info@macguru.org.uk

Printed and bound in Great Britain by
Clays, Bungay, Suffolk

A CIP catalogue record for this book is available from the British Library.

ISBN 978 1 84668 310 7
eISBN 978 1 84765 191 4

The paper this book is printed on is certified by the © 1996 Forest Stewardship
Council A.C. (FSC). It is ancient-forest friendly. The printer holds FSC chain of custody
SGS-COC-2061

FSC
Mixed Sources
Product group from well-managed
forests and other controlled sources
Cert no. SGS-COC-2061
www.fsc.org
© 1996 Forest Stewardship Council

Contents

For Jane

Acknowledgements

This book has benefited from conversations with very many people. Having lived through and reported on the financial crisis and credit crunch since the summer of 2007, I have count of the number of participants and experts I have talked to. There are too many to credit and many would prefer anonymity. My thanks also to fellow journalists and authors for their reconstructions of episodes of the crisis. It goes without saying that any errors are mine alone. The team at Profile Books, led by Andrew Franklin, provided guidance and encouragement throughout the project. My particular thanks go to my editor at Profile, Sarah Caro. She took on the task of recommending thousands of words of cuts and improvements to my original manuscript, when my enthusiasm got the better of me. The book is immeasurably improved as a result. My gratitude, as always, goes to my wife Jane, and my children, Elizabeth, Emily, Thomas and Richard, for their forbearance during the long hours of writing.

Introduction

In the summer of 2004, I went to one of the Treasury's regular drinks parties, to mark the end of the parliamentary term and the start of the few weeks each year in which economic policy goes into hibernation. Treasury ministers and officials were proud of their new building, which had transformed a confusing beehive of interconnected offices, accessed by miles of red linoleum flooring, into modern, stylish, functional headquarters. It had also given them a pleasant courtyard, where we were having drinks in the early evening sunshine. Gordon Brown, who was circulating among the journalists and other guests, came round. He knew I had written a book the previous year and asked me whether I was working on the next one. I should, he said, write one on the 'great stability'. I had, fortunately, already embarked on a different project, which probably saved me from a lot of embarrassment. Given the time it takes to research, write and get a book ready for publication, *The Great Stability* may well have come out in 2007, just before that stability was replaced by the biggest episode of stomach-churning instability most of us have seen. Suddenly, in 2007, the world became a dangerous and alarming place, in a way that made analogies with earthquakes and hurricanes all too apt. I write this not to tell a story against Gordon Brown. The idea of the great stability was an appealing one. Britain, traditionally the most inflation-prone of the big economies, was entering its thirteenth year of sustained, non-inflationary growth. Unemployment, which in the 1980s had seemed destined to be permanently measured in many millions, was heading down towards full employment levels. The long-feared crash in house prices had not materialised. Something had changed, perhaps as a result of a policy framework which included what was then Brown's masterstroke: independence for the Bank of England.

Britain was doing well, but so too was the world economy, which at that stage had embarked on its strongest run of growth since the early 1970s. Perhaps this was the way that globalisation worked; taking the world on to a new plane of rapid growth without inflation. It was the 'China effect' on prices but it was also the impact of new technology and, yes, financial innovation. Most people did well during the boom years but none did better than the investment bankers and hedge fund managers. They appeared to be achieving something rather enviable; using their brains to innovate into new financial products and reinvent traditional finance. Should we have known that all this was dangerously risky? Perhaps we should. Most economists and economic commentators did not delve into such things; it was assumed that the regulators and the banks themselves would ensure that excessive risks were not being taken and the detail could be left to them. Had you asked that evening what a collateralised debt obligation (CDO) or a credit default swap (CDS) was, most would have pleaded ignorance. Credit markets were for the specialists. All that was to change and it was to change very dramatically. The freezing of many of these markets in the summer of 2007 set in train a sequence of events that would include the first run on a British bank since the 1860s; shotgun weddings between institutions previously regarded as almost as safe as the Bank of England; unprecedented government rescues in America, Britain and many other countries; the near-collapse of the international banking system; and the worst global recession since the 1930s. All this did not come out of clear blue sky. It happened, however, while most people's attention was on other things. Few were aware of the approaching storm.

For me, the crisis ushered in the busiest period I have known. Most economic and financial crises follow a set pattern. Either governments and central banks deliberately engineer slowdowns which spill over into recession or there is a big initial economic 'shock', such as a sudden rise in oil prices, followed by a series of smaller aftershocks. This was different. The shocks kept coming and increased rather than decreased in intensity. The initial events, the crisis for some US mortgage lenders, the problems at two Bear Stearns hedge funds followed by difficulties at some European banks and then the run on Northern Rock, almost paled into significance in comparison with what followed. Most crises, too, have a finite sense about them. Even in the darkest days you know the mechanisms exist for getting out. In the 2007–09 crisis, in contrast, the slough of despond seemed never-ending. There were times when, as we shall see, even professionals thought their money was safest under the mattress. In the autumn of 2008, when as we now know the banking system came perilously close to shutting down, the most frequent question I was asked was where people should put their money. There was a straight answer to this, which was that for those who had it, they should divide their savings among different banks, staying within the £50,000 compensation limit at each. Similar guarantees existed in other countries. The truth was, however, that if the banking system went down there would be no compensation. There would be no economy.

How did we get to such a situation? Can we ever rely on our banks again? The near-collapse of the global banking system was not supposed to happen. In an era of financial globalisation and sophisticated modelling of risk, the manias, panics and crashes of the past were thought to have become historical curiosities. Financial derivatives were based on the idea that parcelling up loans and selling them to a wide range of investors across the globe would spread risk – Alan Greenspan said so. Instead these instruments amplified such risk and produced the biggest collapse of financial confidence in the modern era. They also ushered in a new and more uncertain era which would last beyond the immediate crisis. And just as there was nothing new in the nature of the panic – except for its scale and global reach – so there was little new in these kinds of shifts in the economic environment. We get comfortable, then we get complacent, then we panic, then we take years to get over it – as was said during the Asian crisis of 1997/98: 'Confidence grows at the rate a coconut tree grows, but it falls at the rate a coconut falls.' Thus, the golden age of the 1950s and 1960s was followed by the turbulence of the 1970s and 1980s, a period of high inflation and mass unemployment. This appeared to be the new norm. But the 1990s ushered in a new golden age of stability, in which inflation was low, unemployment fell and the world economy enjoyed its best run for decades. It lasted until the summer of 2007, surviving smaller crises, terrorist attacks and political upheaval, when it crumbled abruptly. The new instability meant the world could face years of adjustment to the biggest financial shock since the Great Depression.

The aim of this book is to set the events of 2007–09 in a wider context, partly picking up from where an earlier book of mine, *From Boom to Bust*, left off in the early 1990s. For Britain, that coconut tree of confidence grew over many years – a sixteen-year period in which the UK did not experience a single quarter of falling gross domestic product – giving rise to Britain's own version of hubris. The long time span is appropriate; the development of the so-called shadow banking system began in the early 1980s, while the era-defining events of 1989 also set in train new economic forces. I have looked at those events, together with the Asian, Russian and hedge fund crises of 1997/98, and the extent to which they were a dress rehearsal for the much bigger crisis a decade later. There is the story of Britain leading up to the crisis and that famous (now plain embarrassing) phrase beloved of Tony Blair and Gordon Brown, 'no return to boom and bust'. How could they have been so bold, or so foolish? No account would be complete without examining the housing boom, both in Britain but also America's subprime boom. In telling the story of the crisis itself, I have tried to steer a course between detailing every takeaway pizza and expletive as bankers negotiated to save their skins with governments, central bankers and regulators, and not getting too bogged down in the minutiae; there is always a risk of not seeing the wood for the trees. Each one of those crisis weekends probably merited a book in itself. There was high drama and there was plenty of it. The book also examines where the crisis leaves the subject of economics and where it leaves the world. The short answer to the second is tilting even farther to the East, but there is a longer answer towards the end of the book.

This book has been written at a moment in history; it was completed late in 2009. The verdict then was that the worst of the crisis was behind us, though the full economic repercussions had still to play out. You will know as you read this whether that was a reasonable assessment.

1

Out of the Ashes

The end of economic history?

Where did it all begin? How far do we have to go back to find the roots of the crisis? A powerful belief in the superiority of market economics led naturally to a belief in the infallibility of markets. If there was an alternative, it was not obvious what it was. If markets created problems, markets could solve them, with only a little help from the authorities. Financial markets are markets in their purest form. It was in financial markets that confidence and self-belief were at their greatest. That confidence has to be a product of its time. Finance came to dominate, in a period some characterise as market fundamentalism. Why did capitalism lose its constraints, and come to be associated with aggressive financial capitalism? Part of the answer lies with the events of one particularly pivotal year.

The years 1989 and 2009 are bookends to a fascinating period in global political and economic history. The former set in motion many of the forces that were to give rise to nearly two decades of stability and rising prosperity. It should have been a time of great optimism, though it did not necessarily feel like it at the time. The end of the cold war and the collapse of communism in the Soviet bloc were followed by the opening-up of China to large-scale foreign direct investment and, soon afterwards, by India's economic reform programme. 'Globalisation' was hardly used as a description of these changes at the time. The term itself, usually attributed to the economist Theodore Levitt in an article in the *Harvard Business Review* in 1983, came into popular usage in the 1990s. The emergence of a global free market as a result of these changes was globalisation's first full flowering in the modern era. Professor Richard Freeman of Harvard University has described[1] as the 'one big fact' about the world economy the doubling of the global labour force from 1.5 billion to 3 billion – and a corresponding increase in the number of consumers with access to international markets – as a result of these changes.

None of this was preordained. In the case of China, the reaction to the international condemnation that followed the bloody putdown of the Tiananmen Square demonstrations could have been very different. Beijing could have looked inward. Instead, under Deng Xiaoping, China decided to look outward, a strategy embodied in Deng's 'Southern Inspection Tour', which took in Shenzhen, one of the country's export success stories, in early 1992. Foreign investment was to be encouraged, to the simultaneous benefit of Western companies and consumers, as well as the Chinese population, which saw large-scale reductions in poverty levels. For now the biggest impact was on firms like Wal-Mart and its customers, who were to be big beneficiaries of the low prices that resulted from low-cost production in China. Some of the other powerful effects, such as the impact on financial markets, were to come later.

In Europe, the eastern bloc's shift to capitalism was far from smooth. It took less than a year from the opening of the Berlin Wall in November 1989 to German unification in October 1990. The strains created by unification, however, persisted for years, with taxpayers in the old West Germany reeling under the burden of supporting a dysfunctional economy in the former German Democratic Republic. The GDR was, however, luckier than most. For many of the old Comecon countries, as well as former Soviet republics and Russia itself, communism gave way for several years to a kind of 'Wild West' capitalism, with scant regard for the rule of law. The debate was over whether this was simply a problem of adjustment. Some were quick to argue that a fundamental shift had occurred. Francis Fukuyama made his name with a 1989 article in *The National Interest*, called simply 'The end of history?' He later expanded it into a best-selling book, *The End of History and the Last Man*. The book, published three years later, was clear on the significance of what had occurred:[2]

We who live in stable, long-standing liberal democracies face an unusual situation. In our grandparents' time, many reasonable people could foresee a radiant socialist future in which private property and capitalism had been abolished, and in which politics itself was somehow overcome. Today, by contrast, we have trouble imagining a world that is radically better than our own, or a future that is not essentially democratic or capitalist. Within that framework, of course, many things could be improved: we could house the homeless, guarantee opportunity for minorities and women, improve competitiveness and create new jobs. We can also imagine worlds that are significantly worse than what we know now; in which national, racial or religious intolerance makes a comeback, or in which we are overwhelmed by war or environmental collapse. But we cannot picture to ourselves a world that is *essentially* different to the present one and at the same time better.

The sweeping global economic and political changes of 1989 had enduring consequences. The supply of low-cost goods from China and low-cost services from India helped destroy the inflation that marred the global economy in the late 1980s. The willingness of the populations of these newly emerging economies to save meant people in the West, and particularly Britain and America, could get by with saving less. The seeds were sown for a long period in which the macroeconomic concerns of the past could be put to one side. New sources of growth would emerge in what we should probably regard as the beginning of the true era of globalisation, both economic and financial. Earlier episodes were more limited in their impact, both geographically and in other respects.

As Alan Greenspan, a firm believer in markets and one of the pivotal figures in this book, put it:[3]

The defining moment for the world's economies was the fall of the Berlin Wall in 1989, revealing a state of economic ruin behind the iron curtain far behind the expectations of the most knowledgeable Western economists. Central planning was exposed as an unredeemable, coupled with and supported by the growing disillusionment over the interventionist economic policies of the Western democracies, market capitalism began quietly to displace those policies in much of the world. Central planning was no longer a subject for debate. There were no eulogies. Except in North Korea and Cuba, it was dropped from the world's economic agenda. Not only did the economies of the former Soviet bloc, after some chaos, embrace the ways of market capitalism, but so did most of what we previously called the third world – countries that had been neutral in the cold war but had practiced central planning or had been so heavily regulated that it amounted to the same thing. Communist China, which had edged towards market capitalism as early as 1978, accelerated the movement of its vast, tightly regulated, then more-than-500-million-person workforce toward the Free Trade Zones of the Pearl River Delta.

This was a huge development, which would have consequences for decades and was what economists would describe as a large and enduring positive economic shock. The International Monetary Fund attempts regularly to assess the 'trend' rate of growth in the global economy, the rate of expansion which is normal and sustainable – not too hot as it generates inflation but not too cold to produce rising unemployment. In the 1970s, this trend rate of growth was 3 per cent a year. By the 2000s it had increased to 4 per cent or more. This may not sound much but for a global economy estimated by the World Bank to have a combined annual GDP of $55,000 billion (in 2007), the difference is equivalent to $550 billion of additional output annually, or adding an economy the size of Sweden, and a little bit more, every year.

The momentous events of 1989 and their consequences also raised another important question, however. Was it possible to have too much of a good thing? Were the forces unleashed then just too big to handle, creating problems unforeseen at the time? Certainly, attitudes on whether these chances were benign or problematical appeared to have varied with the cycle. Initially, as we shall see, the euphoria of 1989 was short lived. Later, it was only after the global financial system hit extreme volatility during 2007 that influential people began to question the benefits of developments they had previously lauded. In the first edition of his memoirs, *The Age of Turbulence*, published just before the crisis, Greenspan celebrated[4] forces that 'largely serendipitously' came together at the beginning of the twenty-first century to deliver low long-term interest rates alongside subdued inflation rates around the world. His main concern then was that these very low interest rates posed a risk of higher inflation in the long run. In the paperback version of his book, updated after the financial crisis had broken, he wrote[5] that these self-same forces had helped create, in the markets, 'an accident waiting to happen'. Policymakers like Greenspan had sometimes warned that it was dangerous for investors to assume that risk had gone away and that the benign conditions of the early twenty-first century were the new permanent condition for the global economy. Such warnings, however, were never loud enough.

The bust before the long boom

While the significance of 1989 was enormous, the optimism was relatively short lived. Even before the fall of the Berlin Wall, strains had been building in the global economy. The stock market crash of October 1987, when Wall Street fell by more than 22 per cent on a single day, 'Black Monday', 19 October, brought powerful echoes of 1929. As the Dow Jones industrial average plunged, the instant prediction from many pundits was that, as in the inter-war years, America faced at best a recession, at worst another depression. Charles Kindleberger, the eminent economic historian, writing a fortnight after the event, took a more considered view, though he was concerned that something was amiss. 'In the cascade of comment on the stock market debacle of the last two weeks, it is hard for an economic historian who has written on 1929 and on eighteenth and nineteenth century booms and crashes to find something to say that is not entirely banal,' he wrote.[6] 'Nonetheless I try.' Kindleberger looked at whether the October crash was another 'made in the United States' event, as in 1929. His conclusion was one of scepticism, though with a significant warning attached:

> Must depression follow a stock market implosion? Not necessarily. The 1929 collapse of stock prices was followed by falling commodity prices which caused banks to fail. As the collapse spread from one national market to another, it produced the Great Depression. This time the

danger seems to lie elsewhere – in luxury real estate, consumer spending for big-ticket items, with companies that have issued junk bond debt, third world debt and consumer debt. But while all of these markets may walk a nice edge, it is quite unpredictable which one or more, if any, may stumble and tip the economy into depression. Watch prayerfully.

Kindleberger died in 2003, otherwise he would surely have been asked to set the events of 2007 to 2009 in historical context. He was right, however, to recognise that even in the 1980s the world had moved on. Stock market crashes were no longer as lethal as in the past. Other things had the potential to be even more lethal. Fears of an imminent depression turned out to be groundless, though the October 1987 crash had more far-reaching implications than it is sometimes credited with. It provided the US authorities in particular with an early test of procedures to ensure financial markets were adequately provided with liquidity and to stand behind brokerage firms and others which risked drowning as the selling wave engulfed them. The procedures worked, though for a time it was touch and go. Importantly, just months into Greenspan's chairmanship of the Federal Reserve, they reinforced the view that crises could be handled, given the right response. The bigger immediate effect, however, was to reverse, if only temporarily, action by governments and central banks to deal with an emerging inflation problem. The clearest such reversal was in Britain.

At the time of the 1987 crash, Nigel Lawson, Margaret Thatcher's second Chancellor of the Exchequer, had been raising interest rates. The Thatcher government, having been re-elected in June 1987, was determined to keep inflation under control. In August he raised interest rates from 9 to 10 per cent. When Wall Street crashed, Lawson dismissed it as 'an absurd over-reaction'. But he responded by reducing interest rates, in an era when such decisions rested with elected politicians rather than the Bank of England. The late Sir Alan Walters, Thatcher's personal economic adviser and a constant thorn in Lawson's side, said later that this response was a mistake. 'One such excuse, according to *The Economist* and many other supporters of the monetary expansion, is that monetary ease was the appropriate response to the 19 October 1987 crash,' he wrote.[7] 'By this means we would then avoid the mistakes made following the crashes of 1929 and 1931. But the appropriate response to a crash is not inflationary expansion.'

The die was cast. Interest rates in Britain were cut to a low of 7.5 per cent in the spring of 1988, even as it became clear that the risks of recession had receded. The reductions in response to the crash gave way to cuts prompted by the strength of the pound. It was, in fact, briefly a time of extraordinarily expansionary economic policy in Britain. Alongside interest rates that were very low for their time, Lawson's March 1988 Budget was the high-water mark of Thatcherism, cutting the top rate of income tax from 60 to 40 per cent and the basic rate from 27 to 25 per cent. The Lawson boom was in full swing, and the man in charge of it declared himself to be untroubled by rapid credit growth and a plunge into large deficit on the current account of the balance of payments. This, he insisted, was not a problem as long as it could be financed by capital inflows. In an echo of what was to happen two decades later, many independent economists argued, in contrast, that it was a sign of an unsustainable expansion. Consumer spending was racing ahead, boosted by low interest rates and tax cuts. Inflation would surely follow. The boom could not last; it could not be allowed to.

In America the Federal Reserve under Greenspan, having responded to the 1987 crash with a response more along the lines favoured by Walters, continued to tighten policy by raising interest rates during 1988, much to the disgust of George Bush senior, then the vice-president, who was campaigning to succeed Ronald Reagan in the White House and made clear that the Fed's efforts, which resulted in rates rising from 6.5 to 9 per cent during 1988, were doing his chances no good at all. In Britain the shift was even more dramatic. Higher interest rates in other countries put pressure on Lawson to act. By the autumn of 1988, UK rates had risen to 13 per cent. Nor was this a temporary measure. A year later they reached an eye-watering 15 per cent, twice their May 1988 level, where they were to stay for a year. In Britain, at least, the recession of the early 1990s was now baked in. The momentous changes of 1989 were still a source of wonderment but for the time being there was only economic pain. For America and Britain this was a classic, policy-driven recession in response to an inflationary boom. Though policymakers will always argue that their aim is always to slow the economy in response to such booms rather than drive it into recession, these things can never be precise. The aim, however, was straightforward enough: induce a period of below-trend growth in the economy, opening up spare capacity and driving up unemployment as a consequence, in order to reduce inflation. As John Major, who presided over most of the UK recession of the early 1990s, had put it, it had to hurt to work. High interest rates were the blunt instrument for inflicting that hurt.

A strange sort of global recession

One striking feature of the global recession of 2008/09, as we shall see, was the extent to which it was 'synchronised', with most of the world, and certainly all the advanced world, sinking at more or less the same pace and at exactly the same time. That made it unusual; normally world recessions ripple between continents. America sneezes and the rest of the world catches a cold, but not straight away. The lags can be quite long and, in limiting the speed of the global fall, rather helpful. But if 2008/09 broke this pattern in one direction, the recession of the early 1990s did so in a very different way. Britain and America fell into conventional downturns, neither of which, with the benefit of hindsight, stands out as particularly deep or long. In Britain, for example, the decline in GDP from peak to trough was 2.5 per cent. In the 2008/09 recession, GDP fell by as much, 2.5 per cent, in a single quarter, the first three months of 2009, according to the early official estimates. This did not stop pundits in both countries predicting the onset of a new Great Depression in the early 1990s. As it turned out, that was a fate which befell Japan, which began to suffer from the bursting of its 'bubble economy' in the late 1980s. Germany, in contrast, was the most obvious beneficiary of 1989, in the short term at least, the fall of the Berlin Wall giving way to a reunification boom. For citizens of the former German Democratic Republic, reunification provided instant gratification, particularly when the West German government was generous enough to convert the currencies of the two parts of Germany on a one-for-one basis. This windfall, together with access to Western consumer goods denied them for more than four decades, produced a short-lived and very powerful consumer boom, even as much of the rest of the world was in recession. The flipside of Germany's boom, which helped lift other economies in Europe, was that when the post-reunification hang-over kicked in it resulted in a drag on global growth. The now unified Federal Republic plunged into recession in 1993 and unemployment in the eastern states soared in what was the start of a long hangover. Both Japan, in its post-bubble era, and Germany, partly as a result of the cost of reunification, entered a new era of slower growth during the 1990s, where 1 per cent became the norm, rather than the 2.5 to 3 per cent characteristic of most advanced economies.

The pattern of the recession and recovery of the early 1990s is impor-tant in what followed. With hindsight, two things can be seen in the data from the period. Individually, most countries experienced rela-tively mild recessions, certainly compared with both the early 1980s and 2008/09. In many cases, too, recessions were fairly short lived; America's lasted for only eight months, though Britain's was longer, 21 months from beginning to end, partly as a result of the constraints on policy arising from UK membership of the European exchange rate mecha-nism (ERM), and in particular the lack of freedom the authorities in Britain had to reduce interest rates at a time and pace of their choos-ing. The other noticeable feature of the period, evident at the time as much as it is from looking at the statistics now, is how long it took for the global economy to regain its composure. At the time the Interna-tional Monetary Fund estimated the trend rate of growth for the world economy to be between 3.5 and 3.7 per cent a year. Its World Economic Outlook database[8] shows that global growth slipped below that trend rate in 1990 and did not get back there until 1996. The three worst years for the global economy in the period were 1991, 1992 and 1993, with growth rates of between 1.5 and 2 per cent, but they were flanked by years when conditions appeared somewhat subdued. Politicians, busi-nesses and individuals do not follow such macro numbers particularly closely, but the data chimes with what was a widespread perception, namely that after the exuberance of the 1980s, the 1990s was a duller, more sober decade. An era the economist Joseph Stiglitz was later to christen the 'roaring' nineties certainly did not feel like it during its first half – 1989 appeared to be more the culmination of a memorable era than an epoch-creating moment.

Apart from the somewhat subdued mood of the period, there was a more direct and obvious economic effect. The recession of the early 1990s, while mild, had the effect of increasing spare capacity in a global economy already on the brink of a huge expansion of capacity as a result of what Richard Freeman estimated to be a doubling of the global labour force, thanks to the opening up of China, India and the Soviet bloc. Six years of sub-trend global economic growth meant that the inflation monster that had emerged during the late 1960s and early 1970s, which policymakers had struggled to slay right up until the end of the 1980s, was now dormant. That was hugely important. From 1970 to the early 1990s, inflation in the advanced economies averaged nearly 7.5 per cent and ranged as high as 14 per cent, with much higher rates in some countries. From the early 1990s through to 2008/09, that average came down sharply, to just 2 per cent, and with much less variation around that average, either from year to year or between countries. The world, it seemed, had become a much more stable place, at least as far as measured inflation was concerned.

The jobless recovery

The world was also a place, however, where jobs appeared to be harder to come by and where the normal processes did not seem to be working. In America the upturn that followed the 1990/91 recession was characterised as the 'jobless recovery', which had political as well as economic implications. It was partly blamed for George Bush senior's failure to win re-election in November 1992, the election in which Bill Clinton's campaign was famously driven by his team's slogan 'It's the economy, stupid'. Though the recession had ended in March 1991, Bush struggled to convince voters that things were getting better as long as the job market remained in the doldrums. The proportion of long-term jobless, people out of work for more than six months, rose to nearly a quarter. The unemployment rate, in fact, peaked at 7.8 per cent in June 1992 and then began to edge down. Voters, however, were far from convinced, a majority telling exit pollsters in November that the economy was in bad shape. Another economic problem for Bush was that he had broken his 1988 pledge not to raise taxes. Even after Clinton was in office, however, the jobless recovery continued to haunt the White House.

In February 1993, nearly two years after the end of the recession, *Business Week*'s cover story was headed 'Jobs, jobs, jobs – it's a recovery without a heart'. The article,[9] typical of many at the time, described the economy as 'erratic and undependable', noting that the recovery was the weakest in 30 years. Its main emphasis, however, was on the weakness of employment growth. 'Corporate America has developed a deep, and perhaps abiding, reluctance to hire,' it stated.

> The spate of downsizing announcements at IBM, Sears and General Motors is just part of the story. The aversion to adding workers has also struck small and midsize companies, which were the mainstay of employment growth in the 1980s. 'The bottom line is that this is not a typical recovery, and the jobs are not coming back,' says Labour Secretary Robert Reich … But even sustained economic growth may only bring the jobs back at half the pace of previous recoveries. It's the lethal combination of global competition, expensive workers and cheap computers that has severed the link between economic growth and job growth.

There are powerful echoes of these 'jobless recovery' fears now. Does the world face years of muted economic growth and even more muted growth in jobs? To a certain extent the questions asked after recessions are always the same. Will there be any jobs? Have companies learned to manage with permanently smaller staffs? And, most enduring of all: where will the new jobs come from? It is not surprising that jobs' growth is weak in the early stages of recoveries. Often companies will go into an upturn with an underemployed workforce after many months of weak order books, so there is no immediate need to take on new people. Firms are unsure an upturn will last and are initially reluctant to go to the trouble and expense of hiring, particularly if they fear they may have to fire again. America's jobless recovery, at least, came to an end and gave way to much more vigorous employment growth later in the 1990s. Europe, with lower labour market participation than the United States (a smaller proportion of the working-age population in jobs), also suffered from significantly higher unemployment. The EU's unemployment rate averaged 10 per cent during the 1990s and, while it fell later, it remained well above US (and UK) levels. Unemployment appeared to be much more enduring, to be 'structural' in nature. OECD data, which is comparable across countries, showed that in the mid-1990s 66 per cent of the EU's unemployed men had been out of work for more than six months, while 47 per cent had been jobless for more than twelve months. The problem of long-term unemployment was endemic. The relevant figures in America were 22 per cent and 14 per cent respectively.

A book of mine written at the end of the decade, *Will Europe Work?*,[10] summed up the problem.

> Since the mid-1970s the US economy has been much more successful at generating jobs, with employment growth averaging 1.8 per cent a year, compared with 1 per cent a year for Japan and just 0.4 per cent for the European Union. Also, in one of the most frequently quoted comparisons in this debate, US employment growth has been predominantly in the private sector, with a net 30 million jobs created, whereas in the EU public-sector employment has risen by around seven million and there has been a 3.5 million decline in private-sector employment. Why is this? What happened to make previously successful European labour markets suddenly become, apparently, no-go areas for private-sector job creation?

In Britain, the picture was somewhat different. Though unemployment rose sharply during the 1990/92 recession, from 1.6 million to nearly 3 million, it peaked in the winter of 1992/93 and then fell steadily but significantly, falling by more than a million over the next four years. That was not enough to remove a strong sense of unease. The equivalent in Britain of America's jobless recovery was what came to be known as job insecurity. It was one of the central themes of Will Hutton's hugely influential mid-1990s best-seller *The State We're In*,[11] which defined Britain as a 'thirty, thirty, forty society', with only 40 per cent 'privileged', their market power having increased under Conservative government policies since 1979; 30 per cent of the workforce disadvantaged and 30 per cent marginalised and insecure. 'This is not the world of full-time jobs with employment protection and benefits such as pensions and paid holidays,' Hutton wrote. 'Instead people in this category work at jobs that are insecure, poorly protected and carry few benefits. This category more than any other is at the receiving end of the changes blowing through Britain's offices and factories; it includes the growing army of part-timers and casual workers.' It was a powerful message, and one that chimed with public opinion. A pamphlet of mine, 'Job insecurity versus labour market flexibility', written shortly after the publication of *The State We're In*, looked in detail at the data on job tenure, the proportion of part-time and temporary workers and survey evidence on worker attitudes. It concluded[12] that it was hard to find evidence for Hutton's thirty-thirty-forty society, and that: 'The notion of generalised job insecurity is a will o' the wisp, unsupported by the evidence. While Britain's labour market has undoubtedly gained in flexibility, there is much more to be done, notably in changing attitudes towards career changes and retraining, in improving the geographical mobility of labour and in further refining the interaction of benefits and entry-level jobs.' One little pamphlet was not going to shift a public mood that had clear political as well as economic consequences. 'The dominant feature of British economic life is widespread insecurity,' Gordon Brown told the Labour Party conference in September 1996.[13] Eight months later he was Chancellor of the Exchequer as the Conservatives slid to a landslide defeat in the 1997 general election. Five years of economic growth and more than four years of falling unemployment failed to rescue a government that had run out of energy and ideas. The prevailing sense of insecurity played a part in that.

Waiting for the cavalry

While it is easy when looking at the statistics to see the two decades from 1989 to 2009 as a period of growth and prosperity broken only by the mild recession of the early 1990s, it did not feel like that at the time in many countries. Some booms you can almost taste and certainly feel. The upturn of the 1990s often felt tentative, certainly outside America, with businesses and consumers waiting for the next downturn, and some of this continued after the year 2000. This kind of mood affects politicians and it affects other policymakers. When did the tentativeness disappear? For Japan it was there throughout the 1990s and beyond, as the 'lost decade', interspersed with brief periods of economic optimism, became a reality. For Europe, blighted by high unemployment, the decade was dominated by slow recovery and preparation for European monetary union and the single currency in 1999. Part of that preparation involved countries reducing their budget deficits and closing in on the inflation rate in Germany, Europe's biggest economy and its benchmark. In America, however, something else was stirring. It had begun to stir well before Bill Clinton's second presidential election victory in November 1996. Clinton won against unconvincing opponents, Bob Dole and Jack Kemp, but was undoubtedly helped by the fact that in America the economic uncertainties were giving way to renewed confidence. The afterburners were switched on. Something happened halfway through the decade to revitalise a ponderous America, until then worried about being overtaken by Japan economically. Nineteen ninety-six was the first of a series of strong years for the US economy, which saw growth averaging 4 per cent annually, well above trend, through to and including the year 2000.

This strong growth in America in this period was in many ways puzzling. Mature economies like those of the United States do not suddenly start to grow more strongly, so the talk was of a new era, of technologically driven productivity growth. The paradox described in the 1980s by Robert Solow, around the time he won the 1987 Nobel Prize for economics, was that you could see computers everywhere but in the productivity statistics. Perhaps this was now changing. This may have helped explain another puzzle about the acceleration of the recovery in America in the mid-1990s, which was that it was not associated with a rise in inflation. If the economy's 'speed limit' had been increased by productivity gains associated with the spread of information technology, it was not surprising that faster growth did not push up inflation. There was another explanation, which was that the China factor – the impact of global competition and the rise in worldwide industrial capacity – was holding down inflation. Either way, it was very good news. Robert Rubin, the first of Bill Clinton's Treasury secretaries, was sceptical about a new era, but he could see that something unusual was happening, as he explained later:[14]

> By mid-1996, the expansion was well established and still going strong. The growth rate was higher, and unemployment lower, than prevailing views would have said was possible. People were throwing around the phrase 'new economy', suggesting that advances in technology had revised the familiar rules and limits. Some investors appeared to be falling prey to the timeless boom-era temptation to believe that the business cycle had been tamed. Yet amid such indicators of what Alan [Greenspan] called irrational exuberance, real signs suggested that something had indeed changed for the better ... The question was whether – as Clinton had intuitively suggested in our internal discussions in 1994 – the American economy could safely grow faster than during the previous few decades. Though there was no real evidence at the time, Clinton's instinct turned out to be correct.

For some critics, this was where the problems really began. At the end of 1996, Greenspan wondered publicly in a speech[15] to the American Enterprise Institute whether the stock market, which had risen sharply, had been 'unduly escalated' by what he famously described as irrational exuberance. He had a point; over the course of 1995 and 1996 the Dow Jones industrial average rose from under 3,800 to more than 6,500. Not for the first time, his comments were widely misinterpreted. His worry was not that there was irrational exuberance in the economy but rather that if a stock market bubble was allowed to build up and burst, this could 'threaten to impair the real economy, its production, jobs, and price stability'. There was no guarantee this would occur, he argued, but it was as well not to underestimate or be complacent about these effects. Greenspan was not so much a cautious central banker as a cheerleader for the new era. As perhaps the most dominant chairman of modern times, he convinced or cajoled his colleagues into agreement. Dean Foust, writing in *Business Week*[16] a few months after the irrational exuberance speech, captured it well. 'By all conventional indicators, an interest-rate increase should have been a sure thing when the Federal Reserve's Open Market Committee (FOMC) met on May 20,' he wrote in the summer of 1997.

> As the 17 central bankers settled around the immense mahogany table in the Fed's conference room, they faced an economy growing at nearly 6 per cent and an unemployment rate below 5 per cent – a level that for the past quarter-century has been a near-certain signal of impending inflation. Indeed, most officials at the meeting seemed to favour hiking rates. Robert T. Parry, the inflation hawk who heads the San Francisco Fed, worried about the low jobless rate. Richmond (Va.) Fed President J. Alfred Broaddus Jr. fretted that inflation could rise if the Fed didn't act. And Fed Governor Laurence H. Meyer – one of the nation's top forecasters – believed that growth was too strong to be sustainable. But after a coffee break, when the group reconvened to decide whether to raise rates, Fed Chairman Alan Greenspan exercised his prerogative to talk first. Speaking from the head of the table in confident, low-key tones, he argued that there was no need for higher rates, noting that the economy showed signs of slowing. More important, he insisted to his colleagues, years of heavy spending on new technology finally could be yielding big productivity gains. When the final votes were cast, the verdict was nearly unanimous: no rate increase. Only Broaddus dissented.

Technology rules

This new era was associated directly with the dotcom boom, which began in August 1995, with the stock market float of Netscape, an Internet browser company. It came to an abrupt end in March 2000, when the technology-heavy NASDAQ index peaked and then began to fall sharply. Along the way, many reputations were made and plenty were lost. The combination of the Internet and investor hunger for what Michael Lewis described as 'the new, new thing' was powerful. Suddenly, young people with IT skills and bright ideas could become paper millionaires overnight. Plenty did so. Such were the attractions of the dotcom world that previously staid institutions such as investment banks (which were later to take their abandonment of staid behaviour to extremes) changed their dress codes and working arrangements to maintain their appeal to the brightest and best young people. The dotcom era, like the railway mania of Victorian England, provided an example of money and new technology coming together with dramatic consequences. Later, technology writers vied to draw up lists of the most spectacular dotcom failures of the era. Most included Boo.com, Pets.com, eToys.com, Webvan.com and Flooz.com. Flooz, promoted by the actress Whoopi Goldberg, had the aim of establishing a new currency for the Internet, to be used for online transactions. By the time it folded in 2001 everybody had realised what they should have done immediately, that credit cards did the job pretty well.

For some, the dotcom era was a time of justified optimism, a sign that there were frontiers of enterprise still to be explored. By the time the boom had turned to bust, the air was thick with recriminations, including those aimed at Wall Street firms that had pushed Internet stocks indiscriminately, in many cases being entirely aware of the shortcomings of the firms they were promoting. There is a direct line from dud dotcom stocks to risky subprime-backed securities, though the extent of mis-selling and misrepresentation was probably greater in the earlier episode. For some observers, such as Robert Shiller and Joseph Stiglitz, there was also a direct line from economic policy to some of the madness of the dotcom era. The NASDAQ composite index, Stiglitz noted, had doubled from 500 to 1,000 between 1991 and 1995, doubling again to more than 2,000 in 1998, before the final exaggerated surge that saw it peak at more than 5,000 in March 2000. These numbers, he suggested, were always 'unreal', though they were seen as part of the triumph of what he describes as 'Economia Americana'. Stiglitz, chairman of Bill Clinton's Council of Economic Advisers from 1995 to 1997, was impressed with Greenspan's irrational exuberance speech at the end of 1996. This, he thought wrongly, was a Fed chairman getting to grips with a bubble before it had a chance to become dangerously overinflated. 'When I approached him after his speech to discuss several of the ideas that he had thrown out, it was clear that he was fixated on the "irrational exuberance" remark,' Stiglitz wrote.[17]

> He knew the pundits would know that it was the United States rather than Japan that he had in mind. He was worried about the stock market, which was having a blow-out year – or so it seemed as the Dow climbed from 5,000 to 6,500 (when it reached 12.000 a little more than three years later, the gains of '96 would no longer be remembered as such a big deal). And if Greenspan was worried, the business and financial world had reason to worry …. And then, nothing happened. The Labour Department released statistics indicating slow job growth; signs of inflation failed to materialise, even later when unemployment continued its downward march; the Fed did not in fact raise interest rates; and the stock market continued to climb, setting records with almost boring regularity for the next four years, until the bubble burst.

Britain booms too

In the UK, it was in about 1996 that things began to turn upwards in more familiar ways. The recession of the early 1990s had produced something not seen since the Great Depression of the 1930s, a fall in actual house prices. The two previous big recessions, in the mid-1970s and early 1980s, had resulted in a fall in 'real' or inflation-adjusted house prices. Because inflation was high, house prices merely had to stagnate, which they did, for their real value to fall. The early 1990s recession was different, pushing actual or 'nominal' prices down by between 12 and 20 per cent, depending on the index used. The aftermath of that slump persisted, with prices remaining flat, 'bumping along the bottom', until late in 1995. Then they began to rise. The Nationwide Building Society measured an 8.5 per cent increase during 1996, the first step towards an increase of more than 60 per cent during the second half of the 1990s. Economists debate the extent to which housing wealth affects spending in the economy, with the Bank of England taking a sceptical view. As in America, however, something was stirring and confidence, the feel-good factor, was returning.

Why did Britain start to do better? While growth rates in the UK did not quite match those in America in the second half of the 1990s, at an average of 3.5 per cent a year they represented a break with the sluggish past. It looked like a triumph of Anglo-Saxon capitalism, the benefits of the Thatcher reforms of the 1980s and the curing of the British disease of excessive union power. In Britain, with a history of economic instability, 'boom and bust', the stability of the 1990s was a welcome contrast. As in America, insecurity began to dissipate as unemployment fell, particularly when that fall was not accompanied by higher inflation. What economists would call the trade-off between growth and inflation improved dramatically in comparison with the 1970s and 1980s. This improvement, evident both before and after Bank of England independence in 1997, was new. Inflation targeting, adopted in the wake of sterling's abrupt departure from the European exchange rate mechanism (ERM) in the autumn of 1992, was working like a dream. It was not just in the UK that perceptions changed. Sterling, which fell sharply in the wake of the 1992 ERM departure, dropping sharply again two years later, suddenly became the poster boy for international investors, beginning a sustained rise in the summer of 1996 that over the next two years was to result in its value rising by 25 per cent. A stable economy and a strong currency suggested, as in America, that something fundamental had changed.

Wealth is good

By the end of the 1980s, attitudes to wealth had changed fundamentally. Even if people were not ready for the 'Greed is good' philosophy parodied by Michael Douglas as Gordon Gekko in the film *Wall Street*, there was an acceptance that exceptional rewards, if justified by performance, were to be applauded. In Britain, indeed in Europe more generally, public responses towards wealth, and conspicuous consumption, had traditionally been more cautious, even hostile. Things, however, were moving. Even in 1989, 40 per cent of people agreed that it was a good thing that some people became very wealthy.[18] The culture of envy was being replaced by a culture of aspiration. Later, Tony Blair was to say that one of his proudest achievements was removing the culture of envy from the Labour Party in a way his predecessors would have found

impossible. Labour politicians were able to stand up at party confer-
ences and defend high salaries. 'Rewards for success' were acceptable
to those on the political left. This was different. 'The issue isn't in fact
whether the very richest person ends up becoming richer,' Blair told
Jeremy Paxman in 2001.[19] 'The issue is whether the poorest person is
given the chance that they don't otherwise have.' For those who were
not convinced, he was famously able to add a real-life example, using
one of Britain's footballing heroes: 'It's not a burning ambition for me
to make sure that David Beckham earns less money.'

Class and financial envy did not disappear during the Blair era any
more that they were absent in twentieth-century America. But they took
a back seat. When most people are doing relatively well they worry less
about those who are doing extremely well. Even studies of long-term
happiness and satisfaction, which show that keeping up with the Joneses
is an important element in people's wellbeing, suggest that it is how
friends and near-neighbours are doing that makes the difference, rather
than distant footballers, investment bankers or company chief executives. It was only when these people, the bankers and chief executives,
came to be blamed for economic misery that attitudes shifted. When
the question about whether it was good for some people to become very
wealthy was asked again in 2009, only 28 per cent agreed; sharply down.
It may have been a temporary backlash, or it may signal a more permanent shift.

2

The Rehearsal

In 1997 and 1998 the world suffered a major financial crisis. The read-across from the Asian financial crisis, and the other crises it triggered, to the global financial crisis that began in the summer of 2007, is not perfect. The parallels, however, are too close to be ignored. What were seen in 1997/98 as vulnerabilities particular to the emerging and newly industrialised economies of Asia later occurred much closer to home, including risky lending practices and inadequate supervision of the banking and financial system. Asian exceptionalism, it seemed, was not so exceptional after all, however convenient it may have been to believe that it was. Many Asians got thoroughly fed up in the years after the crisis with having it blamed on their own faulty business and financial model. There was more than a touch of Anglo-Saxon superiority, if not triumphalism, about it. Most people believed the Asian crisis was the result of factors specific to Asia. Emerging-market crises happened to emerging economies. The big advanced economies, most notably America, the biggest of them all, were as far removed from these new arrivals on the global economic scene as it was possible to be. Surely what happened to Thailand, Korea and others could not happen to America. Or could it? Among those who got the later crisis and the credit crunch more right than most was Nouriel Roubini, professor of economics at the Stern School of Business, New York University, and founder of the RGE Monitor website. The crisis made Roubini a global superstar among economists, but he insisted that all he had done was to apply the lessons of emerging-market crises to the United States. 'I've been studying emerging markets for 20 years, and saw the same signs in the U.S. that I saw in them, which was that we were in a massive credit bubble,' he said.[1]

The lessons of 1997/98, then, were perhaps that Asia was not so different after all, that the vast sums washing around global financial markets have enormous destructive power when directed against anybody, and that Washington, in the form of its twin institutions, the International Monetary Fund and to a lesser extent the World Bank, does not always know best. The Asian crisis was both a rehearsal for and a direct contributor to the turmoil of a decade later.

A financial gale blows

On the evening of 30 June 1997, with the rain pelting down, the ceremony to hand back Hong Kong to the People's Republic of China took place. Tony Blair, Britain's recently elected prime minister, was there, as was the Chinese president, Jiang Zemin. Prince Charles represented the Queen, and he was later to criticise in his diary[2] the 'appalling old waxworks' who were the Chinese leadership. For Britain it was a sombre occasion. Chris Patten, the last British governor of Hong Kong, spoke movingly, the rain soaking his hair and dripping down his face. Britain's contribution to Hong Kong, he said,[3] was 'the rule of law, clean and light-handed government, the values of a free society', and 'the beginnings of representative government and democratic accountability'. Then Patten and the rest of the British party were off. 'My family packed our bags,' he wrote later.[4]

> We embarked on the royal yacht *Britannia*, and sailed through a storm of fireworks out of the harbour into the South China Sea. We joined the largest fleet assembled by Britain east of Suez since the closure of the naval base in Singapore in the 1960s ... We cruised on, accompanied by dolphins, flying fish and seventeen ships of the line, to Manila, where we were greeted by a 21-gun salute from the Philippine navy (using, we were told afterwards, live ammunition).

It was a big moment for Britain and one rich in symbolism, perhaps the final end of empire, and it was a big moment for Hong Kong. Prior to the handover there was a heated debate over whether Hong Kong could possibly thrive under Chinese rule. China's official aim, after all, was to develop Shanghai as a global financial centre. The spirit of Hong Kong, of freebooting market capitalism, sat uneasily alongside the new reality of Chinese communist rule. Some said the talent would leave, particularly in the financial and banking sector, unwilling to contemplate life under Beijing's rule. Others dismissed such fears because of China's commitment to 'one country, two systems' autonomy for Hong Kong. Not only that, but the development of Shanghai into a global financial centre would take years if not decades (a prediction that turned out to be true) and in the meantime Hong Kong would be the beneficiary of the rapidly increasing financial flows between China and the rest of the world. Under British rule Hong Kong had had its fair share of crises, which continued up to the handover, as Patten recalled. The backdrop to the battle over political sovereignty was a constant battle over economic sovereignty. 'I was exposed to other questions of sovereignty during my governorship,' he wrote.[5]

> I remember in particular a couple of hedge fund assaults on the peg that joined the Hong Kong dollar to the American. This was an important foundation of the colony's stability during the years of transition. I did not want Hong Kong to be cast adrift on high seas, blown this way and that by financial gales. But avoiding that fate exposed us to occasional turbulence. With billions in traded currency crashing across the exchanges at the click of computers in London, Frankfurt and New York, I sometimes questioned what it meant to be sovereign in global markets where technology has speeded and amplified every economic activity.

It was a good question, and one that was immediately relevant. The debate over whether Hong Kong could thrive as part of China was one for the longer term. Over the medium term, the answer appeared to be yes. Between 1999 and 2008 the economy grew by nearly 5 per cent a year and the Hong Kong Stock Exchange held on to its position as the world's sixth largest. More immediately, however, the debate was overtaken by events. China assumed responsibility for Hong Kong on 1 July 1997. On 2 July, by a terrible accident of timing (though at the time some claimed a link), the Asian financial crisis started. A financial gale of enormous intensity began blowing and did not blow itself out until it had inflicted enormous damage. Hong Kong was to suffer badly, as was much of the rest of Asia. Political uncertainty was accompanied by enormous economic uncertainty.

Asian dominoes

The first and only time that Thailand's currency, the baht, achieved global importance was on 2 July 1997. It was then that, after weeks of heavy selling pressure, the government in Bangkok decided to float the baht. Just as the decision by the US authorities not to rescue Lehman Brothers in September 2008 sent shock waves around the global financial system, so the Thai government's decision to float the baht had enormous ramifications at the time. The crisis had been building for some time. Even by the standards of Asian economic growth, Thailand's performance was extraordinary. Its growth rate in the ten years leading up to the crisis was 10 per cent a year; if not the fastest in the world, then close to it. Thailand, apparently, was the new miracle economy, a model for successful emerging economies in Asia and elsewhere. 'Although growth at these stellar rates was new for Thailand, sustained economic growth had been the norm throughout the second half of the twentieth century,' wrote the Australian economist Peter Warr.[6] 'Growth of Thailand's real GDP per head of population was positive in every single year from 1958 to 1996, a unique achievement among developing countries. By the mid-1990s, Thailand's performance was being described as an example others might emulate and its principal economic institutions, particularly its central bank, the Bank of Thailand, were cited as examples of competent and stable management.' International capital, short- and long-term, was attracted to Thailand like bees around a honeypot. Real estate and financial assets, including the stock market, soared. The Thai authorities had helped encourage these inflows of short-term international capital by relaxing capital controls. What goes in, however, can also go out, and rapidly. Particularly in the first half of the 1990s, it was hard to explain Thailand's boom without reference to these capital inflows. 'This inflow of foreign capital did not merely fuel the boom,' wrote Warr. 'Its magnitude and its changing composition, combined with the policy environment of the time, also created the foundations for the collapse of 1997.'

All bubbles are different but all have certain common characteristics. The more that short-term capital flowed into the booming Thai economy, the more it encouraged other international investors to pour money in. This was partly the lure of the 'Asia rising' story, partly that as in all bubbles plenty of people can see fundamental reasons for unusual and unsustainable increases, particularly in commercial property prices. Thailand was hot and everybody wanted a piece of it. It had a clean bill of health from the International Monetary Fund. The Thai government encouraged the idea that, with Hong Kong under a cloud because of the handover to China, Bangkok could usurp part of its role as an international financial centre. Even where the Thai authorities tried to do the right thing, they merely fed the boom in capital inflows. The Bank of Thailand, when it raised interest rates to try to quell the inflationary impact of all these funds sloshing around, merely added to the problem by making it even more attractive for overseas investors by raising the return on short-term capital. It had to end in tears and it did. The combination of high wage inflation and a fixed exchange rate meant that the Thai economy rapidly lost competitiveness. When this began to be reflected in a faltering export performance, international investors began to question the miracle. First the capital stopped flowing in, and then it began to flow back out again, and rapidly. On 2 July, the scale of the attack on the baht left no option but to float it. The Asian crisis had begun.

The 'domino theory', that if one country was allowed to fall to communism, neighbours would quickly do so, dominated American foreign policy in the 1950s and 1960s. In the 1997/98 Asian financial crisis, a different kind of domino theory developed, that if one country or currency fell, another was bound to do so. Asian economies, having benefited from capital inflows, now felt the destructive impact of rapid outflows. Some Asian leaders reacted badly. Mahathir bin Mohamad, the controversial Malaysian prime minister, blamed the attack on Asian currencies on 'a worldwide Jewish conspiracy' led by George Soros, the hedge fund billionaire.[7] Mahathir, who also called Soros 'a moron', provoked a high-level battle of name-calling. For his part, Soros said the Malaysian prime minister was 'a menace to his own country' and 'a loose cannon' who should not be taken seriously.[8] Mahathir did, however, take action to stop the damage inflicted by uncontrolled flows of currency across the exchanges. Against the advice of received opinion, including that of the IMF, he reimposed capital controls. What was initially seen as the actions of a maverick with little understanding of international economics was later widely regarded as a far-sighted move.

For the moment, however, Asia had to cope with the domino effect, a contagion of collapsing currencies and financial panic. Bhumika Muchhala, looking back on the crisis ten years later, described the panic vividly:[9]

When the Thai baht was cut loose from its dollar peg, regional currencies plunged in value, causing foreign debts to skyrocket and igniting a full-blown crisis. By mid-January 1998, the currencies of Indonesia, Thailand, South Korea, the Philippines, and Malaysia had lost half of their pre-crisis values in terms of the U.S. dollar. Thailand's baht lost 52 per cent of its value against the dollar, while the Indonesian rupiah lost 84 per cent. During the last stages of the Asian crisis, the regional 'financial tsunami' generated a global one as Russia experienced a financial crisis in 1998, Brazil in 1999, and Argentina and Turkey in 2001 ... The resulting economic recession shocked the world with its staggering economic and social costs. Over a million people in Thailand and approximately 21 million in Indonesia found themselves impoverished in just a few weeks, as personal savings and assets were devalued to a fraction of their pre-crisis worth. As firms went bankrupt and layoffs ensued, millions lost their jobs. Soaring inflation raised the cost of basic necessities. Strapped fiscal budgets imposed a financial squeeze on social programmes, and the absence of adequate social safety nets led to grim economic displacement. Poverty and income inequality across the region intensified, as a substantial portion of the gains in living standards that had been accumulated through several decades of sustained growth evaporated in one year.

There are more lessons to be learned from the Asian financial crisis, including one key development that was central to creating the conditions for the wider crisis a decade later. In the post-1989 era the market was king and the purer and more untrammelled that market the better. The booming economies of Asia were encouraged to make the most of globalisation by allowing the free flow of capital into their countries. That way the world could benefit from their growth and they could benefit from access to international capital. It was the classic win-win situation, except when it turned into a rapid lose-lose. Just as too many controls could stifle growth and restrict investment, so the opposite could occur. Countries could liberalise too much, leaving them prey to wild and sometimes unpredictable market swings. Many countries in Asia did just that.

No early warning

No financial crisis emerges out of a clear blue sky. When a crisis breaks we kick ourselves for failing to spot what, with hindsight, were obvious warning signs. Before any crisis, some are prescient, detecting trouble on the horizon, sounding a warning, and taking action to protect themselves and their finances. The trouble is that such warnings are made all the time, whether justified or not. Nobody gets blamed for predicting a crisis that does not happen; such doom-laden predictions are quickly forgotten. The nature of crises is that they happen only when a critical mass is reached; in the case of Thailand and the other Asian economies enough people lost confidence at the same time to trigger a currency run.

The nearest thing to a prominent warning about Asia came from Paul Krugman, later to be awarded the Nobel Prize for economics (the Bank of Sweden Prize). In 1994 he had an article published in *Foreign Affairs*, 'The myth of Asia's miracle'. It drew the comparison between Western fears of the rise of Asia in the 1990s and similar worries about the strength of the Soviet bloc economies in the 1960s. The apparent

Asian miracle owed more to 'perspiration rather than inspiration', he wrote,[10] adding: 'From the perspective of the year 2010, current projections of Asian supremacy extrapolated from recent trends may well look almost as silly as 1960s-vintage forecasts of Soviet industrial supremacy did from the perspective of the Brezhnev years.' From the perspective of 2010, it is Krugman's article, which was highly sceptical about the rise of China, as well as the Asian newly industrialised countries, which looks a little silly. For a while in 1997/98, however, he appeared to have been one of the few to sensibly question Asia's non-stop rise, though he was modest enough to deny he had predicted the Asian crisis.

Krugman was closer to the mark than the IMF, however, which since 1945 has had a role monitoring the global economy. Its twice yearly *World Economic Outlook*[11] in the spring of 1997, on the eve of the Asian crisis, saw few clouds on the horizon. Asian economies would grow by 8.3 per cent in 1997 and 7.7 per cent in 1998, it predicted. The outcome was rather different. The so-called ASEAN-4 (the biggest four economies then in the Association of South East Asian Nations), Indonesia, Malaysia, Thailand and the Philippines, saw their collective gross domestic product drop by nearly 10 per cent in 1998. The IMF acknowledged that there were growth strains in Asia but remained confident that governments and central banks were dealing with them. 'Among the developing countries in Asia, those that have had to deal with risks of overheating have generally been successful in dampening the growth of domestic demand,' it said. Looking more generally at developing countries, there was plenty to be positive about in Asia. 'Some countries ... have benefited considerably from strong macroeconomic policies and outward-oriented, market-based reforms, which are enabling them to integrate rapidly into the global economic and financial system,' the IMF wrote.

Spotting impending crises is, as noted above, easier said than done. Giving voice to fears of a financial crisis is difficult for organisations like the IMF, which would be immediately accused of sparking panic. Even so, it appears to have been genuinely taken by surprise by the crisis. This was not, however, the biggest criticism of the IMF in 1997/98. For its many critics and most impartial observers, the fault lay with its cack-handed handling of Asia's problems. The situation was already difficult by the time IMF teams flew in from Washington, ready to offer financial assistance but only with substantial strings attached. With few exceptions, those strings, in the form of IMF policy recommendations, made things worse. The Washington 'consensus' that had urged financial and trade liberalisation on Asian economies now forced orthodox policies on recession-hit countries that would only, in the short term at least, make things worse. Interest rates should be raised to stem currency falls, it said, and tough fiscal measures adopted to bring down budget deficits. The contrast between the IMF's response a decade later, when it recommended that advanced economies adopt Keynesian fiscal expansionism and ultra-low interest rates, was striking.

Nobody knows whether, in the absence of the lessons of the Asian crisis, IMF orthodoxy would still have ruled in 2008. Joseph Stiglitz, a vocal critic of the Washington consensus both before and after his spell as chief economist at the World Bank, believed the IMF and the US Treasury, having been imbued with neoliberalism in the 1980s, saw it as their mission to spread the word around the world. Others saw a kind of colonialism in the prescriptions in the IMF's sinister-sounding structural adjustment packages for its client countries. That big mistakes were made is not seriously disputed. 'The IMF recommended a series of policies that evidently worsened the crisis,' wrote Mark Weisbrot, co-director of the Center for Economic Policy Research in Washington.[12] 'Most of these followed a pattern of misdiagnosis that was seen in Argentina and elsewhere, which included high interest rates and a tightening of domestic credit to slow economic growth, fiscal tightening – including cuts in food and energy subsidies in Indonesia, which were later rescinded after rioting broke out – and, amazingly, further liberalisation of international capital flows.'

The effect on Asia of the crisis and the IMF's response to it was profound. South Korea's emergence as an independent economic force had been carefully choreographed and closely modelled on Japan's economic success. South Korea hosted the annual meetings of the IMF and World Bank in 1985 in Seoul, as a kind of financial coming-out party and a prelude to the Olympics in 1988. Pride in the country's economic achievements was enormous, as was the sense of helplessness and shame during the 1997/98 crisis when it had to turn to the IMF for what was then its biggest ever rescue package, totalling $55 billion when additional contributions from the United States, Japan and the Asian Development Bank were taken into account. On a trip to Seoul in 1998, I witnessed the tail-end of an official campaign launched in January of that year, in which ordinary Koreans were encouraged to donate their gold to help the country out of its financial plight. At the time, Koreans were believed to own $20 billion of gold. Tonnes were donated, though the effect on the country's external debt position was more symbolic than real.

Never again

The economic pain and humiliation of the crisis and the fact that countries had to submit themselves to destructive IMF programmes had an effect that went well beyond patriotic donations of gold trinkets and heirlooms. Asian governments asked themselves why they had been so vulnerable. As discussed earlier, part of the answer lay with too-rapid liberalisation of capital controls; fine up to a point when the capital was flowing but deadly when it flowed out again. Another lesson was that when it came to defending their currencies, the Asian countries had insufficient ammunition in the form of foreign currency reserves. The crisis thus had two effects which were to have a very direct bearing on its successor a decade later. The first was that all the affected countries decided that in future they must hold much larger foreign currency and gold reserves. The second effect was on China, whose move towards regional leadership was accelerated. Though China was affected relatively little by the crisis itself, its lessons were not lost on Beijing. China too realised that having a substantial war chest was essential for economic and financial autonomy. Even a controlled currency like the renminbi could be overwhelmed if it did not have the backing of substantial reserves. This desire of Asian economies to 'self-insure' themselves against future crises was a key ingredient in the bigger crisis a decade later. Some say it was the key ingredient. Reserves do not just sit idle, they seek a home. For many Asian administrations that home was in foreign government bond markets and in particular US treasuries. High Asian reserves, coupled with high Asian saving ratios, were both a product of global economic imbalances and a contributor to them. One effect of all these Asian funds sloshing around global markets was to drive interest rates, particularly long-term rates, to extremely low levels.

Between the end of the Asian crisis and 2007, the foreign exchange reserves of Asian economies quadrupled. Not all of this was due to Asian economies taking out insurance against future crises. A substantial part, particularly for China, which was responsible for the lion's share of the increase, was as a result of deliberate action to hold down the region's currencies against the dollar and artificially preserving competitiveness. Even excluding China, however, Asia's currency reserves doubled. Ten years after the crisis, Asia had currency reserves equivalent to 5 per cent of global GDP. How worried should the rest of the world have been about this? In 2005, in a piece called 'Asian squirrels', *The Economist* concluded that there was nothing sinister about the build-up in reserves or the desire of Asian countries to manage their currencies. 'Current policy is largely a response to the East Asian financial crisis of 1997–8,' it said.[13] 'More recently, most countries have allowed some rise in their exchange rates against the dollar, but governments have understandably been eager to rebuild their reserves as ammunition against any future crisis.' *The Economist* did, however, fret about the fact that heavy dollar buying by Asian central banks had inflated the money supply and driven down interest rates, warning that this could lead to 'a misallocation of capital, undermining future growth'.

Low long-term interest rates also exercised Alan Greenspan during 2005. In February of that year he spoke of a bond market 'conundrum'. Even as the Federal Reserve was raising interest rates, the bond markets were delivering low long-term interest rates, a key influence on, for example, US mortgage rates and the cost of corporate borrowing. Greenspan, in testimony to Congress,[14] went through the various possible explanations, including the fact that 'a larger share of the world's pool of savings is being deployed in cross-border financing of investment', but concluded that none fitted. The bond market's performance, he suggested, was an aberration. 'None of this is new and hence it is difficult to attribute the long-term interest rate declines of the last nine months to glacially increasing globalisation,' he said. Others disagreed, most notably Ben Bernanke, the man who was to succeed him within months as chairman of the Federal Reserve. Greenspan and Bernanke were very different in background, style and temperament. Greenspan was a numbers man, who had made his reputation in the commercial world running his own economic consultancy before entering public service. His method was to scour the statistics, however obscure, to come up with the answers. Bernanke, quiet and softly spoken, some-times known as 'Gentle' Ben, was an academic who once occupied a room at the Massachusetts Institute of Technology (MIT) next to a young British academic, Mervyn King. Neither would have expected to become heads of their respective central banks. Bernanke's area of particular expertise, which subsequently became eerily appropriate, was the Great Depression.

He identified a 'global saving glut' that was having a key influence on the world economy in general and America in particular. The strat-egies of the East Asian economies, and China, had been built around export-led growth, surpluses on balance of payments current accounts, high savings and accumulating 'war chests' of currency reserves. Asian governments effectively acted as financial intermediaries, he suggested, channelling the high savings of their citizens into the international capital markets.

What was the effect of this global saving glut, and why did it matter for America, which, in contrast, was running with very low savings and a large deficit on its current account? 'After the stock-market decline that began in March 2000, new capital investment and thus the demand for financing waned around the world,' Bernanke said.[15]

Yet desired global saving remained strong. The textbook analysis sug-gests that, with desired saving outstripping desired investment, the real rate of interest should fall to equilibrate the market for global saving. Indeed, real interest rates have been relatively low in recent years, not only in the United States but also abroad. From a narrow US perspec-tive, these low long-term rates are puzzling; from a global perspective, they may be less so. The weakening of new capital investment after the drop in equity prices did not much change the net effect of the global saving glut on the US current account. The transmission mechanism changed, however, as low real interest rates rather than high stock prices became a principal cause of lower US saving. In particular, during the past few years, the key asset-price effects of the global saving glut appear to have occurred in the market for residential investment, as low mortgage rates have supported record levels of home construction and strong gains in housing prices.

This was a direct line from one from crisis to another. Though some struggled to see it, including Greenspan, the policies adopted by Asian countries in the wake of their crisis in 1997/98 helped create conditions for the bigger crisis that followed a decade later. The big global imbalances; America's deficit versus Asia's surpluses; high Asian savings versus low Anglo-Saxon savings, and exceptionally low interest rates; all developed during this period. What was a conundrum for Greenspan was also a ticking time bomb.

3

Long-Term Capital
Mismanagement

Robert Rubin, Treasury secretary under Bill Clinton, was, like George W. Bush's Treasury secretary Hank Paulson a decade later, a Wall Street veteran from Goldman Sachs. In Paulson's case, that may have turned out to be a disadvantage, particularly when he was trying to seek approval from Congress for taxpayer funds to bail out the banks. For Rubin, his intimate knowledge was an advantage. In September 1998, as he was enjoying a weekend away from Washington at his home in New York, he had the first of a series of calls from Gary Gensler, another former Goldman Sachs partner who was also working in the Clinton administration as assistant secretary for financial markets. The calls concerned Long-Term Capital Management (LTCM), one of Wall Street's biggest and most pivotal hedge funds. 'Gary called again on Sunday evening, to tell me what he had learned,' Rubin wrote.[1]

LTCM had taken vast positions financed by billions of dollars in loans from major financial institutions – positions that would work out only if the financial markets calmed down and the spreads reverted to more normal relationships. Now LTCM was facing massive losses, and its imminent bankruptcy portended uncertain effects on the financial markets. My first reaction was to say to Gary, 'I don't understand how someone like John Meriwether – who was thought of as such a sophisticated and experienced guy when he worked at Salomon Brothers – could get into this kind of trouble.' Before founding LTCM, Meriwether had run a massive trading operation at Salomon and had done very well over a long period. He had some of the top names in finance – Nobel Prize winners Robert Merton and Myron Scholes – working with him at LTCM. I was amazed that they had done what it seemed they had, betting the ranch on the basis of mathematical models, even ones built by such sophisticated people.

Rubin was not alone in being amazed. Myron Scholes and Robert Merton were the most respected figures in financial economics, winning the 1997 Nobel Prize, the Bank of Sweden prize, for their work on modern finance. Paul Samuelson, an earlier Nobel winner, described Merton as the Newton of modern finance. Along with the late Fischer Black, they were the people who had done more than anybody else to bring economic science to bear on the pricing of risk. When they were recruited by John Meriwether, a Wall Street legend, investors were rightly impressed. Meriwether was following a long Wall Street tradition. In the late 1920s, ahead of the 1929 Wall Street Crash, American investment trusts, then a new and, as it turned out, disastrous vehicle, rushed to get some academic respectability on board. It was, as J. K. Galbraith pithily recorded,[2] 'a golden age for professors'. Thoughts of 1929 were, however, a long way from the minds of LTCM's investors.

Operating from offices in Greenwich, Connecticut, LTCM seemed to be the epitome of modern, intelligent finance; smart people using scientific methods to generate healthy returns. Meriwether, despite having been forced to quit Salomon Brothers in 1991 following irregularities surrounding bids by his senior bond trader in US treasury auctions, was hugely successful in attracting investors, including wealthy individuals and most of the big Wall Street names, to his new venture LTCM, on its launch in 1994. It was not just the big academic names; investors knew that Meriwether's team at Salomon had been hugely profitable. The minimum LTCM investment was $10 million, though most of its 80 initial investors subscribed much more. With more than $1 billion in capital, LTCM was well set up, and its investors looked to have made a wise decision. In both 1995 and 1996 it achieved returns of more than 40 per cent, slowing to a still-impressive 17 per cent in 1997. LTCM was a phenomenon, the envy of its competitors. By early 1998 this relatively new venture had become a big player, with an investment portfolio of more than $100 billion, a net asset value of $4 billion (compared with an initial capital of $1.3 billion) and an outstanding position in derivatives markets, mainly interest-rate swaps (instruments used to hedge against interest-rate changes) of $1.25 trillion.

LTCM's initial trading approach was simple enough. Government bonds are among the safest and most analysed investments in financial markets. Within government bond markets, however, LTCM's founders recognised that there will always be discrepancies in pricing; such discrepancies providing the opportunities for financial arbitrage. These discrepancies could occur within an individual government bond market, for example the US treasury market, or between them, when there was mispricing of US, European and Japanese bonds in comparison with one another. A typical LTCM deal was a 'convergence' trade, which assumed investors would spot these differences and they would then disappear and prices converge at the right level. There was nothing unusual in LTCM's approach. What was different was that its mathematical models were well ahead of rivals in detecting these arbitrage opportunities.

LTCM did not confine itself to simple trades, which Scholes described as picking up the nickels other investors chose to leave on the sidewalks. Gradually it became more ambitious in search of bigger returns, to further differentiate it from competitors. Some of these trades included so-called risk arbitrage, essentially betting on the outcome of corporate takeovers. It also traded on what it saw as discrepancies in the pricing of individual equities. One such trade sought to profit from differences in the pricing of the stocks of Royal Dutch and Shell, essentially the same company but quoted in different markets. It invested in bond markets in Russia and emerging economies. Through it all, LTCM increased its leverage sharply, borrowing more than $120 billion from the banks to better take advantage of investment opportunities. LTCM became around thirty-five times leveraged, similar to Wall Street's most vulnerable investment banks a decade later. This was not a problem, however, as long as its trading strategies were sound, which for the most part they were. An additional confidence boost was provided by the fact that the firm's strategists themselves believed fervently in the business. By the summer of 1998, $1.9 billion of LTCM's capital, which by then had grown to $4.8 billion, was from the firm's own partners and employees, their own initial investments multiplied many times over by reinvested profits and bonuses. Nearly half the business, in other words, was owned by the people who ran it and who generated the returns. It looked perfect. Until, that is, it went badly wrong.

Genius fails

LTCM's magic touch began to desert it in the summer of 1998, when its monthly returns began to turn sharply negative, partly as a result of more volatile markets, partly because of bets that went wrong. The end came as a result of something that few had thought remotely possible, Russia's decision to simultaneously devalue the rouble and default on more than 280 billion roubles ($13.5 billion) of debt on 17 August 1998. During the 2007–09 crisis the phrase 'Black Swan event', popularised by Nassim Nicholas Taleb, was thrown around freely, meaning high-impact events outside the normal range of predictions. Just as Europeans had assumed all swans were white until the discovery of black swans by explorers in Australia, so a Russian default was so far outside the range of expectations as to be safely ignored. Russia, after all, had not defaulted through many turbulent years since the revolution of 1917. The Russian economy, which had struggled to adjust to a post-communist era, was caught in the backwash of the Asian crisis. One of its few sources of strength, energy exports, was hit by a collapse in oil prices to $10 a barrel. The backdrop to the crisis was a yawning fiscal deficit, financed by the issue of ever-increasing amounts of government bonds. Russia received support from the International Monetary Fund and the World Bank. By August, however, with the Moscow stock market down 75 per cent since the start of the year, it was clear a crunch was coming. It came in the 17 August announcement.

The Russian default was important in its own right but it was also hugely significant for Western financial markets, triggering the biggest turbulence in half a century. LTCM's problem was not the investments it had made in Russia, though they did not help. It was the fact that its bread-and-butter bond market 'convergence' trades, made on the assumption that pricing discrepancies would be ironed out, were blown out of the water by Russia's action. Suddenly there was a flight to quality, which meant US treasury bonds, and a scramble for liquidity, as happened nine years later in 2007. LTCM's models did not allow for this and the fund began to lose money on an alarming scale. That was not the only problem. Its own 'value at risk' calculations suggested that even in the panic of August 1998 its maximum daily losses would be no more than $35 million. On one single day, 21 August, it lost more than fifteen times that, $550 million. By the end of August, it had lost $2 billion of its $4.8 billion capital. By the end of the third week of September it had lost most of the rest. The fear was that if LTCM folded and defaulted on the many and varied positions it had in a wide range of markets, it would set off a chain reaction of bankruptcies among financial firms and make the market panic up to then look mild in comparison with what could have followed. So, after an abortive takeover attempt by Goldman Sachs, operating in tandem with Warren Buffett's Berkshire Hathaway group, the Wall Street establishment (with what would later turn out to be the interesting exception of Bear Stearns) was persuaded that it was in its own interests to put together a bailout.

As Robert Rubin later described it, it was not quite an official rescue but it would not have happened without high-level involvement by the authorities. 'New York Fed president Bill McDonagh convened the heads of the big investment and commercial banks at the Fed's New York headquarters,' he wrote.[3]

> He walked a fine line, calling the CEOs of the country's biggest banks in but then leaving the room so they could work out the details on their own. After a lot of jockeying, fourteen different institutions agreed to provide a total of nearly $4 billion in additional credit to LTCM, with strict terms attached. This capital infusion gave the hedge fund breathing room to liquidate its positions in a more orderly fashion. Although I did not share the view that a collapse of LTCM was likely to lead to systemic disruptions, I thought the concerns – and Bill's actions – were sensible and appropriate, given the general market and economic duress at the time.

It was indeed in Wall Street's interests to step in and stem the potential LTCM contagion. Fourteen banks put up the funds, most contributing $300 million. As the markets gradually returned to normal, LTCM's trades were unwound and the business gradually run down, formally closing in 2000. It was, it appeared, a costless exercise, with most of the participating banks making a small profit on their contribution, when the alternative would have been eye-watering losses. The mood was one of self-congratulation about a crisis averted. That did not mean, of course, there were no losers. LTCM's partners lost $1.9 billion between them, while UBS, the Swiss bank that also came unstuck a decade later, lost its $700 million investment in the fund. Other losses emerged as the months passed, though on a smaller scale.

Meriwether did not give up the world of investment. Late in 1999, after LTCM had been all but wound down, he launched JWM Partners with some of his former colleagues. It was moderately successful for a period, although, partly because it used far less leverage than his old firm, it was always a pale shadow of LTCM in its glory days. It suffered heavily during the later crisis from 2007 and was shut down in July 2009. Merton also made a comeback, as chief science officer and co-founder of Integrated Finance, a financial advisory firm, which later merged into Trinsum. It filed for Chapter 11 bankruptcy in January 2009. It was easy to spot the pattern. Investment strategies based on complex mathematical models failed when they were needed most, when markets were volatile and economic conditions unusual and uncertain. Like weather forecasters and economic forecasters, they performed best when nothing very out of the ordinary happened. When unusual things happened, they were more badly caught out than anybody.

Lessons unlearned

The failure of LTCM, apparently a monument to modern finance, was important in a number of key respects. It was close to home, in the heart of America's financial system, with some of the most-respected names, and brightest brains, in the field. It came unstuck as a result of a fateful combination of aggressive trading, particularly in financial derivatives, and the use of overly complex 'rocket science' mathematical models.

And it was important because, as Lehman Brothers came even closer to doing exactly ten years later, it came close to collapsing the entire financial system. It also helped reinforce the view that when crises happened reasonable people, acting together, could solve them and prevent them turning into something really nasty. Roger Lowenstein, author of *When Genius Failed*, about the LTCM crisis, looked back on the episode in 2008 on the eve of the collapse of Lehman Brothers, when the failure of Bear Stearns was still the big story. 'A financial firm borrows billions of dollars to make bets on esoteric securities,' he wrote.[4]

> Markets turn and the bets go sour. Overnight, the firm loses most of its money, and Wall Street suddenly shuns it. Fearing that its collapse could set off a full-scale market meltdown, the government intervenes and encourages private interests to bail it out. The firm isn't Bear Stearns – it was Long-Term Capital Management, the hedge fund based in Greenwich, Conn. The Long-Term Capital fiasco momentarily shocked Wall Street out of its complacent trust in financial models, and was replete with lessons, for Washington as well as Wall Street. But the lessons were ignored, and in this decade, the mistakes were repeated. Instead of learning from the past, Wall Street has re-enacted it in larger form, in the mortgage debacle cum credit crisis.

The sad thing is that everybody appeared to be aware of the danger at the time. All the arguments that came to the fore in 2008 were rehearsed in 1998. Alan Greenspan, when told by Bill McDonagh, his colleague at the New York Fed, of the plan to broker a rescue deal for LTCM, confessed he was not happy with the idea.[5] The Fed-coordinated bailout of LTCM was replete with moral hazard and established the principle that some institutions were too big to fail. It also confirmed for many Americans, and many of their congressmen, that finance looked after its own, aided and abetted by the Federal Reserve and the US Treasury. There was, it seemed, one law for Wall Street and another for Main Street. So why, if all this was recognised at the time, did everybody go along with the bailout? There are two parts to the answer. LTCM was not bailed out in the sense that its partners and employees emerged intact; they were the heaviest losers and for some this answered the moral hazard question. The wider point, however, is that it is not in the nature of politicians, central bankers and regulators to stand aside and allow a crisis resulting from the failure of a firm to threaten the system as a whole. Those who live by the market should in theory die by it, but the public would not easily forgive those in authority for standing by while markets plunged and the economy dived into recession if they could prevent it. Had the authorities then argued that they had chosen not to act for fear of creating the conditions for an even bigger crisis a decade later, they would have been given short shrift.

That did not stop the critics. Professor Kevin Dowd, now of Nottingham University, writing a year after the LTCM bailout, was clear on the dangers. 'The Fed's intervention was misguided and unnecessary because LTCM would not have failed anyway, and the Fed's concerns about the effects of LTCM's failure on financial markets were exaggerated,' he wrote in a paper for the Cato Institute.[6]

> In the short run the intervention helped the shareholders and managers to get a better deal for themselves than they would otherwise have obtained … It implies a major open-ended extension of Federal Reserve responsibilities without any congressional authorisation; it implies a return to the discredited doctrine that the Fed should prevent the failure of large financial firms, which encourages irresponsible risk taking; and it undermines the moral authority of Fed policymakers in their efforts to encourage their counterparts in other countries to persevere with the difficult process of economic liberalisation.

Some would dispute certain aspects of Dowd's attack, particularly his suggestion that LTCM could have survived unaided. His general point, however, was well made and was to resurface dramatically later; if firms are allowed to become too big to fail, does this not simply mean that they have become too big?

The caravan moves on

The emerging-market crisis was not over. After Asia and Russia it moved on to Latin America, most notably Brazil and Argentina, which suffered a major financial crisis lasting from 1999 to 2002. These crises occupied politicians and policymakers, and the IMF and the World Bank, and confirmed that the global economy remained a turbulent and unforgiving place. Not, however, that you would have known it in America, Britain or most of the other advanced economies. The danger of serious financial contagion passed, and with it the threat of a major advanced-country recession; and to make doubly sure central banks cut interest rates aggressively. In America, the Federal Reserve cut enough to put the markets back on an even keel, and the concept of the 'Greenspan put', from the language of the financial options market, was established. This was the idea that gained ground among stock traders and investors, that whenever events threatened a significant market fall, Greenspan's Fed would ride to the rescue with soothing interest-rate cuts.

Despite Asia, LTCM and Russia, 1998 was a good year for investors, the Dow Jones industrial average rising by 16 per cent. In Britain, similar developments were occurring. The Bank of England had been raising interest rates until the summer of 1998 but in the autumn began to cut them aggressively. One member of its monetary policy committee (MPC) then, the maverick economist Willem Buiter, was voting to raise rates in August. By October he wanted them brought down aggressively. The Bank cut rates from 7.5 per cent ahead of the LTCM crisis to 5 per cent by the summer of 1999. If there was a threat of recession, it was successfully headed off.

Elsewhere, the crisis was not forgotten but it became easier to think of it as a great escape. Hedge funds, apparently holed below the waterline as a result of LTCM's calamity, retreated for a while before coming back strongly. Financial derivatives, which had caused so much trouble, briefly became a dirty term. For them too it was only a brief setback. In crisis-hit Asia, meanwhile, there was a 'V-shaped' economic recovery, growth in the region bouncing back strongly and defying predictions among economists that the most that could be expected was a painfully slow return to prosperity. From 1999 to 2005, Asia's economies typically expanded at between 4 and 6 per cent a year. This was somewhat slower than the 7 to 9 per cent boom rates recorded immediately before the Asian convulsion of 1997/98, but it suggested something closer to a sustainable expansion. Quietly too, China assumed regional economic leadership, having come through the crisis virtually unscathed. This was the moment, both in Asia and in Western capitals, when China's potential was fully recognised. The emerging economies of Asia, having been seen as production outposts for Japanese and American firms and acutely dependent on Western financial investors, began to look to Beijing. The post-crisis period saw China's growth accelerate from 8 per cent to more than 10 per cent a year.

The crises of the late 1990s were a perfect storm that brought together serious economic and financial turbulence in Asia, Russia, LTCM and Latin America, but they had been tackled. Nobody would pretend that the IMF's handling of Asia had been anything other than clumsy. If the aim of the exercise was to ensure uninterrupted growth in the advanced economies and rising stock markets, however, policymakers had achieved a great success. They could pat each other on the back. Prosperity was protected. The financial system was more resilient than many had feared. There was nothing to worry about. Or so it seemed.

4

No Return to Boom and Bust

On 21 March 2007, Gordon Brown gave his final Budget speech to a crowded House of Commons. After a decade in office, this was a ritual Britain's then Chancellor of the Exchequer was used to. Having helped engineer Tony Blair's early departure, his eyes were on his next job, that of prime minister, to which he would succeed three months later without facing a leadership contest. Brown was on a high, taunting the Conservative opposition with Labour's economic achievements. In ten years he had faced seven shadow chancellors, starting with Kenneth Clarke in 1997 and ending with George Osborne in 2007. Candid Conservatives admitted that as long as the economy was doing well there was little they could do about Labour's political dominance. Though there were signs of fraying around the edges, particularly a series of missed targets for government borrowing, to all intents and purposes the economy was still doing well. Brown had been a phenomenon as chancellor. Three years before, in 2004, he had become the longest-serving holder of the office in the modern era, overtaking David Lloyd George, who did the job for just over seven years from 1908 until 1915, before also eventually becoming prime minister. In the period since the Second World War, only Nigel Lawson, chancellor for six and a half years from 1983 to 1989, came anywhere close. For longer-serving chancellors, it was necessary to go back to the nineteenth century and Nicholas Vansittart, the 1st Baron Bexley, who served from May 1812 to December 1822, or William Gladstone, who did a cumulative twelve years in the post, though that was achieved over a 30-year period in four separate spells. To stay in any political job for a decade represents a considerable achievement. To last so long in one of the most pressured and high-profile roles in government, which had left so many of his predecessors exhausted and demoralised, was Brown's triumph.

So his message was one of overweening pride in Britain's economic achievements under his stewardship. 'I can report the British economy is today growing faster than all the other G7 economies – growth stronger this year than the euro area, stronger than Japan and stronger even than America,' he said,[1] 'and that after 10 years of sustained growth, Britain's growth will continue into its 59th quarter – the forecast end of the cycle – and then into its 60th and 61st quarter and beyond.' There was more. Inflation had averaged just 1.5 per cent since 1997, 'and after examining the historical records, it is Britain's best inflation performance for a century'. All this, he said, was built on the solid foundations of policy discipline: 'Just as our monetary discipline is the foundation of our economic strength, our fiscal discipline is the foundation of the strength of Britain's finances.' In the early 1990s under the Conservatives, he pointed out, the budget deficit had reached the equivalent of more than £100 billion, 8 per cent of gross domestic product. He could look forward, he said, to a future in which annual borrowing would be no more than £35 billion, comfortably less than 3 per cent of GDP. If there were clouds on the horizon, Brown and his officials had not spotted them, or decided they would quickly blow away. The British economy, which in the past had often stood out among its peers for its instability, was now outperforming those peers and growing strongly 'on the foundation of the longest period of economic stability and sustained growth in our country's history'. In case anybody had not got the message, he repeated the New Labour mantra he and Blair had used with great effect since 1997: 'And we will never return to the old boom and bust.'

Abolishing boom and bust

'No return to boom and bust' was the defining slogan for New Labour, more enduring than the party's commitments to education, the National Health Service, social justice and an ethical foreign policy. Economic stability, never before achieved on a lasting basis by a Labour government, provided the basis for everything else. Money for public services flowed from it, as did the government's ability to remain in office and deliver on its other commitments. What is also clear, however, is that 'no return to boom and bust' was more than just a convenient political slogan. The more they said it, the more Gordon Brown and Tony Blair believed it, and the reason they believed it was because they thought the measures they had taken had given the economy immunity from the instabilities of the past. William Keegan, in his 2003 book *The Prudence of Mr Gordon Brown*, traced this line of thinking back to a December 1992 paper by Ed Balls, then a young leader writer on the *Financial Times*, subsequently Brown's key economic adviser and, later as a minister, a hugely influential figure within New Labour. The Fabian Society pamphlet 'Euro-monetarism: why Britain was ensnared and how it should escape' was written in the context of Britain's humiliating exit from the European exchange rate mechanism (ERM) in September 1992. It looked at that policy failure and asked how Britain could avoid such problems in the future. Britain, Balls wrote,[2] had to have 'a credible and predictable macroeconomic policy framework which can deliver economic stability combined with active government measures to promote growth and full employment'. In a key passage, he added:[3] 'Only then can the UK hope to avoid a third, destructive, boom-bust cycle ... Only then can public and international confidence in British policymaking be restored.'

In the absence of a credible framework, in other words, Britain would be vulnerable to the vagaries of the international markets and the whims of foreign investors. Avoiding boom and bust meant gaining the trust of the markets. For Labour in particular, such trust was in short supply; people still remembered the economic turbulence the last time the party was in power in the 1970s and had to turn to the International Monetary Fund to be bailed out. New Labour might be different from 'Old' Labour and ready to assume power in preference to a tired Conservative government, but its politicians were unproven. Overcoming the credibility gap meant, according to Balls, limiting the freedom of action of politicians to mess things up. 'Balls's message was that governments could not achieve economic salvation by relying on macroeconomic instruments alone and that, in the wider public interest, governments had to be constrained,' wrote Keegan.[4]

He was reflecting not only on his observations of the 1980s but also the trend of some of the academic economic literature of the time, in leaning towards 'rules' rather than 'discretion' and questioning the efficiency of decisions made with the short-term political timetable in mind. There was a 'credibility gap' between politicians' short-term desire to stimulate the economy and the public interest in medium-term stability. No-one, he charged, had mastered the art of boom-bust economics better than the British Treasury.

It was logical and it was appealing. As this rules-based approach was disseminated in speeches and interviews in the run-up to the 1997 election, a curious thing happened. The pound, rather than weakening in anticipation of a financially risky Labour government, strengthened considerably. Nor was this a mere flash in the pan. Sterling, having risen, stayed strong for the duration of Brown's chancellorship. It appeared to be an international vote of confidence in Labour's rules-based approach to economic policymaking.

Banking on the Bank

In early May 2007, a few weeks after Brown's final budget as chancellor, Mervyn King was also looking back with a certain amount of pride. The governor of the Bank of England, as important a figure in the design of UK economic policy as Balls and arguably Brown, had been closely involved in the adoption by the Conservative government of Britain's first ever inflation target in the autumn of 1992, as policy was rebuilt out of the wreckage of Britain's exit from the ERM. The idea of inflation targeting, enthusiastically taken up by the Bank, originated from New Zealand's adoption of it four years earlier. Some New Zealand officials were on secondment at the Treasury and, when the search was on for a new policy, were able to advise on the basis of their own first-hand experience. Not all aspects of the New Zealand experiment were imported – it has explicit penalties for a central bank governor who fails to meet the target – but the key aspects were. As the Bank's chief economist, King, a noted academic who in 1981 had joined 363 other university economists in signing a letter of protest against Margaret Thatcher's economic policies, designed the quarterly inflation reports that were the centrepiece of Britain's monetary policy in the run-up to independence. From the autumn of 1992 until the spring of 1997, monetary policy was very different to anything that had gone before. It was transparent and with an explicit and measurable aim, that of keeping inflation (then measured by the retail prices index excluding mortgage interest payments) within a specified range, 1 to 4 per cent, and for it to be in the lower half of that range by the end of the parliament, which at 2.5 per cent in May 1997 it almost was. A monthly meeting between the Bank governor and the chancellor made interest-rate decisions, though the final verdict remained with the politically accountable chancellor. These meetings became known as the 'Ken and Eddie show', after the two main participants, Ken Clarke, the Conservative chancellor, and the late Eddie George (Lord George) from the Bank.

As the years went by, low and stable inflation became unexceptional in Britain. In the early 1990s it was a minor miracle. Most economists thought sterling's downward lurch out of the ERM would be followed by significantly higher inflation as import prices rose. They gave inflation targeting little hope. It was widely seen as a desperate throw of the dice, a strategy to buy some time while the Treasury came up with something else, perhaps even re-entry to the ERM. It did not happen. The spare capacity created by the recession of 1990–92 and a sharp drop in inflation expectations during that recession (explained by some as evidence that Britain had adjusted to the discipline of having to match Germany's inflation performance, it being the benchmark in Europe) kept inflation low. Brown provided the final trigger with his decision in 1997 to grant the Bank operational independence (control over the monetary policy levers to achieve an inflation target set by the government), but much of the preparatory work had been done by King and his colleagues. Independence may have been a bold move for a Labour government – one of its MPs worried out loud about handing over policy to a bunch of 'inflation nutters' – but it was also something of an open goal.

Without that preparatory work under the Conservatives, independence could have taken years.

The fact that it happened at all owed a lot to Alan Greenspan. In February 1997, three months before the Labour landslide, Gordon Brown and Ed Balls travelled to the United States. The trip, which included a Labour fund-raising party in New York organised by Tina Brown and Harold Evans, was partly for fact-finding purposes, partly to raise the international profile of the chancellor-to-be. It was on the Washington leg of the trip that the two discovered real policy gold. After a day of meetings with Greenspan, chairman of the Federal Reserve Board, and Robert Rubin, the then US Treasury secretary, they were driven back to Washington's Dulles airport on 20 February. Brown and Balls realised that the talk at the Fed had been all about monetary policy – interest rates and the control of inflation. At the US Treasury, in contrast, the discussion had been about long-run economic issues such as productivity. Brown knew well the history of previous Labour chancellors, bogged down from the start by sterling crises and a failure to win the confidence of the financial markets. Chancellors of all governments had spent too much time considering and being constantly badgered about interest-rate changes. On arriving back in London he announced new initiatives. Not only would Labour continue to target inflation but it would establish a monetary committee of Bank of England insiders and outside appointees. He tied with it an announcement that a Labour-run Treasury would also have a US-style Council of Economic Advisers. Even then, he still had to win Blair over to the idea of immediate Bank independence. That decision was taken on 28 April, three days before the 1 May general election, though it was not announced until 6 May, five days after Blair was safely in Downing Street.

There was one more element in the decision to give the Bank independence in the area of monetary policy that was to prove controversial later. This was Brown's decision to take banking supervision away from the Bank, hiving it off to a new financial regulator, the Financial Services Authority (FSA). This did not emerge on the day Brown announced Bank independence but two weeks later. Eddie George, the Bank governor, was widely reported to have threatened to resign when told that the Bank was to lose one of its key functions. Later it emerged that George did not disagree with the substance of the decision but its manner, having assured Bank staff there were no immediate implications for its supervisory role from independence. Though at the time relations between Brown and George were frosty – they later improved somewhat – the new chancellor did not set out to embarrass the governor. Brown intended to establish the new FSA somewhat later but was persuaded that for parliamentary reasons (space in the legislative timetable) it was best to do it immediately. Even so, the initial disagreement provided critics of the FSA and the 'tripartite' (Treasury, Bank and FSA) arrangements Brown set up with plenty of ammunition later.

For now, though, and for the next ten years, Bank independence was an essential component in the 'Great Stability', which for policymakers was something like the Holy Grail, and, while it was not confined to Britain, it was a bigger novelty, a greater source of wonderment than elsewhere. 'The behaviour of the UK economy has improved over the past decade, both in terms of its performance and its stability, and that improvement has been more marked in the United Kingdom than in the rest of the G7,' King said in 2007.[5] 'Although structural reforms to the economy over several decades have made the economy better able to respond to economic shocks, the new monetary framework has also played a key role. Inflation expectations have been successfully anchored to the target. And that has meant that cost changes have affected wages and profits rather than prices. As a result, inflation and output growth have been remarkably stable.'

Central bankers are programmed to worry and, to be fair to King, he did not suggest that things had been perfect. He also, in comments that were more prescient than he knew, expressed worries about the money supply. The money supply, having been the centrepiece of economic policy after the election of the Thatcher government in 1979, had gradually been relegated. Even in the City, the number of analysts who pored over the details of the monetary data was in sharp decline. For the Bank governor, this process had gone too far. He did not want to resurrect the monetary targets of the past but he was troubled by the fact that money was being downplayed too much. 'Developments in the banking sector can lead to an expansion of the supply of broad money and credit even while Bank rate remains constant,' he said.[6] 'It is quite possible, in the real world, for there to be unwarranted money supply shocks – whether stimulus or restraint.' Given that the banking system was about to deliver a shuddering and negative money supply shock, he was right to be concerned.

Britain's housing boom

Housing and house prices are national obsessions in Britain. The two most popular house price measures in Britain are those produced by the country's two biggest mortgage lenders, the Nationwide Building Society and the Halifax, now part of the Lloyds Banking Group. In October 2007, before prices started to fall, their average level was £186,044, according to the Nationwide. Compared with their most recent trough, in December 1995, when the average price was £50,798, this represented an increase of more than 260 per cent. After twelve years of rises, prices were more than 3.5 times where they had started. Moreover, this was an era of relatively low inflation. Even adjusted for inflation, prices were more than 2.6 times where they started. There were extenuating circumstances. One was that the starting point for the boom was a significant undervaluation of prices in the mid-1990s. They fell sharply in the recession of the early 1990s before slipping more gently for several years to produce a cumulatively very large 'real', or inflation-adjusted, price fall. Even so, the boom in prices from 1995 to 2007 was the longest and largest on record, bigger than the Lawson–Thatcher era of the 1980s and, indeed, any period of rising prices in the twentieth century, all of which had been brought to a halt by deliberate policy, usually higher interest rates or the imposition of lending controls. Nor was it confined to the Nationwide's statistics. The Halifax's measure peaked at £199,614 at the start of the financial crisis in August 2007, 3.3 times as high, in cash terms, as its low point in 1995.

Neither the Treasury nor the Bank of England was prepared for sustained rises in house prices of this kind, stretching over more than a decade. Brown commented on the rise in house prices that had occurred in the year leading up to his maiden Budget speech in July 1997. Prices had increased by between 7 and 11 per cent, depending on measure, and to the new chancellor this was evidence of the unstable, unbalanced, consumer-led economy he had inherited from his predecessor, Kenneth Clarke. Labour would deliver stability to the economy and, though he did not spell it out, stability for house prices. Why, instead, did prices boom? There are many influences on house prices but one of the most important in Britain is the level of short-term interest rates. There is strong evidence that the key calculation for potential home-buyers is the 'front end' cost of ownership. If they can afford the initial monthly repayment, almost irrespective of the price of the property in relation to their income, they will buy. For existing homeowners on variable-rate mortgages, the level of interest rates is the main mechanism through which the free income of households (the amount left after spending on essentials) is raised or lowered. Mortgage rates are thus a highly sensitive instrument, economically and politically, and, more than in countries such as the United States with a tradition of fixed-rate mortgages, are in the gift of policymakers. When Blair and Brown handed independence to the Bank, they were giving up a very important lever of power. At first, the Bank appeared to be doing its best to ensure that the housing market followed the stability script. At the time of the May 1997 election Bank rate was 6 per cent. By June 1998 it had been raised to 7.5 per cent, its highest for six years and, as it turned out, the highest to date in the independence era. The Bank's untried monetary policy committee had a job to do in establishing its credibility and it did not mind if it upset homeowners and dragged down house prices in the process. By late 1998 house price rises had slowed to near zero and some judged that the mini-boom was over.

Then, however, in what advocates of a more stable housing market and limited price rises would see as the first of a series of fatal diversions, the Bank started cutting interest rates in response to the financial crisis of autumn 1998, the coming together of the Asian, Russian and LTCM (Long-Term Capital Management) crises. For the next few years Bank rate was mostly kept below 5 per cent. Each time the nine members of the Bank's monetary policy committee appeared to be in the middle of a process of tightening policy, which might have cooled the housing market, something else cropped up. These events included the bursting of the dotcom bubble, the 9/11 attacks on America and the mini global recession of 2001 and the uncertainties leading up the beginning of the Iraq war in 2003. All, it could be argued, pushed the Bank into setting interest rates at a lower level than was justified by the state of the domestic economy and, in particular, the housing market. In 2003 rates were reduced to what was then a 50-year low of just 3.5 per cent, a powerful 'buy' signal for the housing market. Moreover, the Bank's strategy of boosting domestic spending, if not the housing market, was deliberate. Though it had long expressed unease at the unbalanced nature of the UK economy, with too big an emphasis on the consumer, when the global economy turned down, it felt obliged to boost domestic demand to maintain economic growth. Had growth weakened too much, inflation would have undershot the official target. The late Eddie George, Lord George, was explicit about this. 'We knew that we were having to stimulate consumer spending,' he said after retiring from the governorship of the Bank in 2003.[7] 'We knew we had pushed it up to levels that couldn't possibly be sustained into the medium and long term.'

Supply, demand and the fundamentals

Throughout the period of rising prices, almost from the moment they started to rise after the slump of the early to mid-1990s, a debate raged about whether they would come crashing down again. The farther prices rose, the more intense the debate was. House prices were what the middle classes talked about when they gathered for dinner parties. Now they became the subject of dozens of websites, of varying quality. Economic journalists quickly became aware that if they wanted to elicit a response from readers, which could quickly turn into an e-mail torrent, they should write about house prices. Debating house prices, either in print, online or in public, became a significant part of the job. My general position during the boom was that, while house prices had clearly risen hugely, and were clearly overvalued on most measures, house prices crashes were rare in Britain. Only in the 1930s and early 1990s had house prices fallen significantly in 'nominal' or money terms, though there had been substantial real price falls in the 1970s and early 1980s. There were good reasons for this. In normal circumstances sellers who do not have to sell will not cut their prices to do so; only when there is economic distress are people forced to do so. So, adapting Keynes's view of wages, house prices were likely to be 'sticky downwards' in the absence of big economic shocks. In Britain it typically took a big, recession-inducing event to produce a large housing market correction or crash, not spontaneous house-price combustion. The big recession-inducing event was, of course, the credit crunch, aimed like a guided missile at a market dependent on the continued supply of mortgage finance for its wellbeing.

That was for later. In the meantime, when house prices failed to follow the general stability story, economists and officials looked for other reasons why prices were rising so strongly in a low-inflation era. There were many. One was low short-term interest rates, variable mortgage rates, described above. Another was the low level of long-term interest rates, perhaps a product of the global glut of savings, perhaps a reflection of inflation stability. Mortgage availability and competition in the mortgage market were other key factors. Financial liberalisation and the entrance of the banks into a mortgage market previously dominated by building societies and local authorities had changed the landscape in the 1980s. Gradually, from the mid-1990s onwards but more particularly from the early 2000s, it changed again. Suddenly, mortgages were on tap. Arranging a mortgage, which in the past had involved a lengthy interview process, could be done in half an hour on the phone, or online. The mortgage industry grew with the entrance of new players, some from overseas, and it became more aggressive. Lenders wanted to lend, and they relaxed their lending criteria. Though data from the Council of Mortgage Lenders showed that the average mortgage-to-income ratio for homebuyers rose only to around 3.3 even for first-time buyers (on average they were borrowing 3.3 times their income), this average concealed a wide range. Many were borrowing on far higher multiples of income and 100 per cent, or more, of the value of their property, and were doing so on very low interest rates, particularly in relation to Bank rate. From 2004 to 2007, in particular, the margin between the interest rate set by the Bank and mortgage rates fell to record lows. That lending, and the source of it, was to lead to many problems later.

In government, the favoured explanation was a straightforward one. Housing was a market and, as in all markets, prices depended on the interaction of supply and demand. Demand was rising because of the annual increase in the number of households in Britain, swelled further after 2004 by the arrival of large numbers of economic migrants from Poland and other so-called accession countries. These joined the European Union in 2004 and their workers were granted immediate employment rights in the UK. Even before that, the government was concerned about the impact of limited housing supply on property affordability. In April 2003 Brown and John Prescott, the deputy prime minister, commissioned Kate Barker, a member of the Bank's MPC and former chief economic adviser at the Confederation of British Industry, to investigate the country's housing needs. Her final report, published in July 2004, was clear on the remedy: more houses. 'I do not believe that continuing at the current rate of housebuilding is a realistic option, unless we are prepared to accept increasing problems of homelessness, affordability and social division, decline in standards of public service delivery and increasing the costs of doing business in the UK – hampering our economic success,' she wrote.[8] For years, additions to the housing stock – new houses and flats – had been running at a slower rate than the rise in the number of households, projected at more than 200,000 a year. To be fair to Barker, she did not argue that the limited supply of new housing was the only factor pushing up prices, though that was probably the interpretation Brown put on it. As in the United States, policymakers were too ready to look for 'fundamental' explanations to justify what with hindsight was an unsustainable price boom.

Buy-to-let and property porn

For critics, there was another fundamental explanation for the boom in house prices. This was that, egged on by an overenthusiastic media, large numbers of people had become speculators in property. This was not just homeowners trading up more frequently and increasing their housing 'equity' at each stage. It was also a new breed of landlords, the buy-to-let investors. In September 2009 it was reported that Fergus and Judith Wilson were quitting the buy-to-let market. The two former maths teachers from Maidstone, Kent, had become landlords by accident in the 1980s when they decided to let out a three-bed semi they were moving from rather than sell it. It was after the slump in prices of the early 1990s that what started on a small scale became a living. In one year, 2003, they bought 180 houses, mainly modest two- and three-bedroomed family houses in Ashford and Maidstone. At its peak, their property portfolio consisted of 900 houses and was worth £250 million, and, after borrowings, they had a £70 million fortune, most of which survived the fall in the market. 'The time is right for us to go,' said Fergus Wilson, announcing his retirement from the buy-to-let business.[9] 'It will break my heart to say goodbye to all the houses we have but you cannot take them to the grave with you.'

The Wilsons were unusual in the scale of their buy-to-let activity but they were part of a national trend. Prior to the 1990s, the private rented sector in Britain had been shrinking for decades, initially a product of rent controls and an increase in the building of council houses, then the rise in owner-occupation. Most remaining landlords were either businesses or relatively wealthy individuals. Buy-to-let landlords were different. Typically they were small-scale private investors who took out mortgages to buy properties with the explicit aim of letting them out. The fact that they could do so was made possible after the launch of specialised buy-to-let mortgages in July 1996, following pressure from the Association of Residential Letting Agents. It was a hugely successful initiative. By September 2007 there were nearly a million such mortgages (991,600), with a combined value of £116 billion. Critics, including frustrated first-time buyers, argued that the activities of this new breed of landlords were creating a 'frozen out' generation. Buy-to-let landlords, with the connivance of the mortgage industry, were depriving young people of access to the housing market in two ways. Their demand was pushing up prices and they concentrated their purchases in the kind of properties, flats and small houses, favoured by first-time buyers. Though there was plenty of anecdotal evidence backing up such claims, the small number of detailed studies carried out suggested the effect of buy-to-let on prices was relatively modest. The National Housing and Planning Advice Unit, a body set up to advise the government following the Barker Review, reported in February 2008 that buy-to-let had lifted prices but by a relatively modest amount. 'BTL has made a small contribution to house price inflation in recent years but rising incomes, low and stable interest rates, household growth and limited supply are much more important factors,' it said.[10]

Almost as much as buy-to-let, the media was widely blamed for stoking up the housing boom. This was despite the fact that crash predictions were fully reported throughout the boom, though they may have lost their impact over time when the market carried on rising. Television programmes on housing, labelled by critics 'property porn', were also accused of stoking the boom. Channel 4's *Location, Location, Location*, presented by Kirstie Allsopp and Phil Spencer, was one. *Property Ladder*, presented by Sarah Beeny, was another Channel 4 programme, featuring amateurs who renovated and developed properties for profit. As with most television programmes, however, they reflected trends rather than creating them. Both series began in 2001, five years into the long boom in house prices and five years after the first specialised buy-to-let mortgages had come on the market. They and similar programmes may have increased interest in the housing market but people in Britain have rarely needed much persuasion where property is concerned.

In the autumn of 2007, after long years of rises, house prices began to fall; at first gradually and then very sharply, eventually dropping by around 20 per cent from their peak. For many in Britain, this was the most visible manifestation of the credit crunch. It was clearly a direct result of it. Falling house prices and slumping consumer confidence went hand in hand, a mirror image of the boom years. Suddenly, instead of 'housing equity withdrawal' – money being taken out of the housing market for other purposes – housing became a drag on the economy. For eighteen months house prices fell relentlessly, before stabilising and starting to rise in the spring of 2009.

Targeting inflation – triumph or disaster?
Inflation targeting changed the nature of monetary policy in Britain. Under targeting, inflation was more stable than for many decades. That

stability, and the fact that it occurred alongside continuous economic growth and falling unemployment, did not exempt inflation targeting from criticism, even before the crisis. Such criticisms became louder when the economy broke decisively out of its apparently stable pattern. Critics argued that the policy had failed at the first serious sound of gunfire, though Bank officials pointed out that it had steered the economy through several potential crises, including the Asian financial crisis, the bursting of the dotcom bubble and the effects of the 9/11 attacks on America. For the most trenchant critics the policy had been instrumental in causing the crisis. Lord Saatchi, the Conservative peer and chairman of the Centre for Policy Studies (CPS), in a CPS paper, 'The myth of inflation targeting', claimed it was 'the largest policy failure of our generation'. To find a culprit for the world's worst postwar financial crisis, one did not have to look at bankers, regulators, borrowers or anybody else. It was the fault of inflation targeting. 'Their mistake was to believe what they were told,' wrote Saatchi.[11]

> They were lulled into a false sense of security by an idea – that if policy makers could maintain low inflation (and more important, low inflation expectations), then all good things would follow – growth, employment, prosperity, stability. Unfortunately, the idea turned out to be a myth – the largest policy failure of our generation ... By first creating the false impression that low inflation meant financial stability, and then measuring the wrong kind of inflation, the inflation targeting policy encouraged the view that it was safe to borrow, safe to invest. The Myth led bankers to lend more, traders to risk more, homeowners to borrow more, regulators to relax more, and politicians to boast more – about the end of boom and bust. When the Myth collapsed, it took all of us down with it – academics and auditors, bankers and bakers, economists and electricians. We all went into the dark.

Though Saatchi's comments were extreme and not taken very seriously, they included two common criticisms of inflation targeting in the UK. The first was that since 2003 the Bank had been required to target a measure of inflation, the consumer prices index, that nobody recognised and, crucially, did not include most housing costs, including house prices and mortgage rates. The Bank was initially tasked in 1997 with targeting the familiar retail prices index (RPI), though excluding mortgage interest payments. This target, called RPIX, worked well, and the decision to change it, by Brown, was not popular at the Bank. 'When defending a free kick from David Beckham, you don't expect someone behind you to move the goalposts,' said King.[12] There was little evidence, however, that the change in the target had a significant impact on the Bank's interest-rate decisions. The second criticism was that the Bank should have done more to puncture the house-price boom, by raising interest rates even when its target measure of inflation was comfortably under control, a strategy known as 'leaning against the wind'. Spencer Dale, the Bank's chief economist in 2009, responded directly to the argument that decision-makers should have deliberately aimed off the inflation target if, by doing so, they could have prevented house prices rising so much, leaning against the wind. 'The practical difficulty of implementing a policy of "leaning against the wind", where the main policy instrument is short-term interest rates, should not be underestimated,' he said.[13] 'If, as policymakers, we were successful in preventing a bubble from inflating, it might appear as if we were responding to phantom concerns. The bubble or imbalance would be nowhere to be seen, but interest rates would be higher, inflation would undershoot the inflation target and we would appear to have inflicted unnecessary economic hardship.' It was a good argument. When house prices start building momentum, it takes more than an interest-rate nudge to slow them down.

Inflation is not enough

Though central bankers had a reasonable response to most of the criticisms, they could not escape a central fact. The stability created by targeting inflation both enabled asset prices – mainly housing and commercial property – to boom, while concealing the build-up of enormous instability below the surface. The Bank of England's monetary policy committee went from congratulating itself, and being congratulated, for presiding over the most stable period in Britain's modern economic history to firefighting the biggest economic and financial conflagration in decades. Ahead of the crisis, one particular development should have rung more alarm bells than it did. During 2006, the rate of growth of the money supply accelerated sharply. The M4 money measure of 'broad' money – cash plus most bank and building society deposits – was a direct descendant of Sterling M3, targeted by the Thatcher government in the 1980s. Perhaps because of this, or perhaps because the acceleration of M4 to its fastest growth rate since 1990 did not chime with other statistics showing inflation stable and growth steady, its significance was played down. Minutes of the meetings of the MPC during 2006 show that discussions about the money supply were cursory. The Bank had an inflation target and the question that mattered was whether this rapid growth in the money supply would be inflationary. The Bank, after deciding that it mainly reflected lending within the financial system, by banks to their subsidiaries, decided it would not be. The question of whether that lending was worrying in itself, because it suggested risky and unsustainable developments in the financial system, did not long detain the Bank's interest-rate setters.

Paul Tucker, then the Bank's executive director for financial markets, was more concerned about monetary developments than most of his colleagues. Even he, however, concluded that there was probably not too much to worry about. 'As has recently attracted a good deal of attention, UK broad money is up around 15 per cent on a year ago, and more than 25 per cent since the beginning of 2005 – much more than elsewhere in the G7,' he said in a speech in 2006.[14] 'Of this increase, almost half – or around £140 billion – is accounted for by the money holdings of so-called Other Financial Corporations (OFCs). Central bankers have to ask whether that represents a threat to inflation and stability or, rather, a shift in the demand for money that is a symptom of structural change in the financial system.' After mulling it over, he decided structural change was probably the explanation and that 'essentially, some types of non-bank financial intermediation have become more significant, and seem to have entailed higher money holdings on the definitions currently employed' and 'if so, recent OFC money growth does not of itself obviously have malign implications for money spending and inflation'.

Seen through the prism of the inflation target, there was no problem. Looked at in the round, there may have been.

Perhaps the most honest subsequent response was provided by Sir John Gieve, a deputy governor of the Bank of England whose career at the Bank was brought to a premature end by the crisis. Having joined at the beginning of 2006, he left at the end of February 2009, after pressure from the Treasury. After leaving the Bank, he was more open about the limitations of inflation targeting. In a speech to the David Hume Institute a few months after he left the Bank, he admitted that what was seen to have worked flawlessly from the early 1990s to 2006 was exposed by the crisis. 'The prevailing wisdom – which seemed to be confirmed by the LTCM [Long-Term Capital Management] crisis and dotcom bubble – was that it was difficult to identify bubbles in advance, probably counterproductive to try to prick them early, and – most important – possible to limit any damage to the wider economy if or when they did burst,' he said.[15] 'The last two years have shown the limitations of the approach … It had little place for the long build-up of global imbalances and of the credit and asset price bubbles in the West which have exploded with such devastating force … We have learned the hard way that we need to prevent the build-up of chronic imbalances and asset price bubbles; mopping up after they burst won't do.'

This is anticipating what will come later but it underlines an essential point. It is possible for the economy to appear stable for very long periods, as Britain was, even when dangers are building. During those periods, not only does confidence build but it becomes hard to argue for change. If it ain't broke, why fix it? Only after the crisis broke would it become clear that Britain's economic and financial framework needed fixing.

Spending fit to bust

If the inflation target was left bruised by the financial crisis, the other key plank of Labour's macroeconomic framework, the fiscal rules, were destroyed by it. One important issue is whether any fiscal arrangements could have done anything about the lurch into record deficit that occurred from 2007 onwards. This, according to David Cameron, who became Conservative Party leader in 2006, was Labour's key error, of 'failing to fix the roof while the sun was shining'. 'It's easy to forget that we actually entered this recession with one of the highest budget deficits in the developed world too,' he said in 2009.[16] 'That is Labour's record. Borrowing in the boom – so when the tough times did come, they had run out of money with which to help people.' Brown was accused of gross fiscal irresponsibility, of a devil-may-care attitude to public and private debt. It had all started so very differently. For two to three years after the 1997 election victory, some Labour MPs and many of the party's supporters openly wondered what the victory was for, so fiscally conservative was the man running the economy. Brown had determined that he would be tied to the mast of his fiscal rules, ignoring siren calls from inside and outside his own party. The first rule was the 'golden rule' of balancing the current budget over the cycle, in other words borrowing only for investment. The second, the sustainable investment rule, was to keep the public sector's net debt below 40 per cent of GDP. The rules, while self-imposed, and self-policed (though the Treasury checked its assumptions twice a year with the National Audit Office), were intended to be met.

This meant, initially at least, higher taxes and no spending bonanza for the public sector. Brown in 1997 had inherited public spending plans described by Kenneth Clarke, his Conservative predecessor, as 'eye-wateringly tight'. He raised taxes in his first budget, including a £5.2 billion windfall tax on the privatised utilities and a £5 billion annual 'raid' on pensions through the abolition of the dividend tax credit. He also increased personal taxes by stealth, partly by abolishing well-established reliefs such as the married couples' allowance and mortgage interest relief. The aim was clear. Brown and Tony Blair had learned from the history of previous Labour governments, which, on taking office, typically relaxed government spending, thus cheering supporters in the public sector unions. The problem with spending first and asking questions later was that it usually ran into financial trouble, as the devaluation crisis in the 1960s and the IMF crisis in the 1970s clearly showed. So Brown went about it in the opposite way. First he raised the taxes and squeezed spending, to provide the cushion of very healthy public finances. These were helped by the April 2000 auction of third-generation (3G) mobile phone licences, which raised an astonishing £22.5 billion; £380 per head of the UK population. Then, and only then, did Brown relax spending. He had been prudent for a purpose (the title Brown gave to his 2000 Budget document) and that purpose was a prolonged increase in spending. The spending increases announced in the 2000 Budget, partly foreshadowed in Tony Blair's January interview that year with Sir David Frost – in which he pledged to raise health spending in Britain to the EU average – took Britain into new territory. It was also an example of the often destructive nature of the Blair–Brown relationship. Prior to Blair's admission on Frost's Sunday morning television sofa, Brown had been happy with the commitment simply to raise National Health Service spending to the European average. After it, he wanted to go significantly farther, and did.

In the case of the NHS, founded in 1948, Brown delivered the biggest sustained increases in its history, averaging 6.6 per cent a year in real terms from 2000 to 2010. 'In many ways the NHS in England is more robust and better prepared than ever to deal with the downturn,' wrote Niall Dickson,[17] chief executive of the King's Fund, a health charity, in 2009, ahead of an expected future squeeze on spending. Health was not alone. Calculations by the Institute for Fiscal Studies[18] showed that overall government spending rose by 4 per cent in real terms between 1999/2000 and 2007/08, with the increase split between a huge 16.4 per cent annual rise in investment spending (schools, hospitals, roads, etc.) and a 3.6 per cent average increase in current spending. The increases for health were outstripped by transport, 8.4 per cent a year. Education, 5.4 per cent, law and order (the Home Office), 4.8 per cent, and housing, 4.3 per cent, were also significant winners.

To put these rises into perspective, the Treasury's estimate of the long-run rate of growth of the economy, its trend rate, was 2.75 per cent a year. Over a sustained period, therefore, public spending was being increased at a much faster rate than growth in the economy's productive potential. To those looking to a Labour government to make good what they saw as years of neglect for public services, it was impressive. The question was whether it was ever affordable. Though the crisis marked the formal abandonment of Brown's fiscal rules, the writing had been on the wall for some time. With hindsight, the turning point came in November 2002, when Brown was forced to announce big increases in public borrowing. The episode, which gave him some of his worst headlines (up to then), was the moment when 'prudent' Brown started to take risks with the public finances. Prudence was replaced by a steady stream of upward revisions to the official borrowing forecasts. Even with the economy growing strongly, the budget deficit was high, though a fraction of what it was to lurch into later. Sensible management of the public finances would not have prevented the swing into deficit but would have helped persuade the financial markets that it was a temporary aberration. Borrowing should have been lower.

Thanking the City

Before he left the Treasury, Brown had one bit of unfinished business. His relations with Britain's financial district – the City's Square Mile and Canary Wharf – had not always been smooth. While bankers and brokers applauded some of his policies, in particular his 1997 decision to give the Bank of England control over interest rates, an air of suspicion persisted. They suspected his instincts were to tax, redistribute and regulate, and many were concerned about the large-scale increases in public spending he had presided over. One of his first policies, introduced at much the same time as Bank independence, had been to remove the favourable tax treatment previously accorded to company dividends. This became known as the infamous £5 billion annual 'raid' on pension funds, for which many in the City had never forgiven him. Brown, in turn, took some time to overcome his doubts. He suspected that most people working in the financial markets were instinctively Conservative, and he was too much of a student of history not to be aware that, sooner or later, every previous Labour government had seen the markets turn against it, sometimes with devastating consequences. On a trivial level, Brown refused to wear evening dress when addressing the annual Mansion House dinner (the Lord Mayor's Banquet for Bankers and Merchants of the City of London), his aides arguing that it was a working occasion and, as such, he was wearing his working clothes.

By 2007, however, such hostilities had been forgotten. Brown, while sticking with the lounge suit, gave his final Mansion House speech as chancellor on 20 June, a week before becoming prime minister. 'Over the ten years that I have had the privilege of addressing you as chancellor, I have been able year by year to record how the City of London has risen by your efforts, ingenuity and creativity to become a new world leader,' he said,[19] before listing its achievements. They included a 40 per cent market share in international equity trading, 30 per cent of global foreign exchange and first place in a league table of the top 50 financial centres in the world. It was nothing less than 'an era that history will record as the beginning of a new golden age for the City of London'. Nor was this success merely significant for the City itself. Its achievements reflected the ambitions Brown had for the country as a whole. 'The financial services sector in Britain, and the City of London at the centre of it, is a great example of a highly skilled, high value added, talent driven industry that shows how we can excel in a world of global competition. Britain needs more of the vigour, ingenuity and aspiration that you already demonstrate that is the hallmark of your success,' he said.[20]

Such words were to return to haunt him. The picture painted by Brown, of an economy apparently immune from the forces that in the past had generated extreme turbulence, was by 2007 free of any caveats. Boom and bust, it seemed, had been consigned to the history books. The City, meanwhile, was the test bed of a new type of British economy, bursting with talent and innovation, meritocratic and fiercely competitive. London was where the world came to do business. The rest of the economy could and should take a leaf out of its book. Building on this success was Brown's agenda for his premiership. Events, of course, proved otherwise.

5

Subprime Follies

In the early months of 2006, there was plenty to occupy the thoughts of Americans. There was relief when the hurricane season came to end, without a rerun of the Hurricane Katrina disaster, which a few months earlier had brought devastation to New Orleans. Investors were cheered by the Dow Jones industrial average rising above 11,000. From the Middle East there was a rising US casualty count in Iraq and the worrying development of Mahmoud Ahmadinejad, the Iranian president, announcing that his country had successfully enriched uranium. The Pittsburgh Steelers beat the Seattle Seahawks in the Super Bowl. Quietly, however, something else was happening that, for the next three or four years, was going to have a more profound effect. The country's housing boom was coming to an end and it was doing so quite abruptly. According to the Case-Shiller home price index, published each month by Standard & Poor's, house prices in America peaked in the first quarter of 2006, before beginning a gentle slip that quickly turned into a full-blown slide. At first it was far from obvious that a turning point had been reached in a trend that had seen US house prices rise in every quarter since late 1992, during which time the value of the average American home had increased by more than 150 per cent. A turning point was reached in 2006, however, and there were solid reasons why. From mid-2003 to mid-2004 the Federal Reserve under Alan Greenspan had kept short-term interest rates, the Fed Funds rate, at just 1 per cent, their lowest for decades. Gradually, however, the Fed moved towards a more normal interest rate as worries about the economy subsided. By 2006 the rate was moving to 5.25 per cent. For those who believed the era of ultra-low interest rates was permanent it was an abrupt awakening. The sheer scale of the house price rises over the preceding period had, in addition, left potential buyers seriously stretched. Estimates of the overvaluation of the US housing market varied, but the International Monetary Fund suggested that by 2005 prices were 10–15 per cent higher than justified by fundamental factors. In the light of the subsequent correction, that looked like a conservative estimate.

Any fall in US house prices was unusual. America's housing market is highly regionalised, so booms in certain regions and states can coexist with busts elsewhere, making it harder for national house prices to fall. Regional busts were common, large national ones rare, the previous one dating back to the Great Depression. At first the correction that began in 2006 appeared to be following a similar pattern, with California in the grip of a severe adjustment. Where California was leading, both in foreclosures and prices, other states and regions were to follow. While prices nationally slipped only modestly in 2006, soon what many people had thought was impossible was happening before their eyes. Home prices nationally dropped by 9 per cent during 2007 and by a further 18 per cent in 2008.

Irrational exuberance in America

Robert Shiller, the Yale economist described by his publishers as 'the sage of New Haven', came to prominence with the publication of his book *Irrational Exuberance* in 2000. Though Shiller had warned of the unsustainability of the stock market boom of the 1990s for some time, his book, which took its title from a phrase used by Greenspan in a famous 1996 speech, established him as an economic voice to be listened to. It came out at a time when stock market euphoria about technology stocks was at its height, the peak of the dotcom boom, when Wall Street was promoting a new era for the US economy, with the support of many leading economists. Shiller warned that the boom in the share prices of technology stocks, and in the wider market, had no basis in economic fundamentals. It was, instead, a speculative bubble of the kind seen time and time again throughout economic history. Each time people had argued that this time it was different and each time they had been wrong. What was true of railway stocks in the Victorian era in Britain was true of technology stocks in America in the late 1990s. People were buying on hope rather than economic reality. When the dotcom bubble burst in 2001, Shiller was hailed as a prophet, guaranteeing him air time on Bloomberg TV, CNBC and the other financial channels.

Even so, when a second edition of *Irrational Exuberance* appeared in 2005, warning of a real estate bubble in America as troubling as the one in the stock market a few years earlier, he was still something of a voice in the wilderness. He wrote that the consequences of real estate values continuing to rise and then falling back sharply would be a steep increase in personal bankruptcies, which could lead to failures for financial institutions, hitting personal and business confidence hard and threatening a recession, possibly a worldwide one. That, however, was a long way from being the mainstream view. In the year that the second edition of Shiller's *Irrational Exuberance* was published, Ben Bernanke was chairman of George W. Bush's Council of Economic Advisers. On 20 October 2005 he testified to Congress on the White House's view of the economic outlook, four days before being appointed to run the Fed with effect from early 2006. In the autumn of 2005 the main economic concern was the impact of Hurricane Katrina, which had devastated New Orleans in August and pushed oil prices to record highs because of the damage to oil installations in the Gulf of Mexico. There were also concerns about overheating in the housing market. Such concerns, said Bernanke,[1] were misplaced:

> House prices have risen by nearly 25 per cent over the past two years. Although speculative activity has increased in some areas, at a national level these price increases largely reflect strong economic fundamentals, including robust growth in jobs and incomes, low mortgage rates, steady rates of household formation, and factors that limit the expansion of housing supply in some areas. House prices are unlikely to continue rising at current rates. However, as reflected in many private-sector forecasts ... a moderate cooling in the housing market, should one occur, would not be inconsistent with the economy continuing to grow at or near its potential next year.

So, while Shiller was warning of an unsustainable bubble in US house prices, the main worry for the chairman-designate of the Federal Reserve was that slower growth in the value of housing would slow the economy. Such a difference of views was fundamental and reflected different ways of analysing the economy. Many economists have had to accept that their inability to spot the crisis coming reflected serious shortcomings in their models, something that will be examined in more detail later in the book. According to Shiller, however, it was staring them in the face all the time.

Bubble mentality

How do we understand bubbles and booms? Why do people apparently behave irrationally when, after the episode is over, they are perfectly capable of recognising that irrationality? The study of financial manias and panics is almost as old as investment itself. For Shiller, explaining America's housing bubble, the key was what he described as a kind of social contagion, which leads to boom or 'new era' thinking becoming the accepted norm. As he described it in a later book, *The Subprime Solution*:[2]

> Every disease has a contagion rate (the rate at which it is spread from person to person) and a removal rate (the rate at which individuals recover from or succumb to the illness and so are no longer contagious). If the contagion rate exceeds the removal rate by a necessary amount, an epidemic begins … So it is in the economic and social environment. Sooner or later, some factor boosts the infection rate sufficiently above the removal rate for an optimistic view of the market to become widespread. There is an escalation in public knowledge of the arguments that would seem to support that view, and soon the epidemic spirals up and out of control.

To demonstrate that his views on social contagion were more than mere supposition, Shiller and his long-term collaborator Karl Case – they developed the Case-Shiller index of house prices in major US cities, which subsequently told the story of the housing bust in all its gory detail – carried out some market research. They asked San Francisco homebuyers what their expectations of house price increases were for the following ten years. The median expectation was 9 per cent, so as many people expected annual increases above 9 per cent as below it, while the mean was 14 per cent, showing that price expectations were heavily skewed to the upside. Included in the sample were people who genuinely believed that home prices in their part of California could rise by 50 per cent a year. Shiller's social contagion has another important element, which could be characterised as suspension of disbelief. Even people who know instinctively that home prices cannot rise indefinitely for 9, 14 or 50 per cent a year begin to doubt themselves when so many other people appear to believe it. What behavioural economists describe as 'information cascades' occur, in which people disregard their own information in favour of the general view. Any caution is squashed in the stampede. Extreme views, whether they are excessively optimistic or pessimistic, become the norm.

Economists will debate whether US housing was a true bubble, with market participants driven by unrealistic price expectations and interested only in short-term gains, or whether something different but no less dangerous was happening. The alternative view is that it was a boom brought about by the interaction of a set of specific and unusual conditions but not necessarily a speculative bubble. Homebuyers, in other words, were what economists would call 'price takers', buying at high prices because as individuals there is no alternative to paying the market rate and, crucially, because they were able to obtain the mortgage finance, on affordable terms. In practical terms, the difference between a bubble and a boom may be semantic. In both cases, the situation is unsustainable. Equally important, however, may be the fact that in all bubbles/booms, the market's ability to go on rising, even when there are warnings of its imminent demise, has the effect of adding to confidence and the belief that 'this time it is different'.

In 2002, John Cassidy, a writer with the *New Yorker*, visited the Long Island suburb of Levittown, built in the years immediately after the Second World War to offer attractive, affordable housing. Coincidentally, it was where Alan Greenspan first set up home half a century earlier after marrying his first wife. For $58 a month, just under $8,000 in total, the developer Levitt & Sons offered 'the whole works', fully fitted, ranch-style houses built on farmland, housing for ordinary people looking to move out from the city, or step up. By the time Cassidy visited, $8,000 was a distant memory for Levittown prices, and so was $200,000. Prices had dropped to that level in the aftermath of the bursting of the dotcom bubble and the share-price crash on the technology-heavy NASDAQ. The 9/11 attacks on New York and Washington sapped confidence further. Even so, by 2002 prices were between $275,000 and $300,000, and rising strongly, surprising even local real estate agents. The result was that those who wanted to buy were forced to stretch themselves to do so. As Cassidy wrote:[3] 'By and large, the kinds of people buying houses in Levittown are the same as they have always been: cops, fire-fighters, janitors, retail workers, and others for whom fifty thousand dollars a year is a good salary. But now many of them have to apply for jumbo mortgages – loans of more than three hundred thousand dollars – which used to be reserved for the well-to-do.' What this meant, according to local real estate agent Richard Dallow, was that for a typical couple to keep up the mortgage payments and other housing costs, it not only required a joint income but, in many cases, second 'moonlighting' jobs. The days when such houses were affordable on a single breadwinner's income were long gone.

Cassidy spoke to economists, including Frank Nothaft, chief economist at Freddie Mac, one of the two government-sponsored mortgage finance and guarantee companies (the other being Fannie Mac). Nothaft said the rise in US home prices was largely driven by fundamentals, including low mortgage rates, the limited stock of new homes for sale, rising housing demand from immigrants and so-called 'echo boomers' – the children of baby boomers who were old enough to buy homes and start families of their own. These fundamentals would offer support to housing, even at these elevated price levels. Nothaft expected the rate of US house-price inflation to slow but nothing worse. 'We are not going to see the price of single-family homes fall,' he said. 'It isn't going happen.' It did not, at least not for several years. Part of Cassidy's concern was what would happen to the 'ordinary Joe' buyers in Levittown and places like it when mortgage rates rose. Thanks to Alan Greenspan and his colleagues at the Federal Reserve, that did not happen. In 2003 the Fed cut short-term interest rates, the Fed Funds rate, to just 1 per cent, the lowest since 1958. Though US mortgage rates reflect long-term interest rates, the effect was to lower rates for all maturities.

In other respects, however, the piece was remarkably prescient. He quoted William Poole, president of the Federal Reserve Bank of St Louis, who warned that problems at Freddie Mac and Fannie Mae, because of their sheer size, could cause huge disruption in credit markets. It was probably the first explicit warning that if the US housing market did fall, the effects would go well beyond housing. As Cassidy put it:[4] 'If Fannie or Freddie did get into serious trouble, the repercussions would dwarf the problems at Long-Term Capital Management in 1998, when buyers and sellers withdrew from the credit markets and the financial system almost seized up.' Fannie or Freddie did get into trouble, and in September 2008, a week before the collapse of Lehman Brothers, had to be bailed out by the American government. Well before then, however, the writing was on the wall.

The lessons of history

Shiller had another important string to his bow in determining that US housing was in a bubble. This was that from about 1997, just over halfway through Bill Clinton's eight-year stint as president, house prices had begun to move outside the range of previous experience. Though there was plenty of anecdotal evidence that something different was happening in housing markets across America, proving it was not so easy. In particular, he discovered that reliable long-run data on house prices was not readily available. So Shiller put together his own long-run price index, dating back to 1890, by linking together previously available but separate series and by getting his research assistants to fill in the gaps by extracting price information from old newspapers. What he found was that real house prices, adjusted for consumer price inflation, had shown at best a gentle upward trend for most of the twentieth century. The level of real house prices, having fallen in the inter-war years, rose steadily in the 50 years after the Second World War, but only in line with building costs and population growth. These appeared to be the important determinants of real house prices; the fundamentals. From 1997 to 2006, however, house prices broke free from these fundamentals, rising, as Shiller put it, like a rocket taking off. Real house prices rose by 85 per cent over the period, easily the biggest sustained rise in nearly 120 years of US house-price history. Individual cities and states had experienced such price booms in the past. The difference this time was that very many cities and states rose together. This was the biggest-ever US national house-price boom.

While Shiller was constructing his data to show that US housing was out of line with all previous experience, others took a different view. Housing bulls in America had two important strings to their bow. The first was the fact that, with the exception of the very special conditions of the Depression era, there had not been a national housing crash in the United States. Not only that but economic conditions were unusually benign, with mortgage rates low and set to remain so. Even a conventional recession did not appear to be on the horizon, let alone a rerun of the Great Depression. Equally powerful, for the housing bulls, were the 'fundamentals' of persistently strong demand for housing, partly based on demographics. One of the most prominent bulls was David Lereah, chief economist at the National Association of Realtors (NAR). Lereah, whose 2005 book, *Are You Missing the Real Estate Boom?*, came out at the height of US housing fever, was a true believer, investing in his own real estate portfolio. Articulate and telegenic, he became a regular fixture on American television. Interviewed[5] by *Realtor* magazine, he explained why everybody should try to get a piece of the rise in home prices. 'It's never been simpler to buy and sell real estate, and there's never been a better market for it,' he said.

> We're in the middle of a boom, not at the end of one. That opens the
> door for consumers to make real estate investments just as much a part
> of their financial planning as stocks and bonds ... We'll continue to
> see strong demand for properties thanks to a confluence of once-in-a-
> lifetime demographic trends: baby boomers in their peak earning years;
> their children, the echo boomers – also a huge age cohort – starting to

form their own households; retired people living longer and healthier lives; and immigrant households – a record number over the last 30 years – now ready for homeownership. When you combine these factors with the increasing ease of buying and selling thanks to technological advances and an array of mortgage products, you have the recipe for a long-term boom.

Lereah became notorious as the biggest cheerleader for the US housing boom, though the views he expressed were echoed by many others, including America's most senior policymakers. In February 2009 he was named[6] by *Time* magazine as one of the 25 people to blame for the financial crisis. What is the role of those, like Lereah, who talk up an already booming market? Some would argue that if enough people have already been infected by Shiller's 'social contagion', then the role of pundits and experts, particularly those speaking on behalf of vested interests, is limited. Others would say that Lereah and others like him were instrumental in creating bubble conditions, removing any sense of doubt from buyers and encouraging people with limited experience to invest in residential property. For one particular group of people, as we shall see shortly, that proved to be disastrous. There is another issue, however, related to the role of realtors in America, and estate agents or real estate brokers in Britain and other countries. Who determines the market price for housing? Buyers and sellers have an idea of what properties should change hands for but, in a fast-moving market, that view is heavily influenced by the agents. Add to that the fact that the incentive for agents is to maximise the price for which a property is sold, because their fee is based on a percentage of the transaction, and their role is more than that of the dispassionate broker. In a rising market, they get business by promising vendors a higher price than their rivals can obtain. This competitive bidding process feeds house-price inflation. Even if Lereah was not to blame, members of organisations like the NAR and their equivalents elsewhere helped stoke up the bubble. In a falling market, the incentives for agents run in the opposite direction. They are desperate for sales and commission and know that the best way of securing them is by persuading sellers to reduce prices aggressively.

The agent can put up with the reduced commission on a lower price as long as he has some cash flow coming in to keep the business ticking over. The role of agents is to extend market extremes, extending the scale of both rises and falls.

The rise and fall of the ninjas

In 2006 Aquila Eberhardt, then a 27-year-old single mother living in Slavic Village, Cleveland, noticed an advertisement in a local newspaper offering mortgages to potential borrowers with poor credit histories. She fitted the bill perfectly. Living on social security benefits of $1,400 a month, she had not worked for three years and struggled to keep up with her credit-card payments. Her savings were just $1,300. Eberhardt was, however, apparently a perfect candidate for a mortgage industry keen to lend. Wooed with the offer of a night in a nice hotel, she soon had an offer of a mortgage of nearly $104,000, enough to buy her a three-bedroomed house in Slavic Village, named after Czech and Polish immigrants who came to the area in the nineteenth century to work in Cleveland's wool and steel mills. As in many such areas, industrial decline had taken its toll on Slavic Village, which had serious problems of crime and drug abuse. By 2006, though, it appeared to be on the up again, partly as a result of rising home ownership. Eberhardt's first shock was to discover that her monthly mortgage payments were nearly $700 a month, rather than the $400 the real estate agent had said. There were more shocks to come. When Dominic Rushe of the *Sunday Times* visited her in February 2008,[7] her house needed repairs that she could not afford. Many of her neighbours, who had found themselves in a similar position, had moved out and their houses were boarded up. She was facing imminent eviction.

Eberhardt was the classic 'ninja' borrower of the subprime crisis; she had 'no income, no job and no assets', yet was allowed to take out a mortgage. The promise of an easy-to-afford mortgage and a better life had taken just two years to turn sour. Given that her problems were apparent with the arrival on the mat of the first mortgage demand, she did not even enjoy the period of grace of those on initial low 'teaser' rates, where the full extent of the borrowing burden became apparent only later. Though the idea of a ninja loan now sounds like a joke in bad taste it was invented by one American lender, HCL Finance, during the housing boom years, and marketed as such. HCL also advertised itself as the 'home of the "no doc" loan', in other words mortgages for people who could not provide documentation proving income or assets. Astonishingly, perhaps, in the summer of 2009, the California-based lender was still boasting on its website that it specialised in 'minimum documentation loans, i.e. no income, no job and no bank deposit verification loans'. Not all subprime borrowers, of course, fitted into the ninja category, or were obliged to take out so-called 'liar' loans, where, as the name suggests, they invented their own income in order to qualify for a loan. Some of those in the subprime category lacked a credit history for genuine reasons. Many others, however, should not have been allowed to borrow, and the consequences of allowing them to do so were devastating, as Rushe discovered. Slavic Village had street after street of boarded-up houses, their roofs caving in, collapsed balconies hanging from the fronts of buildings. The rats and vandals had moved in.

This was not an isolated example. Across America, from the 'rust belt' of America's industrial north-east to towns bordering the mangrove swamps of Florida, the bursting of the subprime bubble was all too evident. Towns and cities vied for an unhappy honour, that of being America's foreclosure capital. In mid-2008 Stockton in California's Central Valley, a city of just over a quarter of a million people, saw repossession papers filed by the banks on one in every 25 of its homes in the second quarter of that year. The locations may have been different but the story was essentially the same. Many people had been wrongly lured into home ownership, many of them traditionally dismissed as 'trailer trash'. For hundreds of thousands, it was their first experience of the American dream of home ownership. That dream quickly turned into the worst of nightmares.

Blaming Washington

For some economists, particularly American free market economists, the subprime crisis provided a living example of what happens when politicians interfere in the economic process. Their thesis is that the

crisis was the direct result of policies intended to increase home ownership in general, and home ownership among low-income and minority
groups in particular. The seeds of the disaster, on this view, were sown
as long ago as the 1970s, with the passing of the Community Reinvest-
ment Act (CRA) under Jimmy Carter in 1977, supplemented by the
policies of subsequent presidents, particularly Bill Clinton but also
George W. Bush. One of the most articulate exponents of this view was
the veteran economist Thomas Sowell, the Rose and Milton Friedman
Senior Research Fellow at Stanford University's Hoover Institution.
Sowell, Harlem-born and African-American, had little sympathy for
the argument that government intervention was justified because of
systematic bias by lenders against blacks. In his book *The Housing Bust*,
he wrote[8] that 'the idea that lenders would be offended by receiving
monthly mortgage payment cheques in the mail from blacks should at
least give us pause'. He also noted that studies in the early 1990s by the
Federal Reserve, which were used by proponents of political intervention in the mortgage market, contained important caveats and warned
that it was not possible from the data to determine whether there was
unfairness in lending practices. Rather, the research showed that a wide
variety of factors contributed to the success of an individual's mortgage
application, including wealth, income and security of employment. In
any case, was it discrimination to decline a borrower a loan, when to do
so could land unsuitable applicants with huge problems and the agonies
of foreclosure later?

If political intervention was based on a false or naive reading of
the data, how important was it in the subsequent subprime boom and
bust? For Sowell and others of a similar viewpoint, it was very significant indeed, and it is worth rehearsing their arguments. It may seem
strange to blame a law passed three decades earlier for the subprime
crisis but that, according to this view, is when the rot started. The CRA
of 1977 required banks in receipt of Federal Deposit Insurance Corporation insurance, in other words those whose deposits are guaranteed
(currently up to a limit of $100,000), to offer credit to businesses and
individuals in all the communities in which the lender took deposits.
This requirement, subject to the condition that such loans would be

'consistent with the safe and sound operation of such institutions', was not solely designed to increase home ownership, though over time that would be one of its effects. It was designed to address the problem of 'hollowing out' for American cities, brought about by the flight of the middle classes to the suburbs. That problem was exacerbated by the difficulty small and medium-sized businesses found in obtaining credit, as did the mainly low and middle-income households that remained, mainly blacks and Hispanics. The CRA is in many ways a curious target for the critics, and not just because its effects, if they were so damaging, took such a long time to show through. It followed a series of similar legislative moves, some specifically aimed at extending home ownership among lower-income groups, including the Fair Housing Act of 1968, the Equal Credit Opportunity Act of 1974 and the Home Mortgage Disclosure Act of 1975.

For some free market critics, the CRA was, as Eamonn Butler, director of Britain's Adam Smith Institute, put it,[9] 'the final ingredient in this poisonous cocktail'. If it was the final ingredient, however, it required the intervention of later politicians to make it dangerous. Those interventions included, in 1991, an amendment to the Home Mortgage Disclosure Act calling for racial equality in lending decisions. A manual published by the Federal Reserve Bank of Boston in 1992 said that a lack of credit history, typically a problem for poor borrowers, should not necessarily be a barrier to obtaining a loan, and reminded lenders of potential damages from aggrieved applicants as well as penalties of up to $500,000. The Federal Housing Enterprises Financial Safety and Soundness Act of 1992 built on the CRA by requiring Fannie Mae and Freddie Mac, the two government-sponsored enterprises that in 2008 had to be bailed out by the US government, to devote an increasing proportion of their lending to affordable housing. In 1996 the Department of Housing and Urban Development (HUD) set a target of 42 per cent for Fannie Mae and Freddie Mac as the proportion of home loans that should go to people below the median income in their area. In 2000 Fannie Mae disclosed that HUD would soon be setting a target of 50 per cent of loans to go to families on moderate incomes. At the end of 2003, George W. Bush signed into law the American Dream Downpayment

Act, intended to help families on low incomes with the deposits they needed to get on the housing ladder.

'This administration will constantly strive to promote an ownership society in America,' Bush said amid applause at the signing ceremony for the Act at the Department of Housing and Urban Development.[10]

> We want more people owning their own home. It is in our national interest that more people own their own home. After all, if you own your own home, you have a vital stake in the future of our country. And this is a good time for the American homeowner. Today we received a report that showed that new home construction last month reached its highest level in nearly 20 years. The reason that is so is because there is renewed confidence in our economy. Low interest rates help. They have made owning a home more affordable, for those who refinance and for those who buy a home for the first time. Rising home values have added more than $2.5 trillion to the assets of the American family since the start of 2001. The rate of homeownership in America now stands at a record high of 68.4 percent. Yet there is room for improvement. The rate of homeownership amongst minorities is below 50 percent. And that's not right, and this country needs to do something about it. We need to close the minority homeownership gap in America so more citizens have the satisfaction and mobility that comes from owning your own home, from owning a piece of the future of America.

For the critics of government intervention, from George W. Bush back to Jimmy Carter and beyond, such sentiments were about as misguided as it was possible to be. The political imperative to increase home ownership and, in particular, to give low-income, poor-creditworthy, predominantly black families the ability to live the American dream of home ownership, was responsible for a multitude of evils. It stoked up the subprime boom in a way that created the conditions for the worst global financial crisis of the post-1945 era and left most of the beneficiaries of these policies in a far worse position than when they were happily renting rather than owning property.

What's wrong with rising home ownership?

The free market criticism of government intervention has two main strands. The first is that politicians were too ambitious in their goals for home ownership, particularly among minority communities and low-income households. Rather than letting the market decide, government intervention tried to push home ownership too far and too fast. The second criticism is that banks and other financial institutions were forced to lend unwisely, against their will, by intense political pressure.

The bald statistics on American home ownership, compiled by the US Census Bureau, are straightforward enough. In the first quarter of 1965, 62.9 per cent of US homes were owner-occupied. Ten years later home ownership had risen nationally to 64.4 per cent, rising in all regions. It rose further in the late 1970s but then fell back in America's recession of the early 1980s. By 1985 home ownership was marginally lower than in 1975, at 64.1 per cent. There it remained, more or less, for the following decade, so in the first quarter of 1995 it was almost unchanged at 64.2 per cent, though this was in the context of a rising US population, and in particular a rising immigrant population. Even so, on the face of it the various measures adopted in the 1960s and 1970s had at best a marginal impact on the proportion of US households owning their homes.

From the mid-1990s, however, home ownership did begin to rise strongly, hitting 67.5 per cent at the end of 2000 and further, to a peak of 69.2 per cent by the end of 2004. Unlike previous downturns, the recession of 2001 did not reverse the rising trend of home ownership, though the subsequent housing crash and the recession of 2008/09 did. By early 2009 the home-ownership rate was back to 67.3 per cent. The period from the mid-1990s clearly saw a substantial rise in home ownership and, on the face of it, is directly linked to the rise in subprime lending. The numbers are a matter of some dispute. Broadly, however, subprime lending rose from 5 per cent or less of all mortgages in the mid-1990s, to around 9 per cent in the early 2000s (2001–03) and some 20 per cent from 2004 to 2006, with the share averaging between 18 and 21 per cent at the very end of the boom.

The significance of these statistics, and the fact that the real boom in subprime lending came at the very end of the period – only after the sharp rise in home ownership – suggests at the very least that to blame political intervention for driving down lending standards and thus creating the housing crisis is simplistic. Many of the factors that led to rising home ownership were linked to more fundamental economic factors – rising employment and a long, inflation-free upswing that allowed the economy to run on very low interest rates. Indeed, as was clear from Bush's remarks in signing into law legislation intended to boost home ownership further, the concern was that this prosperity was not trickling down sufficiently to blacks and other minority groups, where home ownership rates remained below 50 per cent. Nobody would deny that political errors were made during the housing boom but blaming government intervention and the rise in home ownership is not justified by the facts. Harvard University's Joint Center for Housing Studies[11] listed five factors as explaining the rise in home ownership in the second half of the 1990s, only one of which was increased pressure by federal regulators on lenders to increase loans to low-income and minority borrowers. The others were low mortgage rates, a period of 'unusually vigorous and broad-based growth', the fall in home prices in some parts of the country after the 1991 recession that had made housing affordable, and new automated underwriting and statistical models of loan performance, used by lenders in the prime market, under which a larger number of borrowers qualified as being eligible for prime loans.

Don't blame the CRA

If we accept that the real boom in subprime lending came between 2004 and 2006, just before the crash, does it remain possible that that was the point when the lenders finally cracked and succumbed to pressure from the politicians and regulators to increase lending to poor communities, with devastating consequences? If the Carter-era CRA and subsequent modifications of it is the target of those who would defend the role of markets, such criticisms would appear to be wide of the mark. The fundamental problem for the critics is that the numbers do not support their story. In a speech at the end of 2008, Randall Kroszner, a governor of the Federal Reserve, also absolved the CRA of blame. Kroszner, a University of Chicago economist, might have been expected to side with the free marketeers in their criticisms of government mortgage market intervention. His figures, however, absolved the CRA from blame. As he put it,[12] citing Federal Reserve research:

> The striking result is that only 6 per cent of all the higher-priced loans were extended by CRA-covered lenders to lower-income borrowers or neighbourhoods in their CRA assessment areas, the local geographies that are the primary focus for CRA evaluation purposes. This result undermines the assertion by critics of the potential for a substantial role for the CRA in the subprime crisis. In other words, the very small share of all higher-priced loan originations that can reasonably be attributed to the CRA makes it hard to imagine how this law could have contributed in any meaningful way to the current subprime crisis.

Studies demonstrated that even in the most extreme housing down-turn since the 1930s, default rates on loans covered by the legislation were lower than those from other lenders. The view that it was all the fault of the subprime borrowers, with the connivance of politicians too keen to increase lending to poor communities, was wickedly satirised by the writer Michael Lewis in September 2007. Writing as a Wall Street trader drawing lessons from the subprime crisis, Lewis wrote:[13] 'This is what happens when you lend money to poor people ... I think it's time we all became more realistic about letting the poor anywhere near Wall Street.' It was a parody, but not that much of one.

Nobody would deny that the interventions of politicians and poli-cymakers can have unintended and damaging consequences. Part of the story of the financial boom and bust, and part of the blame, lies in the fact that central banks kept monetary policy too loose and ignored booms and bubbles in asset prices, believing they could be mopped up if and when they burst. Regulators either did not understand what was happening or turned a blind eye to irresponsible and unsustainable behaviour. American politicians helped create a climate in which home ownership became a goal even for families for whom it was never sen-sible. Mortgage brokers and banks could persuade themselves, and their clients, that they were doing good work on behalf of society. For a while at least, the economic force was with them. That, however, is about as far as it goes. Nobody told mortgage brokers to sell loans to people who had no realistic chance of maintaining their payments once the low, 'teaser' interest rate period was over. And nobody told the banks to package up subprime mortgages into complex securities, ensure that they were packaged in a way that would guarantee them Triple-A ratings and sell them to investors or, as it turned out, also hold too many of them on their own books.

Blaming the bankers

So what really happened? The causes of the subprime crisis were many and varied, but a large part of the explanation and the blame has to rest with an unholy alliance of investors looking for yield, or return, in a low-interest-rate environment and banks desperate to provide securitised products, particularly bundles of mortgages, for those investors. 'The origins of the problem in large measure stem from increased institutional demand for higher yielding subprime investments,' said Richard Neiman,[14] New York's Superintendent of Banks, in May 2007, even before the full extent of the crisis was clear.

> As stock values fell earlier in the decade, real estate became an appealing investment alternative and property values increased in response to renewed investor appetite. As a result there was a significant increase in institutional investor demand for higher risk subprime mortgage securities that generate a higher yield. Lenders were quick to respond to this investor interest through the development and marketing of alternative mortgage products. These alternative products contained unique risks, such as the potential for negative amortisation and risk of payment shock as adjustable-rate loans with low initial rates reset. These inherent product risks were combined with underwriting risks, such as 100 per cent loan-to-value financing, no income verification and reduced documentation. These products and underwriting techniques were then applied to consumers with impaired credit histories.

> This was the subprime crisis in a nutshell. Add into the mix mortgage

brokers and salesmen not particularly concerned about whether their customers would keep up the payments – brokers and salesmen would not bear any losses – and it added up to a toxic brew. The role of investment banks is covered in more detail elsewhere, but as an explanation of the main causes of the crisis, this is hard to challenge, despite the determination of some to blame the irresponsibility of low-income borrowers themselves, or politicians pursuing the perfectly laudable aim of wider home ownership.

For years Fannie Mae and Freddie Mac, the two government-sponsored enterprises at the heart of America's mortgage market, had bundled the loans they purchased from banks into mortgage-backed securities to be sold to investors, including pension funds and mutual funds. 'Securitisation' of mortgages made sense and had a good reputation among investors. A bundle of good-quality mortgages, as long as those loans had been made in a way that kept default risk to a minimum, would generate a stream of reliable income. Not only were such securities ultimately 'asset-backed' by bricks and mortar but they were doubly trusted when issued by Fannie Mae and Freddie Mac, for whom a government guarantee was implicit if not explicit. As well as that, mortgages they were allowed to buy had to be 'conforming'. They were limited in size to $417,000, and if the loan-to-value ratio was more than 80 per cent additional insurance had to be taken out to cover the excess.

But the two agencies (not to be confused with the credit-rating agencies), having expanded their share of the mortgage market, ran up against regulatory limits. For markets with an appetite for relatively high-yielding mortgage-backed securities, this was a problem. For the banks, which had created a financial production line running from the provision of mortgages through to the creation of mortgage-backed securities, through to even more sophisticated derivative projects such as collateralised debt obligations (CDOs), CDOs-squared and the rest, it was vital to have a regular supply of new mortgages, the raw material out of which they could generate return, and healthy profits, through the magic of financial engineering. The trouble was, the farther mortgages moved beyond the 'conforming' norm, the more their quality suffered. As John Calverley put it:[15]

From about 2003 the agencies began to take a smaller share of the mort-gage market. In part this was because they did not offer or guarantee large mortgages and with house prices rising they were locked out of the game in an increasing number of areas. But also, they did not do much to provide mortgages for people with low credit scores, despite their origins in the New Deal of the 1930s. Also, questions over account-ing irregularities in 2003–4 meant their regulator forced them to scale back new lending for a while. Private-sector providers quickly filled the gap. Regional banks stepped up lending but also many new institu-tions emerged, specialising in offering mortgages for people who could not qualify for conforming mortgages. These institutions often used the same techniques of originate and distribute that had been developed by banks using Freddie and Fannie as the guarantor, but now with much more relaxed lending standards. Instead of requiring good credit scores from borrowers, detailed and carefully checked income status reports and a significant downpayment, usually 20 per cent, the new lenders demanded much less. Subprime borrowers, defined as those with low credit scores, found that they were being wooed with offers of finance.

The beast had to be fed, even if the diet was of increasingly poor quality. Investors wanted mortgage-backed securities, and were prob-ably unaware that maintaining the supply of mortgages to securitise could be achieved only by a significant erosion of quality. After all, they were buying Triple-A investments. Think of subprime securities as an inverted pyramid with hundreds of billions of dollars of securities resting on the increasingly shaky foundations of irresponsible loans to unsuitable borrowers. America's poor borrowers may not have known it either, but they stood between a world economy apparently running smoothly and the biggest financial crisis of the modern era. Some thought they knew who to blame. In January 2008 Frank Jackson, the mayor of Cleveland, launched a lawsuit against the banks for the damage their irresponsible lending had done to his community, naming Citigroup, Goldman Sachs, HSBC and Greenwich Capital, an arm of Royal Bank of Scotland. Jackson, surveying the wreckage of the subprime crisis in his own city, including the 'ninja' borrowers of Slavic Village described earlier in this chapter, was determined to exact revenge. 'Follow the money,' he said.[16]

> If you ask organised crime figures why they persist in doing what they are doing, knowing the damage they are doing and the risks they are taking if they are held accountable, do you know what they will say to you? The money was just too good. You ask these financiers on Wall Street why they persist in doing this when they know the risks they are running and the damage they are doing to their communities and shareholders, do you know what they will tell you? The money was just too good.

It was a nice try. Had it worked it could have provoked a series of class actions against the banks, adding to their headaches. Cleveland's efforts were, however, in vain. In May 2009 US District Judge Sara Lioi dismissed the lawsuit, saying the city had failed to provide evidence to support its case. The city vowed to appeal but it looked like a long shot. It was an unsatisfactory end to a very unhappy story.

6

Banking in the Shadows

Subprime lending was only one part of a much wider credit boom. The low-inflation stability of the 2000s fostered an appetite for borrowing. Apparently free of fears of a repeat of the shocks of the past, when interest rates often spiked unexpectedly higher, borrowing during this period appeared, for individuals, businesses and the financial industry, to be risk-free. The question was where that borrowing would come from. The answer, to a significant degree, was from what became known as the shadow banking system. The shadow banking system can be defined in a number of ways. One is simply as the supply of non-bank credit to households. Another definition is lending, which, while directed through banks, comes from non-traditional sources. So, instead of funding lending from customer deposits, banks did so from the wholesale markets, in a variety of ways. This was the essence of Northern Rock's business model, as we shall see.

Three decades of shadow banking

How long had this shadow banking system been developing, and why did it do so? In the case of the narrower definition of shadow banking, which applied mainly to America, the answer is that it had developed over nearly three decades. A study by the New York Federal Reserve found that by the middle of 2007 the assets of the US shadow banking system comfortably exceeded those of conventional banks. Shadow banking, consisting of government-sponsored enterprises (GSEs) – notably Fannie Mae and Freddie Mac – mortgage pools backed by these GSEs, finance companies, broker-dealers and issuers of asset-backed

securities, had assets of $16.6 trillion. Commercial banks, savings insti-
tutions and credit unions – the conventional banking system – had
by contrast assets of only $12.8 trillion. The shadow-banking tail was
wagging the traditional-banking dog. Two-thirds of America's stock
of home mortgages was held outside the conventional banking sector.
It was a development that could be traced back to around 1980. Until
then the banks dominated the US mortgage market and most of the
provision of credit in America. Though there was no parallel development elsewhere, at least until considerably later, it fitted the idea of a
'super-bubble', as advanced by George Soros, the hedge fund billionaire.

Soros, whose record at explaining and predicting economic change
has been less good than his record at making money, set out the idea
of the super-bubble in his 2008 book *The New Paradigm for Financial
Markets*. Explaining his theory to a congressional committee later that
year, he said:[1]

> The current crisis differs from the various financial crises that preceded
> it. I base that assertion on the hypothesis that the explosion of the US
> housing bubble acted as the detonator for a much larger 'super-bubble'
> that has been developing since the 1980s. The underlying trend in the
> super-bubble has been the ever-increasing use of credit and leverage.
> Credit – whether extended to consumers or speculators or banks – has
> been growing at a much faster rate than GDP ever since the end of
> World War II. But the rate of growth accelerated and took on the char-
> acteristics of a bubble when it was reinforced by a misconception that
> became dominant in 1980 when Ronald Reagan became president and
> Margaret Thatcher was prime minister in the United Kingdom.

Soros's view was that the growth of this shadow-banking super-bubble was driven by the market fundamentalism of Reagan and Thatcher,
which may be stretching the argument too far. The facts, however, fitted
the idea that the problems that emerged in 2007 did not just reflect very
recent financial developments. Some of them dated back many years.
As the New York Fed put it:[2] 'In retrospect, the boom in the securities
sector ... could be seen as the emergence of a thirty-year bubble that

began in 1980, and which burst with the first outbreak of the subprime crisis in the summer of 2007. We are still feeling the after effects of that bursting.'

On one definition, shadow banking was mainly a US phenomenon, dating back three decades. On a slightly wider definition, however, it occurred in many countries, though later. This was the evolution of a new style of banking, in which banks were no longer constrained in their lending by the amount of customer deposits they could attract. Rather, they obtained funds from the wholesale markets; from other banks and investors. The shift towards increased reliance on wholesale funding, most dramatic in the case of banks such as Northern Rock, took place over a number of years. Some of this was straightforward borrowing but a significant proportion was through the sale of securitized mortgages and other asset-backed securities. Some argue that the driving force was a response by banks to tighter regulation and, in particular, to the attempt to impose international banking standards; the so-called Basel I and Basel II rules. 'International banking regulation encourages the creation of opaque financial instruments,' wrote Philip Booth.[3] 'The increased focus on regulation at international and European Union level necessarily means that regulation either has to be more complex to deal with a greater variety of industry structures and practices or that it is unsuitable in the case of many countries,' he wrote. 'Because gearing and capital are regulated, banks find more and more opaque ways to obtain the effect of gearing without doing the things regulators penalise. This leads to the creation of complex financial instruments and structures that few within, never mind outside, the industry understand. Risk taking is therefore harder for shareholders to monitor and penalise.'

Slapped in the face

One way of measuring the extent of this other form of shadow banking is by looking at the 'funding gap', the difference between the amount banks attract through conventional deposits and the sums they lend out. The Bank of England, in its regular *Financial Stability Reports*, began to monitor this gap for UK banks during the 2000s. In 2001, there was no gap. Even though banks accessed the wholesale markets, some more than others, in aggregate the British banking system was in balance, with deposits and lending roughly equal. Over the next few years, however, driven by relatively low levels of savings and a considerable hunger for borrowing, the gap grew rapidly. By 2007, on the eve of the financial crisis, it stood at £700 billion. A year later, even as the crisis gripped the banks, it grew to £800 billion. About £400 billion of this was accounted for by an excess of lending over borrowing to UK households and firms, the Bank calculated, with the rest mainly the result of lending within the financial system. Its existence ensured that the system was extremely vulnerable when wholesale markets froze in the summer of 2007.

Why was this such a problem? Gary Gorton, professor of finance at Yale School of Management, put it succinctly. This was the moment, he suggested in the title of his paper, when the economy was 'slapped in the face by the invisible hand', and it happened via the shadow banking system. 'The shadow banking system at the heart of the current credit crisis is, in fact, a real banking system – and is vulnerable to a banking panic,' he wrote.[4]

> Indeed, the events starting in August 2007 are a banking panic. A banking panic is a systemic event because the banking system cannot honour its obligations and is insolvent. Unlike the historical banking panics of the 19th and early 20th centuries, the current banking panic is a wholesale panic, not a retail panic. In the earlier episodes, depositors ran to their banks and demanded cash in exchange for their checking accounts. Unable to meet those demands, the banking system became insolvent. The current panic involved financial firms 'running' on other financial firms by not renewing sale and repurchase agreements (repo) or increasing the repo margin ('haircut'), forcing massive deleveraging, and resulting in the banking system being insolvent.

Banks came to regret that they did not rely on a traditional depositor base. People did move money around during the banking panics of 2007 and 2008. In the main, however, retail depositors and business customers kept their heads. Most were content to see the crisis through. The panic was most acute among the professionals and in particular among banks.

How was the shadow banking system allowed to develop in a way that proved to be so destructive? The trouble with it, stating the obvious, was that it was shadowy. Bank shareholders were unaware of its extent, as in some cases were bank boards. Regulators either did not understand the implications of the shadow banking system or decided it was not part of their job to monitor it. The result was that the shadow banking system operated in a regulatory vacuum, expanding even as conventional banking was constrained. Lord Turner, chairman of the Financial Services Authority, described it in his review of the circumstances leading up to the crisis and the regulatory response to it. 'One of the crucial factors in the origins of the crisis was the development of major institutions and financial devices – sometimes labelled near banks or shadow banks – which were performing bank-like functions, but which were not regulated as banks,' he wrote.[5]

> Bank-sponsored (and other) SIVs [structured investment vehicles] and conduits were highly leveraged and performed extensive maturity formation, with liabilities far shorter in tenor than the maturity of assets. US mutual funds had made implicit promises to their customers not to 'break the buck', encouraging investors to treat investments with them as similar to bank deposits in their assurance of capital value, and requiring the funds to liquidate assets quickly in a downturn to meet their promises. US investment banks had developed over several decades into very large, highly leveraged institutions, performing significant maturity transformation, but were not subject to the same regulatory regime as banks.

Leverage

If debt provided the backdrop to the crisis, and the shadow banking system was the vehicle through which much of it was provided, the other key building block was leverage. Without exception, the banks most seriously affected were those that were most highly leveraged. Banks lent, but they also borrowed, and in many cases they borrowed as never before. Leverage, the relationship between bank debt and core capital, or assets to equity, increased everywhere. Though banks may have concealed some of this debt build-up, partly by parking it off their balance sheets, much of the borrowing occurred within the banking system itself. Bank of England calculations[6] show just how widespread the phenomenon was. In 2007 US commercial banks had leverage ratios – debt in relation to core capital – ranging from 30 to around 55. For Wall Street's investment banks, leverage ratios averaged between 40 and 60. Nor was Europe immune from this leverage fever. Its so-called large complex financial institutions had ratios ranging from 35 to 85. Britain's big commercial banks, some of which were to prove highly vulnerable, were not all highly leveraged but some clearly were. Their leverage ratios ranged from a conservative 20 to a risky 60. All these ratios increased further during the crisis as the banks plunged into losses and saw their capital eroded.

How had this rise in leverage come about? The answer is that, even as all the attention was focused on the build-up in household and corporate debt, a far bigger borrowing explosion was happening within the banking and shadow banking sector. The International Monetary Fund found[7] that for the major advanced economies, the ratio of financial sector debt to gross domestic product rose by 154 per cent between 1992 and mid-2007. This rise was to take on huge significance, not just because it was the counterpart of the banks' excessive leverage, but also because some of this debt would have to be assumed by governments as a consequence of banking system rescues. In comparison with the rise in financial sector debt, other sectors of the big economies also increased their debt in relation to GDP, but more slowly. Household debt, for example, rose by 48 per cent on the same basis, government debt by 19 per cent, and corporate debt, excluding the financial sector, by 38 per cent. To put these rises into perspective, by 2007 Britain's private sector indebtedness was equivalent to around four times annual GDP. Most discussions around that indebtedness focused on household borrowing and the country 'living beyond its means'. There was some truth in that. Though the rise in such borrowing was heavily concentrated in mortgages, households owed about the equivalent of annual GDP. A similar amount was owed by companies. The financial sector, however, had borrowings equivalent to twice the level of GDP and, in common with its counterparts in other countries, had increased such borrowings faster than the other sectors. The real debt build-up was within the banks and the rest of the financial sector.

The problem with this leverage was that it assumed the benign conditions in which it had occurred would remain. A thin cushion of capital would be fine as long as the sofa did not suddenly burst a spring. Philip Augar, a former investment banker himself, put the dangers well in his book *Chasing Alpha*. Under the old narrow banking model of matching loans to deposits, bankers knew where the risks lay and, in general, how to manage them. Under the new, highly leveraged model, they faced new and much greater risks. The first was that many of the losses and defaults, on mortgages, credit cards or business loans, ultimately had to be covered by the bank. The bigger the expansion of a bank's loan book in relation to its deposit base, the bigger the risks. The second problem was the 'maturity mismatch' between bank borrowings in the wholesale markets and the loans they were supporting. Even when they bundled up or 'securitised' mortgages, banks borrowed short and lent long. A 25-year mortgage, if it ran to maturity, would need to be rolled over, or refinanced, many times in the markets. These risks were, of course, played down in a climate where not only was it easy to raise funding cheaply but it was also easy to lend to final customers profitably. 'The old discipline of balancing loans and deposits was lost and banks became highly leveraged institutions themselves and vulnerable to either of these risks,' wrote Augar.[8] Investment banks had always operated in this way, lacking a retail deposit base. One way of viewing the developments in banking is that staid commercial banks began operating more like investment banks. In doing so, they pushed the leverage of the banking system to breaking point.

Mervyn King had seen the danger, even if he was slow to react to it when it manifested itself. His June 2007 speech at the annual Mansion House dinner in the City of London, on the eve of the crisis, was explicit about the risks banks were taking through excessive leverage, though by then it was probably too late. 'The development of complex financial instruments and the spate of loan arrangements without traditional covenants suggest another maxim: be cautious about how much you lend, especially when you know rather little about the activities of the borrower,' he said.[9] 'It may say champagne – AAA – on the label of an increasing number of structured credit instruments. But by the time investors get to what's left in the bottle, it could taste rather flat … Excessive leverage is the common theme of many financial crises of the past. Are we really so much cleverer than the financiers of the past?' The answer was no, though few wanted to believe it at the time.

Weapons of financial mass destruction

Warren Buffett has legendary status as an investor, thanks to his record over decades, which turned him into one of America's richest men (at times the richest) and made fortunes for many of his loyal investors. The 'Sage of Omaha', a man of modest tastes, enhanced his reputation further with what were later to be seen as astonishingly prescient comments on the danger of derivatives; contracts that are linked to underlying investments or market indices but which generally multiply the potential gains or losses. Derivatives were traditionally used for hedging purposes; for example, an airline might want to hedge its costs by buying kerosene futures, or an exporter might want to protect itself against currency risk. Increasingly, however, this traditional 'innocent' role was swamped by the use of more complex derivatives for investment. Writing in the annual report of his main company, Berkshire Hathaway, in 2002, using his usual homespun style, he could not have been clearer. The Charlie he refers to is Charlie Munger, his vice-chairman and partner. The context was that the company had acquired a reinsurance business with a derivatives arm and was anxious to wind it down. 'Charlie and I are of one mind in how we feel about derivatives and the trading activities that go with them: We view them as time bombs, both for the parties that deal in them and the economic system …' he wrote.[10]

> For example, General Re Securities [the company Berkshire Hathaway had acquired] at year-end (after ten months of winding down its operation) had 14,384 contracts outstanding, involving 672 counterparties

around the world. Each contract had a plus or minus value derived from one or more reference items, including some of mind-boggling complexity. Valuing a portfolio like that, expert auditors could easily and honestly have widely varying opinions ... The derivatives genie is now well out of the bottle, and these instruments will almost certainly multiply in variety and number until some event makes their toxicity clear. Knowledge of how dangerous they are has already permeated the electricity and gas businesses, in which the eruption of major troubles caused the use of derivatives to diminish dramatically. Elsewhere, however, the derivatives business continues to expand unchecked. Central banks and governments have so far found no effective way to control, or even monitor, the risks posed by these contracts. Charlie and I believe Berkshire should be a fortress of financial strength – for the sake of our owners, creditors, policyholders and employees. We try to be alert to any sort of mega-catastrophe risk, and that posture may make us unduly apprehensive about the burgeoning quantities of long-term derivatives contracts and the massive amount of uncollateralized receivables that are growing alongside. In our view, however, derivatives are financial weapons of mass destruction, carrying dangers that, while now latent, are potentially lethal.

The genie was indeed out of the bottle, even though episodes of derivatives going wrong were plentiful even by then. They included, by the time Buffett wrote to his shareholders, Long-Term Capital Management and Enron. Even before then, there was the extraordinary and notorious case of Orange County, California, whose treasurer, Robert Citron, ran up losses on derivatives trading of $1.6 billion after betting the wrong way on interest rates, forcing it into bankruptcy. So why, if the risks had displayed themselves so often, did derivatives come to dominate the financial landscape of the 2000s? The short answer is that, as long as people were making money out of them, and had the skills and guile to think of ever more innovative ways of spinning complex financial products out of mundane underlying investments, metaphorically turning water into wine, nobody would want to stop the process. Not only that, but individually, each innovation made perfect sense.

A mortgage-backed security was simply that, a pool of mortgages bundled together or securitised, the return on which would be provided by the regular payments of borrowers. Other forms of asset-backed security (ABS) were similar, and they provided a channel of funds from wholesale financial markets to ordinary borrowers. Collateralised debt obligations (CDOs), similarly, the first of which were issued 20 years before the crisis of 2007, provided an extra layer of sophistication. The principle was the same as an ABS, except CDOs were split into tranches, reflecting the different risks of default in the portfolio of underlying assets. Investors could choose the right balance of risk and return for them from a menu of options. Not all CDOs were based on mortgages and not all were divided into tranches of risk. Single tranche CDOs, based on company debt, were popular before the boom in subprime-based securities. CDO-squared (CDO^2) instruments, in effect a CDO consisting of other CDOs, which became initially popular but eventually notorious, gave investors yet another layer of sophistication and, it should be said, even further distance from the underlying asset. It was calculated later that an investor wanting to conduct due diligence on a CDO-squared derivative would have needed to have read tens of millions of pages of documentation.

The alphabet soup of derivatives and related vehicles had two more important acronyms, CDS (credit default swaps) and SIVs (structured investment vehicles). Credit default swaps, invented in the 1990s, can be thought of as a kind of insurance contract, though the analogy is not perfect. A firm wishing to minimise its credit risk gets somebody else to take on that risk, the risk of default, and effectively pays a premium to it to do so. It buys a CDS from another firm, which might in fact be an insurance company (the American insurance giant AIG was very big in CDS). The default risk does not necessarily stay with the original seller. These products, like other derivatives, were freely traded. From small beginnings they developed into an enormous market, estimated at $55 trillion (almost equivalent to the world's gross domestic product) by 2007. The total market in derivatives was estimated to be more than $500 trillion. Finally SIVs, structured investment vehicles, were one type of conduit used mainly by banks to carry out much derivatives activity. SIVs would parcel up and issue debt and in return receive a flow of income on that debt. Most or all of their credit was supplied by the banks themselves – this was a significant part of the lending by the financial sector to itself – and for the banks the beauty was that these entities, and apparently the risk, stayed off their balance sheets.

The popularity of derivatives among those who issued and traded them is unsurprising. There was plenty of money to be made on them. What about those in authority? Here, it is hard to understate the influence and importance of Alan Greenspan, both in official circles in America and globally and in the financial markets. If Buffett was influential as the Sage of Omaha, Greenspan was much more so as the Oracle of Washington. What Greenspan said was always important, so much so that he often prided himself on his powers of obfuscation. What he thought about derivatives, however, was crystal clear. 'What we have found over the years in the marketplace is that derivatives have been an extraordinarily useful vehicle to transfer risk from those who shouldn't be taking it to those who are willing to and are capable of doing so,' he told the Senate Banking Committee in 2003.[11]

> Prior to the advent of derivatives on a large scale, we did not have that capability. And we often had, for example, financial institutions, like banks, taking on undue risk and running into real, serious problems ... The vast increase in the size of the over-the-counter derivatives markets is the result of the market finding them a very useful vehicle. And the question is, should these be regulated? Well, indeed, for the United States, they are obviously regulated to the extent that banks, being the crucial creators of these derivatives, are regulated by the banking agencies, but not beyond that. And the reason why we think it would be a mistake to go beyond that degree of regulation is that these derivative transactions are transactions amongst professionals. And the institutions which are involved have very considerable what we call counterparty surveillance, where, for example, one major bank will know far more about its customer, whether it's a bank or something else, than we could conceivably know as regulators. In a sense, this counterparty surveillance has become the crucial element which has created stability in that particular system.

Unfortunately, the stability that Greenspan thought was guaranteed by the due diligence of professionals was a mirage. He could hardly have been more wrong about derivatives and the fact that, instead of reducing risk, they amplified it.

7

Death of the Rock

Bear's subprime woes

In the early months of 2007, it was becoming clear that America's sub-prime mortgage market was in extreme difficulties. In February HSBC, the UK-based global bank, announced that it was making provision for $10.5 billion of losses by its US mortgage subsidiary, Household, and sacking its two most senior executives. The losses at Household, which had carved out a significant share of the US subprime market, resulted in what was thought to be HSBC's first profits warning in its 167-year history. They were merely the tip of a very large iceberg. Two months later New Century Financial, one of America's biggest subprime lenders, filed for Chapter 11 bankruptcy, having seen its shares tumble 90 per cent before suspension. Despite these obvious signs of distress in the subprime market, on the surface everything seemed fine at Bear Stearns Asset Management, where Ralph Cioffi and Matthew Tannin were running two hedge funds, the High-Grade Structured Credit Fund and the Enhanced Fund (the High-Grade Structured Credit Enhanced Leveraged Fund). Both were heavily dependent on the subprime market, and the ability of borrowers to maintain their payments, through invest-ments in collateralised debt obligations (CDOs). CDOs bundled loans or other assets, or asset-backed securities, into investments that could be traded and rated by the credit rating agencies. Though the Enhanced Fund was riskier than the High-Grade Fund, and marketed as such with the promise of higher returns, both funds invested in securities rated as AAA or AA by the agencies. They were not alone in trusting such ratings too much.

The funds were highly successful, generating the lion's share of the profits of Bear Stearns's asset management business. Cioffi was one of Wall Street's successes, owning five homes with a combined value of more than $20 million, indulging in his passion for rare Ferraris and producing an independent film in his spare time, as William Cohan recounted in his book *House of Cards*.[1] Soon, however, he was facing a crisis that would bring him down, and send shock waves through the global financial system. In February 2007, at just about the time subprime mortgage problems were starting to make headlines, one of the two funds, the Enhanced Fund, reported its first ever monthly loss. It was tiny, 0.08 per cent, so Cioffi decided to ignore it. By e-mail[2] he told Barclays, the British bank that was one of the major investors in the funds: 'You will be happy to know that we are having our best month ever this February.' As so often, the cover-up made the original crime that much worse. Things deteriorated further. In March, during which Tannin warned Cioffi of the risk of meltdown while assuring investors everything was fine and that he was adding more of his own capital (which he did not), both funds fell heavily, the High-Grade Fund by 3.71 per cent and the Enhanced Fund by 5.41 per cent. Cioffi withdrew $2 million of his personal funds from the latter but decided to keep the news to himself. By now it was clear that the funds were on a sickening slide towards collapse. This was not just a falling market of the kind that traders have been familiar with since financial assets were first traded. Rather, the whole basis of the investments that made up the funds was being called into question, as were the AAA ratings that underpinned them. Subprime mortgages were turning sour, and so were the financial assets built on their shaky foundations. However much these mortgages had been sliced, diced and bundled into complex securities, if they were no good, neither were the CDOs and other instruments on which they were based.

Cioffi and Tannin continued to reassure investors while their private e-mails made it increasingly clear that they knew the game was up. Astonishingly, Warren Spector, a senior executive of Bear Stearns, the parent bank, was persuaded to invest a further $25 million in the funds in early May, which turned out to be money down the drain. Much more was needed. In June, in a desperate effort to prevent the collapse of the funds, which Bear Stearns feared would fatally damage its reputation, the bank pumped in $1.6 billion in the biggest hedge fund bailout since Long-Term Capital Management. It did not work, though Bear, as preferred creditor, got its money back. On 18 July, it wrote[3] to investors saying the 'unprecedented declines' in the value of the funds' AAA securities meant there was 'effectively no value left' in the Enhanced Fund and 'very little value left' in the other one. They were to be wound up in an orderly way, it said, adding that it had made the move 'to restore investor confidence' in its asset management division. Petitions to formally wind up the funds, registered in the Cayman Islands, were lodged at the end of the month. Investor confidence was anything but restored. Though few spotted it at the time, this was the start of something very big, and very nasty.

Less than a year later, in June 2008, Cioffi and Tannin were arrested, handcuffed and indicted for fraud, the first prosecution to follow the subprime mortgage crisis. Investors had lost $1 billion directly and much more indirectly. In the indictment they were accused of misleading investors and, in Cioffi's case, insider trading by removing $2 million of his own money from the funds without informing investors. According to the federal indictment,[4] they

> believed that the funds were in grave condition and at risk of collapse. However, rather than alerting the Funds' investors and creditors to the bleak prospects of the Funds and facilitating an orderly wind-down, the defendants made misrepresentations to stave off withdrawal of investor funds and increased margin calls from creditors in the ultimately futile hope that the Funds' prospects would improve and that the defendants' incomes and reputations would remain intact. The subsequent collapse of the Funds during the summer of 2007 resulted in losses to investors totalling more than $1 billion.

The two were acquitted of all charges in November 2009, after a jury trial that was seen as a test case of the ability of prosecutors to punish Wall Street executives for their role in the crisis. The events the collapse of their hedge funds set in train had a lot farther to run.

9 August

Some dates become etched into history, and it is not hard to think of recent examples, most notably 11 September 2001 for the terrorist attacks on New York and Washington, or in Britain 7 July 2005, when Islamic terrorists attacked London's transport network. The collapse of the Bear Stearns hedge funds in July 2007 gave markets a severe dose of the jitters; a sense of impending doom. Writing on 5 August in the *Sunday Times*, I picked up on this nervous mood. 'Sudden mood swings; irrational behaviour; up one day, down the next – no, not this summer's seasonal affective disorder but the financial markets,' I wrote.[5]

> Combine jitters with the fact that many City traders are away on holiday, though no doubt in touch from the beach via their Blackberries, and you have a recipe for volatility. Why now? Problems in the American sub-prime mortgage market – loans to borrowers with dodgy credit histories – have been apparent for months. But the defaults have been getting bigger and more frequent. Think of it as an inverted pyramid, resting on these dodgy, subprime loans, which were sliced and diced and turned into a range of sophisticated financial derivatives, notably collateralised debt obligations (CDOs). If the base is rotten, the pyramid risks collapse, and fears of this have grown, widening spreads (increasing the cost of borrowing) across a range of markets. Deals that looked good when spreads were narrow, such as leveraged buyouts, are no longer viable.

Most episodes of market turbulence pass by fairly quickly. Even those that result in prolonged falls in share prices or extreme currency volatility are not usually powerful enough in their impact to derail economic growth. This bout of turbulence was to turn out to be more than big enough to do so, although not many people spotted it at the time.

On 9 August 2007, the smouldering crisis in the US subprime market became a global event and, in particular, a crisis for Europe's banks. Normally, central banks supply large-scale liquidity to the markets only in extreme emergencies. The aftermath of the 11 September attacks was one such emergency; 9 August 2007 was, for financial markets, even bigger. That morning, from the European Central Bank's headquarters in Frankfurt came a terse announcement[6] that the ECB stood ready to supply liquidity 'to ensure orderly conditions in the euro money market'. Whether officials knew what to expect is not clear but some made no secret of their surprise at the scale of the demand for liquidity; €94.8 billion was demanded by 49 separate banks. Liquidity had dried up in the markets; this was the start of the period characterised in news reports as banks being unwilling to lend to each other. More specifically, banks and other financial institutions lost confidence in counterparties – other institutions – that they had been happy to deal with for years. Markets run on liquidity. When confidence evaporates in the way it did on 9 August, they cease to function. The ECB's dramatic announcement was not the only development in Europe. That day BNP Paribas, France's biggest bank, announced that it was suspending withdrawals from three investment funds, because in current market conditions they could no longer be properly valued. Other institutions took similar measures. A Dutch bank announced it had lost tens of millions of dollars on its sub-prime investments, a drop in the ocean in comparison with what was to follow, but worrying enough in these highly jittery conditions.

The ECB's move was followed, though on a smaller scale, by the Federal Reserve, that same day. On 10 August the ECB was in action again, this time supplying a further €61 billion of liquidity to the markets. The Bank of England, which had not been informed of the ECB's intentions in advance, stayed resolutely on the sidelines. There were mutterings among Bank officials about Europe's central bank having overreacted, panicked even, perhaps because it was inexperienced. Less than ten years in existence, perhaps it lacked the institutional memory of its longer-established counterparts elsewhere. Such mutterings did not last for long; 9 August was the day that marked the start of the crisis and the ECB had recognised the seriousness of the situation early. The excitement died down. Only bankers and those who talked to them knew how serious things were for the next two to three weeks, until the crisis again broke out into the open. Something very significant, however, had happened. 'It was the day the world changed,' wrote Larry Elliott, looking back a year later.[7]

As far as the financial markets are concerned, August 9 2007 has all the resonance of August 4 1914. It marks the cut-off point between 'an Edwardian summer' of prosperity and tranquillity and the trench warfare of the credit crunch – the failed banks, the petrified markets, the property markets blown to pieces by a shortage of credit … With evidence that the crisis is spreading from the financial markets into the economy at large, those who claimed 'it will be all over by Christmas' have fallen silent.

Mervyn's moral hazard

The odd thing about 9 August, and the days that followed, was that the central bank with the biggest financial centre in Europe on its doorstep, in the City of London and its Docklands extension in Canary Wharf, chose to do nothing. Britain's banks were as desperate for liquidity as their European counterparts, as they made clear to their contacts at the Bank of England. Those with euro zone subsidiaries, indeed, took advantage of the liquidity on offer from the European Central Bank. At first they thought officials in the Bank's Threadneedle Street headquarters were weighing up the severity of the crisis in the money markets before deciding on their course of action. As the days went by and conditions in London remained exceptionally strained, with liquidity available only at a very high price, the penny dropped. The Bank had not acted because it was not going to act. Within the Bank, Mervyn King, its governor, took personal charge. As an economist, King was at the top of his trade, having come to the Bank with a glittering academic reputation. Originally a lecturer at Birmingham University, close to Wolverhampton where he grew up, he had spells teaching at Harvard and Cambridge before landing a professorship at the London School of Economics. There, as well as academic papers, he co-wrote a seminal work on the British tax system with John Kay. He also came to the attention of Nigel Lawson, Conservative chancellor from 1983 to 1989, becoming one of a small group of his 'Gooies' (group of outside independent economists) who advised informally on policy. He became a non-executive director of the Bank in 1990, chief economist in 1991, deputy governor in 1998 and governor in 2003, a post he said privately he thought long and hard about before accepting. Eddie George, who he succeeded, said he could have won a Nobel Prize had he stuck with economics, and King saw 2003 as his last opportunity to decide whether to go back into academic economics. He chose to stay with the Bank, though unlike its typical governors he was not steeped in City history and convention. Nevertheless, he became a stickler for Bank traditions and insisted on the dignity of the office of governor. When a journalist accused him of being caught with his trousers down by underestimating the scale of the economic crisis, he was visibly offended.

The question in August 2007 was not whether King was a good economist; it was whether he had the skills to respond to a crisis in the financial markets. Unlike some of his predecessors he was more at home in a university common room than a bank boardroom. The Bank, he believed, should maintain a respectable distance from the money men. He had not sought to develop 'touch' and 'feel' for the markets, skills that in the past were regarded as essential for successful central bankers. Bank officials are famously discreet, adopting the principle that what happens within its four walls stays within those four walls. Even so, it is clear that many within the Bank, including some of his most senior colleagues, disagreed with his tactics as the crisis broke. Neither Sir John Gieve, the deputy governor with responsibility for financial stability, nor Paul Tucker, its executive director for markets, and the Bank's main interface with the City, were comfortable with his approach, but failed to convince him. 'Mervyn did what you would expect him to do,' said one Bank insider.[8] 'He went away and thought about it, discussing it with a small number of close colleagues and made up his mind. And once his mind was made up, that was that.' He could be famously short with those with whom he disagreed, or who disagreed with him, once telling the hedge fund billionaire George Soros[9] that a new book he had written would add 'nothing to the world's stock of intellectual knowledge'. Former Bank staff described him as sometimes 'ferocious'. Why did King fail to intervene in the way the ECB and the Federal Reserve, which extended its liquidity operations during August, had done? One factor may have been that he was unpersuaded of the gravity of the situation. On 8 August, even as the tensions were building in the markets, the governor dismissed suggestions of a global financial crisis at his regular quarterly press conference. The events of 9 August came as a surprise, and he may have thought it would quickly blow over.

The main reason, however, was moral hazard. If the Bank of England stepped in immediately to help the banks out of a mess of their own making, they would assume this would always be the case. Without some sanction against excessive risk-taking the problems would recur. 'The case for caution is, in the jargon, moral hazard,' King said in a speech two months later.[10] 'Put simply, such action by us encourages the very risk-taking that caused the present problems. It is crucial that, in making their lending and borrowing decisions, banks face the right incentives. That is why we did offer to lend in exchange for illiquid assets but only at a penalty rate of interest.' For Britain's banks, this was the worst of all worlds, and they made their feelings known. Not only was the Bank unwilling to provide liquidity on the terms available in Europe and America but any bank applying for it on these onerous terms would be signalling to the markets that it was in difficulty. Barclays had to deny it was in trouble when it tapped the Bank for overnight liquidity, a fairly routine operation, during this period. As for questions of moral hazard, critics argued that while these may have been appropriate for normal times, and for individual institutions getting into trouble because of their irresponsibility, this thing was a lot bigger than that. The entire system was in trouble.

King defended his stance, even as the criticism grew, but he failed to win the argument.

Sir Callum McCarthy, the then chairman of the Financial Services Authority, said that while he acknowledged the governor's arguments about moral hazard, the August crisis had affected those whom he described as 'innocent bystanders'. 'A problem associated with worldwide liquidity drying up affects not only people who have played a part in arguably irresponsible behaviour ...' he said.[11] 'My own view of the balance between the moral hazard arguments and the other instances is slightly different.' McCarthy and Hector Sants, chief executive of the FSA, had pleaded with King to change policy, following pressure from the banks, but to no avail. Others agreed that the Bank's response had been badly handled, including Willem Buiter, a former member of its monetary policy committee. Bank officials, including King, argued that the European Central Bank had injected no net new liquidity during August and that money market operations in Britain, which had been reformed ahead of the crisis, differed in method from those elsewhere.

This cut little ice with the all-party House of Commons Treasury Committee. Its verdict, delivered five months later, was that the Bank, by standing on ceremony and by emphasising its 'moral hazard' concerns, had made a difficult situation worse.

The Bank of England, the European Central Bank and the Federal Reserve each pursued a different course of action in response to the money market turmoil in August 2007,' it said.[12]

> Only the Bank of England took no contingency measures at all during August, in order to protect against moral hazard, that is, the fear that an injection of liquidity would offer incentives for banks to take on more liquidity risk, secure in the knowledge that the Bank of England would step in to resolve future liquidity crises. The European Central Bank appeared to attach far less weight to the moral hazard argument than the Bank of England. Instead, it adopted a proactive approach in resolving what it saw as a practical problem of a faltering market resulting from banks losing confidence in each other. Although the European Central Bank injected no net additional liquidity in August, it did alter the timing and term profile of its regular operations, front-loading its credit supply towards the start of August, and draining this liquidity before the end of the maintenance period. In doing so, the European Central Bank appeared to satisfy the immediate liquidity demands of the Euro zone banking sector, whilst UK banks' sterling demands went unmet. We are unconvinced that the Bank of England's focus on moral hazard was appropriate for the circumstances in August. In our view, the lack of confidence in the money markets was a practical problem and the Bank of England should have adopted a more proactive response.

Some decisions, like those on interest rates, are collective, with the Bank's governor occasionally outvoted by his colleagues. The Bank's tactics as the credit crisis broke, however, were very much King's own. The flak flying in his direction from Britain's banks was echoed, using more restrained language, by MPs. There was worse to come.

The Rock crumbles

On 9 August, as the ECB was flooding the European market with liquidity, financial traders at Northern Rock's headquarters in Newcastle reported a 'dislocation in the market' for its funding.[13] The following day Matt Ridley, its chairman, and Adam Applegarth, chief executive, met to discuss the difficulties in the markets. Ridley was not an obvious choice to be a bank chairman, having made his name as a distinguished science journalist. The Ridleys were, however, one of Northumberland's leading families, local aristocracy, and the post of chairman was almost an inherited one. His father had also been chairman from 1987 to 1992, when Northern Rock was still a building society. Though Ridley was not financially trained, he could quickly see the dangers for the bank of the freeze in money markets. Put simply, its business model relied on a constant flow of funding, not from the savings of retail customers, but from the wholesale money markets. That same day the Financial Services Authority got in touch from London, explaining that it was contacting all banks that it thought might be in difficulty as a result of events in the markets. After a weekend's deliberation, Northern Rock replied on Monday that it was indeed one such bank. The crisis that was to bring down Northern Rock, leading to the first bank run in Britain since the Victorian era, and forcing it into state ownership, had begun.

Until the summer of 2007 Northern Rock appeared to be one of Britain's great banking success stories. Under Adam Applegarth, its youthful, bullet-headed, Sunderland-born chief executive, it had been transformed from a run-of-the-mill, Newcastle-based building society, converting into a public limited company, a bank, or 'demutualised', as recently as 1997. Its growth rate was rapid, roughly 20 per cent a year. In September 2001 its market capitalisation became big enough for it to be admitted to the FTSE-100, as one of country's 100 largest quoted companies. Before then it had been a collection of smaller building societies, the product of a series of mergers. As a bank it grew its mortgage business rapidly and developed a reputation for tight control of costs and the efficiency of its operations, to the extent that other building societies contracted out processing and other back-office functions to its Newcastle operation. Applegarth liked to explain that by keeping the business local he was able to keep a lid on costs – wages in Newcastle were lower than those in London and the south-east of England – at a time when the growth of the business meant that those costs were spread over a larger amount of business. With the exception of one small German bank, it was the lowest-cost operator in Europe. Where there were doubts, and they were frequently expressed in the financial press, they were over Northern Rock's rapid expansion and how it could come undone if the housing market slowed or went into reverse. Applegarth spent much of his time dismissing such fears. 'HBOS – which I happen to think is a really well run company – has 25 per cent of the market,' he said in 2005.[14]

> It has to get one loan in four just to stand still. We only need one loan in 17 to hit high growth targets. Which is why you see them diversify, becoming a much more universal bank, whereas we are very much driven by home loans. People have been saying our success won't last for as long as I can remember. We have delivered. And we're not good proxies for the housing market – we don't compete in the housing market, we compete in the home loan market, which also includes people refinancing, remortgaging; it's investment in residential property, it's older people stripping out equity to support lifestyle.

The irony was that it was not the housing market which proved to be Northern Rock's undoing; it was the mortgage market. It became unstuck before house prices in Britain began to fall in the autumn of 2007. There were two problems for the bank's model. One was that it was expanding rapidly at the point when the crisis struck. While other lenders had begun to take a more cautious view, Northern Rock spotted an opportunity to increase its share of the market. In the first half of 2007 it increased mortgage lending by a net £10.7 billion and took a fifth of the market, well above Applegarth's one in seventeen. For many who knew nothing about the bank's business model, the most obvious sign that it was lending excessively was its notorious 'Together' mortgages. These products, a combination of a mortgage and an unsecured loan, allowed applicants to borrow up to 125 per cent of the value of the property they were buying, thus pushing them instantly into negative equity. The thinking behind them was clear; rising house prices would mean that people borrowing in this way would only temporarily owe the bank more than their property was worth.

An even bigger problem than its aggressive lending, however, was the bank's reliance on wholesale funding. The most straightforward form of banking is one in which banks take in funds from retail depositors, individual savers, and lend it on to borrowers. Building societies, which have a history in Britain dating back more than two centuries, were until the 1980s allowed to lend only in this way. Things changed for building societies and for banks, and they changed in particular for Nothern Rock. At the end of 1997, just after it had converted to a bank, 62.7 per cent of its mortgages were covered by retail deposits. By the end of 2006, this had dropped to 22.4 per cent. By 2007 half of its funding was via securitisation – bundling up its mortgages and selling them to investors – and 10 per cent was in covered bonds, bonds with a flow of income from the underlying mortgages. The remainder not provided by retail depositors was straightforward borrowing from the wholesale markets, some of it of just a few months' duration, some slightly more than a year. This was the funding that Northern Rock would need to roll over at regular intervals.

Applegarth was to insist later that he and his colleagues had spotted the problems emerging in the early months of 2007. A warning from the Bank of England in its April 2007 *Financial Stability Report*, singling out banks excessively reliant on wholesale funding, though without naming names, was duly noted by the Northern Rock board. A new strategy was being prepared, he insisted later in evidence to MPs,[15] which would include selling off some parts of the business and reining back mortgage lending to take account of a tighter wholesale funding environment. Whether it would have worked, nobody will ever know. The problem for Northern Rock was not that funding became tight. It was that it dried up completely.

Asleep on the job

There were three possible escape routes for Northern Rock from its dilemma, none of which was entirely in its own hands. The first was that it would manage its way out of its problems, possibly by selling assets but also by persuading investors to take on more of its 'securitised' debt (bundles of mortgages) as long-term holders. The second was that the Bank of England, with the agreement of the other tripartite bodies, the Treasury and the Financial Services Authority, would provide it with sufficient liquidity, perhaps surreptitiously, to allow it to survive until conditions in funding markets improved. The third was that a behind-the-scenes rescue would be organised, of the kind that has regularly happened for troubled building societies over the years, with the bank being taken over by a larger rival before most people had become aware of its difficulties.

The first route, it quickly became clear, was a non-starter in the market conditions prevailing in August 2007. The difficulty with the second route, particularly for King, was that there was no better example of the kind of moral hazard dilemma he faced than Northern Rock. This was a bank that had expanded aggressively even as its rivals had held back, and which had exposed itself to problems in funding markets by its excessive reliance on them. A response to the crisis which flooded the markets with liquidity and bailed out Northern Rock without penalty would be all the more galling for the governor when it was the failure of regulators, as well as the bank itself, which had landed him with this problem. The Financial Services Authority had contacted Northern Rock as recently as July 2007 to say it was unhappy with its stress-testing procedures – its ability to cope with an adverse change of circumstances. Embarrassingly, it was later revealed that Northern Rock had been one of two banks which was the subject of 'war games' carried out by the tripartite authorities in 2004, in which scenarios of a housing downturn and a freezing of overseas-supplied wholesale funds were played out.[16] In each case it was revealed as the most vulnerable British bank. Subsequent exercises revealed there was no adequate framework in place for dealing with such difficulties. Economists in the Bank of England's financial stability division carried out an exercise in 2006 looking at the vulnerability of UK mortgage lenders to a shift in the wholesale markets. Northern Rock, Alliance & Leicester and foreign players such as GMAC were shown to be particularly vulnerable. The findings were passed on to the FSA but strangely no action was taken.

The FSA's lax regulation of Northern Rock was a key factor in the crisis. The markets sensed that something was wrong from February 2007 onwards and started to sell the bank's shares. By the eve of the crisis, they had lost a third of their value, partly because of concerns conveyed to the market by Northern Rock itself. In late June it issued a profits warning, citing conditions in money and credit markets as creating funding difficulties, noting an 'adverse interest rate environment', and its shares fell by 10 per cent. Not everybody was convinced this was a sign of trouble. Ray Boulger, a prominent mortgage market commentator, accused[17] the City's 'teenage scribblers' of failing to understand the mortgage market or the strength of Northern Rock. His, however, was an untypical response and the FSA was roundly criticised for failing to spot the warning signals. It even allowed Northern Rock what was known as a 'Basel II waiver', permission to temporarily avoid tighter international capital rules. 'The FSA did not supervise Northern Rock properly,' concluded the Commons Treasury committee.[18]

> It did not allocate sufficient resources or time to monitoring a bank whose business model was so clearly an outlier; its procedures were inadequate to supervise a bank whose business grew so rapidly. We are concerned about the lack of resources within the Financial Services Authority solely charged to the direct supervision of Northern Rock. The failure of Northern Rock, while a failure of its own Board, was also a failure of its regulator ... In the case of Northern Rock, the FSA appears to have systematically failed in its duty as a regulator to ensure Northern Rock would not pose a systemic risk, and this failure contributed significantly to the difficulties, and risks to the public purse, that have followed.

No means no

This was the backdrop to Mervyn King's response to a formal request from Matt Ridley, the chairman of Northern Rock, on 16 August. King and his Bank colleagues had been aware of the bank's difficulties for some days. Sir John Gieve, the deputy governor for financial stability, had direct discussions on 14 August and was liaising with the FSA and the Treasury. Chancellor Alistair Darling, on his return from a holiday in Majorca, where he had been kept in touch with developments, was told a major British bank was in difficulties. King's response to Ridley, as it had been to banks in general pressing for him to flood the markets with liquidity, was to say no. Though the FSA was in no position to lecture, having fallen down on the job in regulating Northern Rock, its chief executive, Hector Sants, argued privately, and later publicly, that the Bank should have provided the markets with liquidity during August. By easing conditions in the money markets generally, and by helping out Northern Rock in particular, it might have staved off the subsequent crisis, he argued. King disputed this strongly, saying the scale of liquidity support Northern Rock needed was so large that it would not have been practicable to conceal it from other market participants. He also revealed that he would have preferred a 'covert' operation to rescue the Rock, of the kind that his predecessors would have revelled in, but that he was prevented from doing so by disclosure rules and, in particular, the European Union's 'market abuses' directive.[19] Though it was true that he received legal advice to this effect, EU officials expressed their bafflement at this interpretation of the directive. One puzzle is why Northern Rock, with a subsidiary in Ireland, within the euro zone, did not take advantage of the liquidity available from the European Central Bank. The other route typically adopted by King's predecessors, getting the City's big hitters around the table and making them come up with the funds, was not open to him. Not only were his relations with the banks very poor but they were also short of liquidity and capital, as would later become clear.

The crisis in the markets continued for the rest of August, and not just for Northern Rock. Countrywide, America's biggest independent mortgage lender, revealed large-scale foreclosures and defaults on its subprime lending and had to raise an $11 billion loan from a consortium of leading US banks to see it through its funding difficulties. The Federal Reserve announced a cut in its discount rate on 17 August to demonstrate that it stood ready to provide help to the markets. Barclays pumped in $1.6 billion to bail out Cairn Capital, one of its clients, a so-called structured investment vehicle (SIV), invested heavily in mortgage backed securities. IKB, a specialist German lender to small and medium-sized businesses, revealed it was carrying significant subprime-related losses and was bailed out by KfW, the state development bank. The prompt rescue of IKB, which many believe prevented the banking crisis spreading in Germany to the same extent it did in Britain (though bank exposures were also lower), was handled smoothly. A year later it was sold on to Lone Star, a US private equity firm.

How serious were these problems in the markets regarded at the time? Many market participants thought the freeze in credit availability was the end of their world, and in some cases it was. Policymakers and economists had difficulty, however, in gauging whether this was one of those periodic and necessary bouts of market turbulence vital in pricking bubbles. Many shared the view of Michael Mussa, former chief economist of the IMF, who took part in the annual gathering of central bankers and economists at Jackson Hole, Wyoming, in August 2007. 'There are a lot of investors who invested on a leveraged basis in high-risk assets,' he said.[20] 'They are going to have to eat substantial losses. And as far as I am concerned the proper policy response is "Bon appetit!"'

Back at Northern Rock, meanwhile, the bank's board was hard at work on Plan C; the 'safe haven' option, a takeover by a friendly rival. Through August and early September, Northern Rock negotiated its own sale. At first there were two potential bidders, then one, which was said to have shown only a slight interest, dropped out. This left Lloyds Bank, one of Britain's 'big four' banks, and at the time regarded as the safest and most conservative. Lloyds, run by Eric Daniels, a softly spoken American, had to protect its own shareholders. Protecting shareholders in August and September 2007 meant taking over Northern Rock at what looked like a knockdown price of £2 a share and securing some £30 billion of credit from the Bank, on commercial terms, for two years. Again, however, King emerged as the main obstacle to a rescue, making clear his opposition in advice to Alistair Darling. The chancellor could have taken a different view, though it would have been difficult to over-rule the Bank on this. Northern Rock misread the situation again, as it had on 16 August in requesting support from the Bank. Gieve, the deputy governor, telephoned Applegarth to tell him, to his surprise and disappointment, that the Lloyds takeover was a non-starter. Instead of announcing a private sector rescue on 10 September – with official support – Northern Rock had to accept that it was on its own.

King insisted that official funding was not the only obstacle to a deal. It would have been impossible, he suggested, to put a takeover together quickly enough to satisfy the markets, though this was achieved, initially at least, a year later when the Lloyds–HBOS merger was announced. King's view was also disputed by Applegarth,[21] who argued that an 'announceable offer' would have provided the markets with confidence and eased the pressure on Northern Rock. King, however, dismissed outright the possibility of official funding. 'The idea that if [the chancellor] stood up and said, "I am willing to lend £30 billion to any bank that will take over Northern Rock" – that is not the kind of statement that would have helped Northern Rock one jot or tiddle,' he said.[22] 'It would have been a disaster for Northern Rock to have said that.'

We will never know exactly how provision of large-scale liquidity to the markets or a takeover by Lloyds Bank with a multi-billion credit line from the government might have changed the course of events. Either could have made a significant difference. When it came down to hard negotiation, Lloyds could probably have been knocked down from its £30 billion. Nobody took it that far. King may have been right in theory to emphasise his moral hazard concerns in general, and to veto help to Northern Rock in particular. The practical effect was to make a bad situation worse. The strong sense was of an inexperienced chancellor – Alistair Darling was only weeks into the job – a governor who failed to appreciate the financial consequences of his obduracy and a set of regulators at the FSA who, having failed in their job, neglected to push through a sensible solution. Gieve, who was closer to the situation than most, said just before leaving the Bank at the end of February 2009 that the footwork of the authorities during the episode owed more to John Sergeant than Fred Astaire, a reference to the former BBC political journalist's inelegant performance on the TV show *Strictly Come Dancing*. 'We did it clumsily,' he said.[23] 'We did not need two days of queues in the streets.' Queues in the streets were, however, what they got. Northern Rock was about to make history.

A rational run

On Thursday, 13 September, at around 8.30 in the evening, the BBC's business editor, Robert Peston, reported the first in what was to be a series of scoops during the financial crisis. Northern Rock, he said, was to be given emergency support by the Bank of England, acting as lender of last resort. Only the previous day, in a letter to the Treasury committee, King had set out the terms under which he would provide such support, but few expected him to be exercising it so quickly. The Bank had been quietly working on it all week, having effectively vetoed Northern Rock's 'safe haven' option with Lloyds, and the secret almost held. Rumours began to circulate in the market on Thursday afternoon and the BBC was able to confirm them that evening. Peston insisted that Northern Rock's depositors had nothing to fear, a message he was to repeat at regular intervals over the following months for other banks. His reports that evening, while momentous in their implications, were measured and responsible. They were also hugely damaging, prompting attempts to unmask his source, which proved unsuccessful, he insisting he had pieced together the story from a range of sources. Had the lid been kept on the news, the original plan was to make an official announcement first thing the following Monday morning, 17 September. When rumours began to circulate, the timing was brought forward to Friday, 14 September. That announcement would have taken a while to digest and would have been the main news for the following day's newspapers. As it was, most led on Friday with the story of the bailout of the Rock. By Saturday, they had another story; the run on the Rock. It is impossible to know for certain whether the early disclosure resulted in the run, though many of those closely involved firmly think so.

There were, in fact, two runs on the Rock by retail customers. The first, which began almost as soon as Peston's report was broadcast, was an electronic run, as Internet customers rushed to transfer their funds to other banks. Many, however, were frustrated as Northern Rock's website frequently froze or crashed, unable to cope with the demand. A plan to increase the site's bandwidth over the weekend, ahead of the originally planned announcement, was thwarted. The more difficulty customers had getting access to their funds online, the more the panic began to spread. Rather than difficulties with the technology, could it be that the Rock had already run out of money? With only 72 branches, only four of them in London, the bank was ripe for a run. Internet customers, frustrated by their inability to get at their funds online, turned up in person. So did many of the bank's traditional passbook customers. Assurances that they had nothing to fear, from Darling and others, fell on deaf ears. People saw television pictures of savers lining up to withdraw their money and decided that there was no smoke without fire. The run lasted all day Friday and continued on Saturday morning, when the bank traditionally stayed open until noon. A report in one of the North-East's own newspapers was typical. 'Hundreds of Northern Rock customers besieged their branch in Hartlepool to take out cash amid fears the bank would go bust,' it said.[24] 'Staff in the firm's York Road outlet struggled to cope as punters queued before opening to withdraw their savings – despite being told: "Don't panic". Staff were forced to usher the gathering crowd outside desperate to take out their money before the branch closed at 12 pm on Saturday. But branch manager Evelyn Clark made a decision to keep the branch open until customers were served. She said: "We won't turn anyone away."' Just as the circumstances leading up to the run on the bank were badly handled, so was the event itself. Most Northern Rock branches were lightly staffed and the bank failed to make provision for the surge in customers, adding to the queues. Its Internet system proved inadequate and so did its branch network. The response of the authorities, similarly, was ponderous.

Before the run began, most savers thought their deposits were subject to some kind of protection. When financial journalists pointed out the limits of that protection, it added to the worries. Only the first £2,000 of an individual's deposits in any institution was fully guaranteed at the time, together with 90 per cent of the next £33,000. Above £35,000 there were no guarantees. Some of Northern Rock's savers, attracted by its market-leading interest rates, had substantially more than that invested. Nor were those who rushed to get their money out being irrational. 'Once they learned that there was concern about Northern Rock it is not that surprising that they thought perhaps it might be safer to take some money out,' said King.[25] Applegarth also refused to criticise the bank's depositors. 'I can understand readily the logic of somebody who has their life savings invested in an institution and who sees pictures of people queuing outside the door and they go and join that queue,' he said.[26] The run continued on Monday, 17 September, losing steam only that evening, when, during a joint press conference with Hank Paulson, the US Treasury secretary, who was in London on a scheduled visit, Darling announced that all existing deposits with Northern Rock would be guaranteed by the authorities, with no limit. Four days after news of its difficulties was broken, the run on the Rock was stemmed. But it had taken far too long.

Running back to the 1860s

As the run on the Rock dominated the headlines and news bulletins, journalists looked for historical precedents. The 1991 collapse of Bank of Credit and Commerce International (BCCI) and the 1995 failure of Barings, following fraud by Nick Leeson, one of its traders in the Far East, were huge events that resulted in years of litigation, particularly in the case of BCCI. Neither, however, led to bank runs. Smaller building societies had got into difficulty over the years, including, in 1983/84, the New Cross, which had to be rescued by the Woolwich, its bigger rival. In 1978, Harold Jaggard, the 79-year-old chairman and secretary of the Grays Building Society, committed suicide in his bath. He was discovered to have defrauded the society of millions over four decades, to satisfy his twin appetites for women and racing. In these cases, and others, some worried investors rushed to get their money out, though their efforts fell short of a proper bank run. For that, said economic historians, it was necessary to go back to the Victorian era and, in particular, the run on Overend, Gurney and Co., in May 1866. Though it was a wholesale operation, a discount house, whose depositors were other banks, its failure threatened the banking system. Its problems were also the result of overambition and over-expansion. The failure of Overend, set up by members of two prominent Quaker banking families, took dozens of companies down with it and for decades was etched on the City's folk memory. Reflecting on it, Walter Bagehot wrote[27] in his book *Lombard Street* in 1873 that 'there is no country at present, and there never was any country before, in which the ratio of the cash reserve to the bank deposits was so small as it now is in England'. The parallels with 2007–09 were obvious.

Banana republic

The run on Northern Rock marked a sudden and serious loss of reputation for Britain. Television pictures of depositors queuing around corners to get their money out of the troubled bank were transmitted around the world. For a fund manager in Tokyo, the West Coast of America or even New York, bank runs were something that happened in Latin America, not well-run economies. The pictures could not lie, and they suggested the UK was going down the pan. By coincidence Richard Lambert, the former *Financial Times* editor who became director-general of the Confederation of British Industry, Britain's biggest business organisation, had a speech scheduled in Newcastle in the final week of September. Lambert, who also had a spell at the Bank of England as a member of its monetary policy committee (MPC), did not spare his former organisation in attacking what had been allowed to happen. The Bank of England, the Financial Services Authority and the Treasury, the three pillars of Britain's previously admired tripartite system, should have prevented it from happening. 'We do, I think, know enough to say that the crisis has not been well handled by those responsible: the Government and the City authorities,' he said,[28] adding: 'The tripartite system has failed to deliver the goods. Perhaps there are just too many conflicts inherent in a system where three different institutions, with three different policy priorities, have to come together to tackle a fast-moving crisis.' Lambert was speaking to an audience shell-shocked by the near-collapse of one of its most important businesses, perhaps the most important local business, sponsor of the Newcastle United football team, the Newcastle Falcons rugby union club and Durham County

Cricket Club. His anger and bemusement were palpable. 'It's not just the North East that has been damaged by this episode,' he said. 'The reputation and standing of the UK as a world financial leader has also been tarnished. Outside the movies, a run on a bank is something that happens in a banana republic. That one should have happened, under our noses, in a mature and prosperous country like the UK, is almost unimaginable.'

This was not just talk. The economic consequences of the run on the Rock were genuine. The episode marked the end of the long period of strength for the pound. Its average value began to slip, gently at first but then more sharply, in a fall that was to see it eventually lose 30 per cent of its pre-crisis value. Consumer confidence also began to slide, and proved to be a more accurate predictor of recession than most economists. Individuals, even those with no knowledge of banking or finance, sensed that something serious was up. House prices began to fall almost immediately, both because of the drying up of mortgage supply (and the loss of a major player) and because confidence weakened. More so than the crisis unfolding on the markets, the run was the event that transmitted the severity of crisis to the public.

Nationalising Northern Rock

After the extreme turbulence of August and September, conditions in the financial markets improved. When finance ministers and central bankers of the G7 met in Washington in October 2007, they could report that conditions in the financial markets were picking up, though pledged that they would continue to be closely monitored. It was too much to hope that the crisis was over, but there was optimism that it was manageable. The International Monetary Fund, in its usual forecasting update for the annual meetings in Washington, revised its forecast for 2008 only modestly lower, and predicted that the world economy would grow by 4.8 per cent, followed by 5 per cent in 2009.[29] It had certainly been a storm, but perhaps in economic terms it was a storm in a teacup. In Britain, meanwhile, the government pondered what to do with Northern Rock. Vince Cable, the Liberal Democrat shadow chancellor, urged immediate nationalisation, as he subsequently urged the full nationalisation of Royal Bank of Scotland and Lloyds Banking Group. For Labour, however, nationalisation smacked too much of the party's past. A Labour government facing a financial crisis carried enough historical resonance, without a return to nationalisation, something Tony Blair had symbolically steered the party away from by getting it to revoke the Clause 4 commitment to public ownership in its constitution.

As the crisis appeared to ease, it was easy to think that Northern Rock represented the extent of Britain's banking crisis. That itself was bad enough, Labour having presided over the first serious banking run for more than a century. If, however, the ailing bank could be disposed of quickly, even after it had been kept alive with tens of billions of pounds of liquidity support and lending, all might still be well. It was a tall order. Though the Bank of England did not disclose the precise figures, the authorities kept Northern Rock afloat only with tens of billions of pounds of support between September 2007 and February 2008, raising questions of how much support even an ailing financial institution could receive without contravening European Union state aid rules. At one stage during this period, the Treasury underwrote £51 billion of Northern Rock's liabilities. What was still notionally a private company was being propped up to an unprecedented extent by taxpayers. In the meantime, the Treasury and Northern Rock looked for a 'white knight', a private sector buyer to take on the bank. As for the business itself, its strategy was a curiously inconsistent mix. The official aim was to run down the bank's mortgage book (which had the effect of further starving an already severely squeezed home loan market), and this was achieved. But Northern Rock, fully backed by the government, was attractive to savers.

During this period the aim was to sell Northern Rock to a private bidder. There was intense interest in buying all or part of the business, including from some names that would soon be in no position to acquire anything. Lehman Brothers and Bradford & Bingley, for example, wanted to buy part of the mortgage portfolio. AIG was part of the consortium headed by Sir Richard Branson, who wanted to merge Northern Rock with his Virgin Money operation. This became the government's preferred bidder. Olivant, headed by Luqman Arnold, former head of the Abbey, dropped out towards the end of the bidding process. So did J. C. Flowers, the buyout specialist, and Cerberus, the private equity firm, which also explored acquiring the bank. All this interest was to no avail, mainly because of the same stumbling block that had prevented the Lloyds takeover. Bidders wanted a dowry from the government to see the bank through credit market difficulties. Critics of the private sector bids said that even temporary support of this kind would give a successful private sector buyer all the potential upside, while leaving taxpayers carrying the risk. Alistair Darling agreed, announcing on 17 February 2008 that Northern Rock would be taken into temporary public ownership, following an assessment by Treasury officials that neither of the private sector bids represented good value for the taxpayer. It was a low moment for the government, one of many in what would turn out to be a long sequence. The Conservatives, who had opposed nationalisation, went on the attack. George Osborne, the Conservative shadow chancellor, said Darling was 'politically, a dead man walking'.[30] David Cameron, the Conservative leader, said 'the nationalisation of Northern Rock is a disaster for the British taxpayer, a disaster for this government and a disaster for our country'.[31] Darling did not lose his job, not least because his departure could have increased the pressure on Brown, and he fought off an attempt by the prime minister to shuffle him into another job sixteen months later, in the summer of 2009. What had started badly in September 2007 had, however, become worse. The chancellor insisted that the bank's mortgage book was of good quality, a claim that was soon to come unstuck as a falling housing market pushed Northern Rock heavily into loss. In August 2009 it reported a loss of £724 million for the first half of the year and a 3.92 per cent arrears rate (customers more than three months behind with their payments), nearly double the industry average. Past nationalisations had often been associated with heavy losses for the taxpayer. Northern Rock was proving to be no exception. In October 2009, the European Commission approved a plan to split Northern Rock into a 'good bank', which would operate normally, with its toxic assets hived off into a taxpayer-owned 'bad bank'.

There was a postscript. As the crisis deepened in the autumn of 2008, and the US authorities were forced to bail out AIG, America's biggest insurer, the state's hands became plunged more deeply into the world of finance than would have seemed possible. State involvement also threw up other oddities. At one stage British ministers could joke that via Northern Rock nationalisation they were sponsoring Newcastle United while the American government was sponsoring Manchester United. There was a difference. At the end of the 2008/09 season, just before AIG gave up its sponsorship, Manchester United were crowned champions of the Premier League. Newcastle, however, were relegated. It was perhaps a fitting epitaph for the handling of Northern Rock by the UK authorities.

8

The Demise of Bear

The nationalisation of Northern Rock in February 2008 was a sign that the crisis was far from over. In fact, it was just about to enter a new and more deadly phase. Two months later, at the spring meetings of the International Monetary Fund and the World Bank in Washington, the International Monetary Fund warned of the severity of the crisis and its consequences. 'The financial market crisis that erupted in August 2007 has developed into the largest financial shock since the Great Depression, inflicting heavy damage on markets and institutions at the core of the financial system,' it said in its twice-yearly *World Economic Outlook*[1] Simon Johnson, its chief economist at the time, was if anything even more colourful in his assessment, warning that

> the world economy has entered new and precarious territory. The US economy continues to be mired in the financial problems that first emerged in subprime mortgage lending but which have now spread much more broadly. Strains that were once thought to be limited to part of the housing market are now having considerable negative effects across the entire economy, with rising defaults, falling collateral, and tighter credit working together to create a powerful and hard-to-defeat financial decelerator.

Earlier hopes that the crisis would prove short lived, as happened in 1998 following the near-collapse of Long-Term Capital Management, had been dashed. Credit markets froze in August 2007 and for the most part they remained frozen eight months later. Most of all, Wall Street had a tumultuous month in March 2008. Bear Stearns, whose hedge fund difficulties marked the start of the crisis, had been sold at a knock-down price to JP Morgan, a takeover made possible only by the provision of tens of billions of dollars of government money, via the Federal Reserve. Bear was the biggest casualty of the crisis so far, and its death throes had coincided with, and added to, the powerful sense that what started as a financial crisis was turning into a full-blown credit crunch, with consequences stretching deep into the economy. The IMF, for all its gloomy tone and dramatic language, was not pessimistic enough. It said in April 2008 that there was only a one in four chance of a global recession and that losses for financial institutions would total $1 trillion. Within six months the global recession was a reality and estimates of banking losses had multiplied even from the IMF's apparently very high figure. Why was this crisis so large and enduring in its effects? It was because of the dangerous interaction, established over years, not months, of rising debt and increasingly complex derivatives.

Bust follows boom, as sure as night follows day. The problem for policymakers was that the boom that preceded the 2007–09 bust was an unconventional one. Normal booms are characterised by runaway economic growth and sharply rising inflation, providing a clear signal to put the brakes on, usually through higher interest rates. Most recessions, after all, are the result of deliberate acts of policy, engineered to squeeze inflation out of the system. What began to unfold in the summer of 2007, and continued, was therefore different. Andrew Sentance, a member of the Bank of England's monetary policy committee (MPC), put it well in a speech at the end of 2008. He was describing Britain but his comments could have applied to any advanced economy. 'Viewed through the lens of the classic inflationary boom-bust cycle, we appear to be experiencing a bust without having experienced a preceding boom, at least in terms of short-term measures of the growth of UK demand and domestic inflationary pressures,' he said.[2] He then went on to examine features of the recent experience that did, in a wider sense, meet the characteristics of a boom. One was the length of the upturn, certainly in Britain, which had experienced 16 years, 63 consecutive quarters, of economic growth, which was unprecedented. Another was the sharp rise in global commodity prices, the most obvious evidence of which was a rise in the price of crude oil to a record $147 a barrel in July 2008. Five years earlier oil prices had been between $20 and $30 a barrel. A third factor was the global credit and housing boom, in which Britain had played a full part. There was a boom, in other words, but most policymakers were looking in the wrong places for it.

The problem was a tricky one. It was not that people were unaware of the lessons of history; it was just that they were looking at the wrong sort of history, at the policy-driven recessions of the relatively recent past. Boom and bust was, however, known to earlier generations. They, perhaps, would have been better at spotting that something was seriously awry. 'If we take a longer view of economic history, stretching back to the Industrial Revolution, financial and commodity booms and busts were the predominant drivers of economic cycles,' said Sentance.[3]

> The characteristics of the current cycle have much more in common with cycles experienced before the First World War and even pre-industrial economic history than they do with post-war inflationary cycles. We are now appreciating that the earlier years of this decade saw an expansion of various forms of financial market activity which have subsequently proved unsustainable. The rapid correction we are now seeing is spilling over into the real economy – creating recessionary forces. This is not the unwinding of a classic inflationary boom-bust cycle that we have seen before in postwar Britain. But it is nevertheless creating equally severe consequences as it unwinds.

Sentance and his Bank of England colleague Michael Hume, in a paper,[4] tracked the global credit boom. A mainly US corporate lending boom in the 1990s gave way to a boom in household lending after 2000. Why did the credit boom last so long, and not result in higher inflation? They offered a couple of explanations. The first was that much of the credit was used to acquire assets, particularly housing but also new financial instruments, rather than being spent directly on goods and services. The second was that there were elements of the long economic upturn, particularly in America and Britain, which were unsustainable, such as widening current account deficits. Nobody, it seemed, worried too much about that.

A patriotic duty to spend

Alan Greenspan opened his memoir *The Age of Turbulence* with an account of his experience of the al-Qaeda attacks on New York and Washington on 11 September 2001. He had been attending a meeting of central bankers in Switzerland when the news of the attacks was conveyed to the pilot of the commercial plane he was on, and his flight back to Washington was turned back to Zurich in mid-Atlantic. There, the news of the attacks, in which nearly three thousand people died, including the hijackers of the four planes, sank in. For Greenspan, who had divided his career between New York and Washington, it was devastating news. It was, however, imperative that he get back quickly. He feared the collapse of the American economy, and he was its pivotal player. 'This was meant to be a symbolic act of violence against capitalist America – like the bomb in the parking garage at the World Trade Center eight years earlier,' he wrote.[5]

> What worried me was the fear such an attack would create ... If people withdraw from everyday economic life – if investors dump their stocks, or business people back away from trades, or citizens stay home for fear of going to malls and being exposed to suicide bombers – there's a snowball effect. It's the psychology that leads to panics and recessions. A shock like the one we'd just sustained could cause a massive withdrawal from, and major contraction in, economic activity. The misery could multiply.

Greenspan managed to get on to a US Air Force tanker flight back to America, flying over the smouldering rubble of the Twin Towers in New York on his way back to Washington. Then it was into action, ensuring that funds flowed around the economy (the suspension of air travel was a problem for cheque-clearing and postal payments), lowering interest rates aggressively and supporting emergency action by the Bush administration to support and boost the economy through fiscal measures.

The danger of a collapse of America's economic and financial system passed but, as Greenspan recorded, the world had entered a new age. The complacency that had followed the end of the cold war had been shattered. This was a moment when terrorists had hoped to derail the US economy. Had they succeeded, perhaps pushing America into a new Great Depression, it would have been a much greater victory than even inflicting the loss of thousands of innocent lives. The former Federal Reserve chairman was never explicit about the necessary economic response to this threat but others were, including President George W. Bush. He urged Americans to carry on spending, rather than stay at home. Preserving the American way of life meant preserving the US economy. After the attacks, unsurprisingly, people were unwilling to fly. Bush urged them to do so. On 27 September 2001, after taking a flight to Chicago's O'Hare airport, the president spoke to airline and airport staff. 'One of the great goals of this nation's war is to restore public confidence in the airline industry and to tell the travelling public, get on board, do your business around the country, fly and enjoy America's great destination spots,' he said.[6] 'Go down to Disney World in Florida, take your families and enjoy life the way we want it to be enjoyed.' In the patriotic fervour, with the crowd chanting 'USA, USA, USA', it was a message people wanted to hear. It was repeated many times by Bush and by others such as New York's then mayor, Rudolph Giuliani, in the months that followed. The best way for America to demonstrate that it was undefeated was not just by military means. It was also to show that it remained a formidable economic power.

Except in the immediate aftermath of the 9/11 attacks, nobody sat down and thought explicitly about how they could use economic growth as a weapon in the 'War on Terror'. A defeat for Bush in the presidential election in 2004 would have been seen as a verdict both on the Iraq war (which began in March 2003) and his response to 9/11. In the same way, a prolonged US recession during that period could have been interpreted as a success for America's opponents. Just as it was the patriotic duty of Americans to spend immediately after the attacks, so it seemed important to keep the economy growing subsequently, even if this meant growing indebtedness, significant imbalances and other

potential dangers, including the housing boom. Andrew Bacevich, professor of history and international relations at Boston University, has put
it succinctly, tracing it back to Bush's declaration of the 'War on Terror'
immediately after 9/11. 'Senior officials routinely described the war as
global in scope and likely to last decades, but the administration made
no effort to expand the armed forces,' he wrote.[7]

> It sought no additional revenue to cover the costs of waging a protracted
> conflict. It left the nation's economic priorities unchanged. Instead of
> sacrifices, it offered tax cuts. So as the American soldier fought, the
> American consumer binged, encouraged by American banks offering
> easy credit. From September 2001 until September 2008, this approach
> allowed Bush to enjoy nearly unfettered freedom of action. To fund the
> war on terror, Congress gave the administration all the money it wanted.
> Huge bipartisan majorities appropriated hundreds of billions of dollars,
> producing massive federal deficits and pushing the national debt from
> roughly $6 trillion in 2001 to just shy of $10 trillion today. Even liberal
> Democrats who decried the war routinely voted to approve this spend-
> ing, as did conservative Republicans who still trumpeted their prin-
> cipled commitment to fiscal responsibility and balanced budgets. Bush
> seems to have calculated – cynically but correctly – that prolonging the
> credit-fuelled consumer binge could help keep complaints about his per-
> formance as commander in chief from becoming more than a nuisance.
> Members of Congress calculated – again correctly – that their constitu-
> ents were looking to Capitol Hill for largesse, not lessons in austerity. In
> this sense, recklessness on Main Street, on Wall Street and at both ends
> of Pennsylvania Avenue proved mutually reinforcing.

The binge meant more than just taking holidays at Disney World or
buying new cars; it took in the housing boom and a rapid rise in corporate borrowing, including breakneck growth in private equity.

Would things have been different had the 11 September attacks and
the Iraq war not taken place? It is impossible to say. We cannot know
whether there would have been other events instead. It is quite possible
that the exuberance of American consumers, and bankers, would have

been even greater, though that exuberance would probably have been met with a more forthright response than the decisions of the Greenspan Federal Reserve to reduce its main interest rate to 1.75 per cent in the aftermath of the 9/11 attacks and to 1 per cent in June 2003. Keeping the economy growing in spite of these events was important. It helps explain why policymakers took their eye off the ball.

A ratings breakdown

In 2003, Greenspan should have been more aware than he was of the extent to which the banks were starting to push the envelope of derivatives out so far that the quality of the underlying asset, subprime mortgages, was suspect enough to almost guarantee disaster if there was a change in economic circumstances. His best excuse is that he, along with others in authority, probably had little idea how rapidly the financial market innovations he was praising were growing. 'One of the truly staggering things about this boom in newfangled credit investment products was that very few non-bankers had any idea that SIVs and CDOs even existed,' wrote Gillian Tett.[8]

> Even regulators seemed only vaguely aware of what the banks were really doing. Yet SIVs were proliferating like mushrooms after a rainstorm. Some of that frenzy was occurring in New York and Connecticut. The main concentration of SIVs and other related vehicles, though, was found in London. In part, that was because a body of legal and financial expertise had grown up in the City to service these financial beasts and all the mutations that they spawned. The legal and regulatory framework was also very favourable since – in keeping with the 'light-touch' mantra that drove British regulatory policy – the UK government saw little reason to monitor what these entities were doing. They were rarely mentioned in any official reports produced by the Bank of England or Financial Services Authority, the entity that had inherited the main regulatory mantle. Nor were SIVs mentioned in the mainstream British press. The financiers had created a vast shadow banking system that was out of sight of almost everybody outside the specialist credit world.

The fact that this activity was difficult to monitor was one problem, and regulators may have been happy to turn a blind eye to a phenomenon that did not cause them any difficulties. Another was that, contrary to Greenspan's assertion that 'counterparty surveillance' rather than regulation would keep derivatives on the straight and narrow, many investors relied on the rating agencies – Moody's, Standard & Poor's and Fitch – to do it for them. An AAA (Triple-A) rating was a guarantee of the saleability of a product. Even before the crisis, however, some experts were sceptical about the agencies. They were, said critics, fatally compromised by conflicts of interest, being paid by the issuers of the securities they were rating. They were also, according to some, never really up to the job of properly assessing complex financial instruments. The smart money was in the investment banks, as were the smartest people. The rating agencies could never really keep up with the complexity, even if it was their aim to do so. Frank Partnoy, a professor of law and finance at the University of San Diego, whose earlier career was as an investment banker specialising in derivatives, had long been a critic. In a paper written in 2001,[9] Partnoy had noted what he described as the paradox of rating agencies, that increased reliance on them in the market and by regulators ran counter to what he described as their 'limited informational value'. The agencies, in other words, could not or did not tell anybody very much, yet their words were treated as gospel. They were soon to be treated differently, with deep suspicion.

In the autumn of 2008, Henry Waxman, chairman of the House of Representatives Committee on Oversight and Government Reform, gave it to them with both barrels. 'The leading credit rating agencies – Standard and Poor's, Moody's, and Fitch – are essential financial gate-keepers,' he said.[10]

They rate debt obligations based on the ability of the issuer to make timely payments. A triple-A rating has been regarded as the gold standard for safety and security of these investments for nearly a century. As our financial markets have grown more complex, the role of the credit rating agencies has grown in importance. Between 2002 and 2007, Wall Street issued a flood of securities and collateralized debt obligations backed by risky subprime loans. These new financial inventions were so complex that virtually no one really understood them. For investors, a triple-A rating became the stamp of approval that said this investment is safe. And for Wall Street's investment banks, a triple-A rating became the independent validation that turned a pool of risky home loans into a financial goldmine. The leading credit rating agencies grew rich rating mortgage-backed securities and CDOs. Total revenues for the three firms doubled from $3 billion in 2002 to over $6 billion in 2007. At Moody's, profits quadrupled between 2000 and 2007. In fact, Moody's had the highest profit margin of any company in the S&P 500 for five years in a row. Unfortunately for investors, the triple-A ratings that proved so lucrative for the rating agencies soon evaporated. S&P has downgraded more than two-thirds of its investment-grade ratings. Moody's had to downgrade over 5,000 mortgage-backed securities ... The story of the credit rating agencies is a story of colossal failure. The credit rating agencies occupy a special place in our financial markets. Millions of investors rely on them for independent, objective assessments. The rating agencies broke this bond of trust, and federal regulators ignored the warning signs and did nothing to protect the public. The result is that our entire financial system is now at risk.

One of the features of the financial crisis was the close relationship between announcements by rating agencies and the pressure on institutions, and in some cases countries. That relationship was unsurprising. In some cases downgrades by the agencies had an automatic impact, requiring investors to reduce their holdings of the downgraded securities and requiring banks and other institutions to bolster their capital from other sources. Those downgrades were dramatic in scale, often coming at times when the system was least able to cope with them. In November 2007, when hopes were starting to emerge that the worst of the crisis was over, the agencies downgraded more than two thousand mortgage-backed securities, and in a quarter of cases the downgrades were more than ten notches, a sudden dive from high-quality to something like junk status. The crisis of September 2008, and in particular the convulsions at AIG, were partly prompted by ratings downgrades. On 16 August 2008, for example, Moody's downgraded 691 mortgage-backed bonds at a stroke. This, of course, is what agencies are supposed to do, and had been doing for a hundred years since Moody's came into being in 1909 to rate railway bonds. When circumstances change, the agencies are supposed to warn investors of such changes. If they did not do so, they would be falling down on the job. It was not, however, the conduct of the agencies during the crisis for which they were blamed but their conduct before it. How had the agencies contrived to give top AAA ratings to securities that in many cases turned out to be virtually worthless?

Compared with the system prevailing before around 1970, when the big institutional investors paid the agencies to rate bonds and other securities, in the modern era the agencies received their fees almost exclusively from the issuers. The argument that this leads to an inevitable slide in standards is not entirely clear cut. 'Payment by issuers for their own ratings generates an obvious conflict of interest,' wrote Alan Morrison.[11]

> When a ratings agency relies for fees upon the firm whose creditworthiness it evaluates, one might expect it to lower its standards so as to increase the level of business it generates. The counter-argument rests on reputational considerations. Agencies have nothing to sell if they lose their reputation for honesty in ratings and hence, goes the argument, they will resist the short-term incentive to race their competitors to the bottom in order to protect their long-term revenue stream. Whether this short-term race-to-the-bottom effect or the long-term reputational effect dominates depends on the power of the short-term incentive to burn reputation. If the immediate profits from doing so are large enough, and the long-term profits to be obtained from maintaining a good reputation are sufficiently small, then it is rational to run down a reputation. On the other hand, it would be surprising if rational investors did not anticipate the trade off faced by the ratings agencies.

There was a race to the bottom, and it appears to have been created by the desire to keep these businesses expanding in the face of competition, as much as by the flawed models used by the agencies, which failed every bit as badly as those of the investment banks. Waxman's congressional committee obtained evidence from within the rating agencies showing that they had been aware of the conflicts between maintaining standards and market share. Ray McDaniel, chairman and chief executive of Moody's, was explicit in a memo to his board in October 2007. 'The real problem is not that the market underweights ratings quality but rather that, in some sectors, it actually penalizes quality by awarding rating mandates based on the lowest credit enhancement needed for the highest rating,' he wrote.[12] 'Unchecked, competition on this basis can place the entire financial system at risk. It turns out that ratings quality has surprisingly few friends: issuers want high ratings; investors don't want rating downgrades; short-sighted bankers labour short-sightedly to game the rating agencies for a few extra basis points on execution. Moody's for years has struggled with this dilemma.'

The agencies' methods were flawed and the nature of the competition between them meant that standards were always likely to suffer. In the blame game that followed the crisis, they got off relatively lightly. Their role lived on. That role in the boom years had been to help inflate a credit bubble that was about to claim its biggest victim.

Bear's death throes

That victim was Bear Stearns, though few in the markets or outside had much sympathy for its plight. Bear, as it was known, had a lengthy Wall Street pedigree. Founded in 1923 by Joseph Bear, Robert Stearns and Harold Mayer, it had survived any number of market and other traumas, including the 1929 crash and the Great Depression. Though by size it was a member of Wall Street's elite – it was America's fifth-largest investment bank in 2007 – it also had a reputation as an aggressive outsider, more ruthless than others in its willingness and determination to do rivals down. Jimmy Cayne, its boss, exemplified that attitude. In 1998, when the authorities arranged a rescue for Long-Term Capital Management, Bear Stearns was the only one of the big investment banks not to contribute. At the key meeting when banks were asked to chip in to bail out LTCM, Cayne uttered the immortal line: 'Don't go alphabetically if you want this to work.'[13]

One theory behind its humiliation in March 2008 was that the Federal Reserve wanted revenge for Bear's unwillingness to help out ten years earlier, though that theory received a knock a few months later when Lehman Brothers, which had joined in with the LTCM bailout, suffered an even greater humiliation. Bear in 2007/08 had all the vulnerabilities that were to prove its downfall rolled into one. It had been aggressive in expanding its mortgage business in general, and subprime mortgage business in particular. It was highly leveraged. Even more than most of its investment banking peers, it was largely reliant on the continued confidence of the markets. Like all non-deposit-taking banks, it raised its funding on the wholesale markets. Unlike others, Bear's funding was particularly short-term in nature, so needed to be rolled over more frequently, and it used mortgage-backed securities as its main collateral. The biggest vulnerability of all was that Bear had already flagged up its difficulties. The failure of two of its highly rated hedge funds in July 2007 had been the first solid sign of the impending crisis. It raised questions about the parent company which proved fatal.

In December 2007, Bear reported the first ever quarterly loss in its 84-year history, $854 million, together with write-downs of $1.9 billion on its assets. Cayne, at that time both chairman and chief executive, said the bank was 'obviously upset' with the loss but emphasised the strength of many areas of its business.[14] The markets did not agree. A month later Cayne, under pressure from investors, stepped down as chief executive though continued as chairman. With a 5 per cent stake in the company, which was worth over $1 billion at the peak, he remained hugely influential, at least for the next couple of months. The writing, however, was on the wall. The previous October Cayne had arranged a share swap with Citic Securities, a Chinese investment firm. Bear was not alone in turning to China for help during this period, but in February Citic announced that it was renegotiating the terms of the agreement as a result of a slump in the Bear Stearns share price. Later that month some investors who had lost money in the collapse of the Bear hedge funds the previous summer announced that they were seizing them in an attempt to get back $1.6 billion they had lost. March 2008 proved to be Bear's undoing. Carlyle Capital Corporation, a $22 billion hedge fund to which Bear Stearns was significantly exposed, collapsed, knocking 17 per cent off Bear's share price. Other hedge funds which Bear had lent money to, including Peloton Partners and Thornburg Mortgage, were also in difficulty. Bear was the equivalent of a heavyweight boxer taking a repeated pummelling. Over ten months since the problems had emerged in the summer of 2007, the blows had rained down. Each time a little more investor confidence evaporated.

Bailing out Bear Stearns

Not everybody was convinced that Bear's problems were terminal. On 11 March 2008 Jim Cramer, the energetic and excitable host of CNBC's *Mad Money*, on the financial cable news channel, told a concerned viewer that the bank was not in trouble and that he should leave his money in it. Over the next few days, as the value of Bear's stock slumped by more than 90 per cent, Cramer was panned for one of the worst bits of investment advice in history, though he insisted he was addressing the question of whether money in a Bear Stearns investment account was safe. Even so, he could be forgiven for not believing that one of Wall Street's investment banks was about to disappear from view, absorbed by one of its rivals with the help of official guarantees worth tens of billions of dollars. Bear's final collapse began on Monday, 10 March, when market rumours began to circulate that it was having severe liquidity problems. Ironically, within the bank itself this was a time when executives believed they were putting the worst behind them. The previous quarter's loss had been turned into a small profit. The new chief executive, Alan Schwartz, had flown down to Palm Beach for the firm's annual media conference. To this day, many of its former executives believe the liquidity rumours were started by malicious rivals. They were, however, believed by the markets. Selling of Bear shares continued on the Monday. On Tuesday, 11 March, when Cramer made his comment about Bear Stearns being 'not in trouble', hedge funds queued up to dump its stock and, most worrying of all, there was a scramble to get out of credit instruments that were exposed to its possible failure. That scramble involved somebody else taking on that risk, for a fee, and initially Deutsche Bank, Credit Suisse First Boston and Goldman Sachs were willing to do so. Then, under instruction from their credit departments, traders at Credit Suisse and Goldman Sachs were told to stop.

On Wednesday, 12 March, Schwartz did a live television interview to try to calm the markets, though the fact that he did it from Palm Beach, before his return to New York, hardly helped inspire confidence. The following day Bear's management received the news it had been dreading. The so-called repo lenders who rolled over the bank's short-term borrowings in the market indicated that they were no longer prepared to do so. Without this, and with $30 billion of borrowings due to be rolled over on Friday, 14 March, Bear would be bust. It was saved from collapse that day by the announcement of a 28-day $30 billion credit line from the Federal Reserve but channelled via JP Morgan Chase, a commercial bank (but with a big investment banking arm) which was entitled, unlike Bear, an investment bank, to access funds at the Fed's so-called discount window. There was no provision, at the time, for direct Fed assistance to Bear Stearns. As soon as the markets closed, Fed officials, led by Tim Geithner, then the president of the Federal Reserve Bank of New York, later Treasury secretary under Barack Obama, made clear that the announcement of a 28-day credit line was a device to get through a difficult day. Bear's management had the weekend to find a buyer.

On Wednesday Alan Schwartz had been in Palm Beach, assuring the world that Bear Stearns was safe. By Saturday morning he was negotiating its sale, at a knockdown price. His chairman, Jimmy Cayne, meanwhile, was at a bridge tournament in Detroit. When he broke off from bridge to take part in telephone discussions, his expletive-filled contribution was to bellow at the board that the bank should file for bankruptcy rather than accept a deal that, in his view, undervalued his company. Bridge was an important part of Cayne's life and he was very good at it, having contemplated turning professsional when younger. It had helped promote his career during his early years at Bear Stearns, when a mutual love of the game allowed him to form a bond with 'Ace' Greenberg, his predecessor as chief executive. During the hedge fund crisis the previous summer, he was at a tournament in Nashville, Tennessee, and out of contact for hours on end. The *Wall Street Journal* reported[15] a conference call with investors in August 2007 when, after a few opening words, he disappeared from the conversation. It also reported allegations, which were not denied, that Cayne relaxed by smoking cannabis with fellow players at bridge tournaments and that he spent days out of contact with the office on the golf course. The reporting of these allegations, just as Bear Stearns was plunging into loss in November 2007, had helped push down the company's share price. Until a few months after March 2008, when Lehman Brothers' Dick Fuld gained even more notoriety, Cayne was ahead of the field as the unacceptable face of Wall Street.

In 2007, the bank's share price had been as high as $170. By the time the weekend was over, it had been sold to JP Morgan for just $2 a share, though that was subsequently increased to $10 under pressure from the bank's investors, including the British-born, Bahamas-based billionaire Joe Lewis, who continued to build a stake in Bear even as its woes mounted, and ended up losing almost a billion dollars. Even the initial $2 a share offer did not tell the full story. JP Morgan and its chief executive Jamie Dimon were concerned about being contaminated by Bear's tarnished reputation, mainly arising from Cayne, and they were concerned about the toxic debt on the bank's books, only agreeing to take it on if the Federal Reserve agreed to set up a vehicle that would ring-fence – remove the risk from JP Morgan – of $30 billion of Bear's most toxic assets. A deal was done, because it had to be done. 'Geithner believed he couldn't let Bear die,' wrote Bryan Burrough in a detailed reconstruction.[16] 'The repercussions were unthinkable. For the first time in history the entire world was looking at the failure of a major financial institution that could lead to a run on the entire world financial system, a Fed official recalls. It was clear we couldn't let that happen.'

Staff who worked at the bank were stunned. More than half, 8,000, were to lose their jobs over the next three months. One shouted 'This is rape!' at Schwartz when he explained the deal to them at a mass meeting of staff. Cayne was also outraged, though far from impoverished. He and his wife sold their shareholdings in Bear Stearns for $61 million shortly after the JP Morgan offer had been raised to $10 a share. Those holdings had once been worth over $1 billion. At the shareholder meeting on 29 May 2008 to approve the sale of the company, an angry Cayne grabbed the microphone and blamed a conspiracy of rival investment banks, acting in consort with hedge funds, for bringing Bear Stearns down. Later he was to insist that he had tried to limit the bank's excessive leverage and risk-taking, but to no avail. The anger did not abate. Versions of an extraordinarily crude rant by Cayne, directed at Geithner, who he clearly believed did not have the authority to sell his bank from under him, began to circulate on the Internet. It was, however, an old man raging against the dying of the light. Cayne, who turned 75 in 2009, would never work again on Wall Street. He was an example of a certain type of old style, cigar-chomping investment banker. The world had changed dramatically and it had left him behind.

Controversial though the bailout of Bear Stearns was, it appeared to have established a principle. That principle was that big and important banks would not be allowed by the authorities to go under, though they and their employees would not be spared the pain and humilation in any rescue. Wall Street would not be bailed out but it would be prevented from inflicting damage on the wider economy. Or so it seemed for a few months.

9

The Weekend That Changed the World

In the autumn of 2008, the world economy went into a nosedive. Every indicator turned down simultaneously and sharply, including global gross domestic product, world trade, business investment, industrial production, retail sales, new car registrations, business sentiment, consumer confidence, jobs, housing transactions, air travel, commodity prices and the stock market. House prices in Britain were down by 10 per cent in six months, their fastest fall on record. Meanwhile, tension in the financial markets, which had been unusually heightened since the summer of 2007, gave way to fear and panic. What started as a financial crisis had become, with dizzying speed, the biggest economic crisis of the post-war era, or so it appeared. Alistair Darling, who had the misfortune to take over as Chancellor of the Exchequer in June 2007, just weeks before the financial crisis broke, invited a journalist a year later to spend a couple of days with him and his wife on the family croft on the island of Lewis in the Outer Hebrides. There, he offered the view[1] that the economic times the country was facing 'are arguably the worst they've been in 60 years', adding: 'And I think it's going to be more profound and long-lasting than people thought.' When the interview was published, in August 2008, he was accused of spreading unnecessary gloom and did a round of radio and television appearances to insist that he was referring to global economic conditions and the scale of the challenges faced by policymakers, A few months later, presenting his April 2009 Budget, he was able to report, though with little satisfaction, that his unguarded predictions had turned out to be right. 'A crisis that started in the developed economies has spread to emerging and developing countries,' he said in the House of Commons.[2] 'Industrial production has fallen and unemployment is rising – by 5 million in the US alone. In the last few months, world trade fell – and while our exports are down 14 per cent, exports in Germany are down 21 per cent, in China 26 per cent, and in Japan 45 per cent. For the first time since the Second World War, the world economy is expected to contract this year.'

Falling off a cliff

Policymakers normally try to walk a fine line between providing reassurance and appearing complacent, not disguising the extent of the difficulties but not overdoing the gloom either. In the autumn of 2008, and for several months afterwards, however, it was hard for them not to sound gloomy. The data did not lie and the mood was bleak. The world economy was falling off a cliff. 'The financial crisis intensified considerably in the fall,' Ben Bernanke told a congressional hearing in March 2009.[3]

> Real gross domestic product (GDP) is reported by the Commerce Department to have declined at an annual rate of 6.2 percent in the fourth quarter of last year, with nearly every major category of final sales contributing to the drop. Businesses shed 600,000 jobs in January, about the same pace of job loss as in November and December, and the unemployment rate jumped to 7.6 percent. Moreover, the number of claims for unemployment insurance has moved higher since mid-January, suggesting that labour market conditions may have worsened further in recent weeks. In reaction to the deteriorating job market, the sizable losses of equity and housing wealth, and the tightening of credit conditions, households have continued to rein in their spending. Home sales and new construction have continued to decline. The manufacturing sector has also deteriorated further so far this year. Manufacturing output fell sharply again in January, bringing the rate of capacity utilisation to its lowest level in the post-World War II period.

Every aspect of America's economy was being affected by the slump in activity, and the story was repeated the world over. Those that were weak before the crisis were finished off by it. In Britain, the Woolworths retail chain, brought over from America in 1909 by Frank Woolworth as a variation on his US 'five and dime' operation, limped through Christmas 2008 before finally closing the doors of its more than eight hundred shops. Some were bought by 'pound' shops; others remained boarded up and empty. In America, the 'Detroit Three', General Motors, Ford and Chrysler, lobbied Congress in November 2008, and again in December, pleading for aid to prevent collapse. Their first trip to Washington was a public relations disaster, their arrival by executive jet going down badly with the politicians they were hoping to obtain aid from, but their message was clear. 'What exposes us to failure now is not our product line-up, or our business plan, or our long-term strategy,' said Rick Wagoner, the chief executive of General Motors.[4] 'It is the global financial crisis, which has severely restricted credit availability, and reduced industry sales to the lowest per-capita level since World War II. Our industry, which represents America's real economy, needs a bridge to span the financial chasm that has opened before us.' Without such a bridge, he warned, the 'societal costs' of the failure of America's car giants would be colossal, including 3 million jobs lost in the first year, a $150 billion drop in US personal incomes and a tax loss for the US government of $156 billion over three years. Consumer and business confidence would be shattered. Even without the executive jet, Wagoner was already damaged goods by then. President Barack Obama insisted on his resignation a few months later as the price of government aid, aid which did not prevent GM's temporary bankruptcy.

Wagoner's message was, however, consistent with those of the other executives. Alan Mulally, president and chief executive of Ford, who had joined the company after a career with Boeing, offered a similarly gloomy assessment. The previous month's business, he said, told the story. 'In October, the annualized sales rate for the US industry was only 10.5 million units – compared to over 16 million units just last year,' he said.[5] 'This means the industry has lost over 5 million vehicle sales – the equivalent of two companies the size of Ford in North America – in a single year. October was the worst auto sales month the U.S. industry has seen in 25 years, and we expect it will not be the weakest result we see over this economic cycle.' Robert Nardelli, his counterpart at Chrysler, had a similar message. 'We are asking for assistance for one reason,' he said.[6] 'To address the devastating automotive industry recession caused by our nation's financial meltdown, and the current lack of consumer credit, which has resulted in the critical lack of liquidity within our industry.' Congress and many American voters were sceptical about bailing out the auto industry, which for years had been criticised for producing fuel-inefficient vehicles and for loading itself down with high costs, particularly for its employees' healthcare plans. The plight of the car industry was real, however, and not just in America. Toyota, the world's biggest car company, announced in May 2009 that it had made its first annual loss in 59 years. Governments responded to the plight of the global car industry with both aid and special incentive schemes, called 'cash for clunkers' or 'scrappage', in which buyers were given a taxpayer-provided discount if they traded in old cars for new.

Something had sent the global economy into a downward spiral, and the effects were being felt from the boarded-up Woolworths stores in Britain's high street, to the icy winds blowing through Detroit, and to Toyota City in Japan. The economic numbers for the slide into recession in 2008/09 were striking. The International Monetary Fund reported that advanced economies, taken as a whole, were contracting at a 7.5 per cent annual rate in the final three months of 2008, with a similar decline expected in the first quarter of 2009 (in the event it was worse for most economies). Industrial production, heavily reliant on trade, was hit particularly hard. Trade itself collapsed. In March 2009, the World Trade Organisation (WTO) produced a strikingly gloomy forecast. Previous global recessions had resulted in a sharp slowdown in world trade growth, or occasionally a modest contraction. This time it was different. Trade, said the WTO, would slump by 9 per cent in 2009 compared with 2008, easily a post-war record decline. The globalisation era, by creating so many linkages around the world, had spread economic growth far and wide during the upturn. Now, just as financial globalisation had spread America's subprime problems to countries many thousands of miles away, so trade linkages were magnifying the downturn in economic activity. 'For the last 30 years trade has been an ever increasing part of economic activity, with trade growth often outpacing gains in output,' said Pascal Lamy, the WTO's director-general.[7] 'Production for many products is sourced around the world so there is a multiplier effect – as demand falls sharply overall, trade will fall even further. The depleted pool of funds available for trade finance has contributed to the significant decline in trade flows, in particular in developing countries. As a consequence, many thousands of trade related jobs are being lost.'

Why had the world economy suddenly plunged into its steepest dive in living memory? One explanation was that it was just the grinding effect of a financial crisis that by the autumn of 2008 had been going on for more than a year. Limit the supply of credit in modern economies for a prolonged period, and this is what you get. That did not explain, however, why the relatively gentle downturns of the spring and summer of 2008 suddenly turned very nasty. Advanced economies, it seemed then, were heading for 'technical' recessions, defined by two or more quarters of economic contraction. There was nothing technical, however, about the recession that followed. A second explanation rested with oil prices, the culprit in so many previous post-war recessions. In the summer of 2008, driven in large part by a shift of speculative investment into commodities, the oil price had hit an extraordinary high of $147 a barrel, almost six times its level five years earlier. Perhaps this was the straw that broke the camel's back, which tipped the world into recession, although the remarkable thing about the high oil price was how most economies appeared to be coping with it, though some central banks were distracted from responding to the credit crisis by the effect on inflation of soaring oil. By September 2008, however, economies were undoubtedly weakened by the ongoing credit crisis and a conventional oil price shock. It needed only another shock to push the world economy over the edge. That was provided by the collapse of Lehman Brothers. Before the weekend of 13/14 September 2008, there was a reasonable chance that the world could escape serious recession, despite the formidable challenges posed by the twin shocks existing at that time. After that weekend, there was no chance. This was when

Wall Street's problems also became those of Main Street, and it was when, for a few weeks, there were serious doubts about the survival of the global banking system. Those responsible for the failure of Lehman had a lot to answer for.

The Gorilla

Lehman Brothers owed its origins to Henry Lehman, who emigrated from Germany in 1844 to Montgomery, Alabama. There he set up a general store, selling groceries, dry goods and household equipment to local farmers. It was a success, and six years later his brothers, Emanuel and Mayer, joined him in the business, which became Lehman Brothers. Henry died in 1855 at the young age of 33, but his brothers continued to run the firm for the next four decades. The arrival of the brothers changed the business, which expanded into cotton trading, buying and selling locally produced cotton. It established a New York office in the late 1850s, trading in commodities and later being instrumental in setting up the New York Cotton Exchange. The firm expanded beyond commodities trading and into securities, becoming a member of the New York Stock Exchange in 1887. Until the 1920s, only family members were allowed to become partners. Richard 'Dick' Fuld joined Lehman Brothers in 1969. He climbed rapidly through the ranks, becoming chairman and chief executive late in 1993. Fuld, tough and physically imposing, acquired the nickname 'The Gorilla' inside and outside the firm. Having been dismissed as a college army cadet for a fist fight with a senior officer, he acquired a reputation for taking matters into his own hands. Dotted throughout his later life were episodes when he did so, though he always claimed, as with the fight as a cadet, that when he fought it was to protect the underdog. Even so, the word on Wall Street, and within Lehman, was that you crossed Dick Fuld at your peril.

He was also hugely successful. In his first full year in charge at Lehman, the firm made a profit of $113 million. In 2007, before the financial crisis hit hard, that had multiplied to a record $4.2 billion. As the man who had delivered that performance, Fuld inspired a combination of fear and respect. 'Fuld had made a lot of people fabulously rich – shareholders, employees and of course himself,' wrote Andrew

Gowers,[8] the former *Financial Times* editor who worked at Lehman Brothers in the period leading up to its demise.

> In the eight best years he had taken home a cool $300m – funding five residences, his wife Kathy's passionate interest in modern art and a host of philanthropic activities. To say he was surrounded with a cult of personality would be an understatement. He was the textbook example of the 'command-and-control CEO'. More than that, to many employees and to the outside world, he was Lehman Brothers – his character inextricably intertwined with the firm's. Fuld inspired great loyalty and, on occasion, great fear. Those closest to him slaved like courtiers to a medieval monarch, second-guessing his moods and predilections, fretting over minute details of his schedule down to the flower arrangements and insulating him from trouble – from almost anything he might not want to hear. His ferocity could be intimidating, his eyebrows beetling tight over his hard eyes, his brutally angular brow appearing to contort in rage. He would regularly upbraid colleagues for minor wardrobe malfunctions – in Dick's book, that tended to mean anything other than a dark suit and a white shirt or, in my case, a beard. Even when in a relatively upbeat mood he seemed to take pleasure in violent imagery. Lehman was 'at war' in the market, he would say. Every day was a battle, employees were troops. At an investment banking conference in London last spring, I saw him astonish several hundred of his managing directors with a blood-curdling threat aimed at investors who were selling Lehman shares short – depressing the price. 'When I find a short-seller, I want to tear his heart out and eat it before his eyes while he's still alive,' the chairman declared. Histrionics, maybe – but with a purpose. Fuld had used this aggression to consolidate his reputation as the most successful chief executive in the banking business and one of the most respected corporate leaders in America.

Plenty of people had reason to fear Fuld's ire in 2008. Though he had given a warning at the annual Davos world economic forum in the Swiss Alps in January 2007 that markets faced a difficult year, this did not temper his aggressively expansionary strategy for the bank. When the immediate crisis of August and September 2007 appeared to fade, he was among the first to call the crisis over. 'The worst of this credit correction is behind us,' he said in early October 2007.[9] It was wishful thinking and it was not the first example. As soon as Bear Stearns had been rescued by JP Morgan in March 2008, with the considerable help of the Federal Reserve, market attention switched to Lehman, which was seen as the next weak link in the chain. Lehman was everything that Bear Stearns was except, if anything, its expansion into mortgages and the mortgage-backed securities that were rapidly turning toxic was even more aggressive. Even when the US housing market turned down in 2006, Fuld drove its expansion into big commercial property deals. Lehman, in other words, was running fast, and into all the wrong places, when the crisis broke.

By March 2008, the bank was having to face up to the fact that its unblemished record under Fuld was rapidly becoming tarnished. Its published results had been deteriorating since the impact of the freezing of credit markets the previous summer came through, Fuld's optimism about the 'correction' having proved unjustified. Lehman, having been identified in the markets as having many of the vulnerabilities of Bear, found its shares under attack. Fuld, however, was convinced that the markets had got it wrong because the action of the authorities, while focused on Bear, would also help Lehman. 'The Federal Reserve's decision to create a lending facility for primary dealers and permit a broad range of investment-grade securities to serve as collateral improves the liquidity picture, and from my perspective, takes the liquidity issue for the entire industry off the table,' he said a few days after the Bear Stearns rescue.[10] He may also have thought that his own particular qualities would protect Lehman from harm. 'People stopped doing business with Bear at the end,' said one Wall Street executive.[11] 'I don't think they would do that with Lehman because they wouldn't want Dick to come crashing through the window to rip their arms off.' Nevertheless, Lehman's shares had a torrid time. At one stage on 17 March, just after the Bear bailout, the shares were down 48 per cent on the day. The cost of insuring Lehman debt against default rose sharply. Whenever rumours about Lehman's liquidity surfaced, Fuld and his senior team, including Erin Callan, the firm's chief financial officer, would seek to counter them. A set of 'talking points' was circulated to anybody in the markets doubting Lehman's financial position.[12] It compared Lehman's capital and liquidity positions favourably with those of Bear Stearns, Goldman Sachs, Morgan Stanley and Merrill Lynch. Fuld, who had to make a hurried return from a trip to India to handle the crisis on the advice of Henry 'Hank' Paulson, the US Treasury secretary, insisted that the markets had not taken on board the implications of the Federal Reserve's actions in providing liquidity to the markets. 'People are betting that the Fed can't stabilise the market and I don't think that is a very good bet,' he said.[13] While Fuld was making these public attempts at reassurance, his colleagues were working furiously behind the scenes to ensure that the big banks, particularly international banks such as ING, did not pull the funding plug on Lehman. Most did not, though they warned that they were exercising more vigilance.

Fuld's moral hazard

During the spring and summer of 2008, Lehman's troubles deepened. Insiders say Fuld was always confident enough in his own abilities, and the strength of his firm, to believe he would never need a government bailout, though if it ever came to it, he was confident that the authorities would never let Lehman fail. 'It was certainly at the back of his mind,' said one former Lehman insider.[14] The rescue of Bear Stearns had, in effect, created the moral hazard that central bankers worry about. Fuld could walk tall, and be choosy about who he was prepared to sell all or part of his business to, knowing that the outright collapse of Lehman was unthinkable. Or so it seemed. In April, Lehman tried to shore up its capital by raising $4 billion from the sale of convertible preferred shares. The funding was expensive, with the shares carrying a 'coupon' of 7.25 per cent, but was seen, temporarily at least, as a vote of confidence in the firm. Erin Callan was unusual on Wall Street for having broken through the 'glass ceiling' at a relatively young age, having been appointed to the post of chief financial officer in September 2007, at the age of 41. She was particularly bullish about the April fund-raising, saying, 'it provides us with dry powder to take advantage of some of the opportunities in the market'.[15]

Two months later, however, her short career at Lehman was at an end. When Lehman published results showing a huge loss of $2.8 billion for the second quarter, both Callan and Joe Gregory, the company's president, were forced to quit. Fuld, however, held on. His task, said experts, was to sell the firm while he still had the opportunity to do so. Fuld was made of sterner, or perhaps more foolish, stuff. 'I have said many times that I very much believe that, with this franchise's strength and power, we can go it alone,' he said on 18 June[16] At least he was consistent. In December 2007 he had said that as long as he was alive Lehman would never be sold, and if it was sold after his death, he would return from beyond the grave to buy it back. Going it alone did not preclude him talking to investors, or trying to sell off parts of the business. Lehman's asset management business, Neuberger-Berman, was touted for sale, at a price of up to $10 billion, which would have gone a long way to solving the bank's problems. In June, news emerged that Fuld and senior executives had flown to Seoul for talks with the state-owned Korea Development Bank about taking a stake in Lehman. Had a deal been concluded quickly then, and had the sale of other parts of the business been speedily concluded, events could have turned out very differently. There was no announcement, however, even though Fuld continued to talk to the Korea Development Bank, and had exploratory discussions with Citic, another state-owned company, this time from China, and with Tokyo Mitsubishi Bank. Lehman's plight, on the face of it, offered a canny international investor a wonderful deal, even the opportunity of a lifetime.

Perhaps because Fuld never really wanted to cede even a degree of control of his bank, or perhaps because potential investors were justifiably wary of what they might be getting into, Lehman's last week began on Monday, 8 September 2008 with reports citing South Korea's banking regulator saying that the Korea Development Bank had pulled out of the talks. The reports, while denied, led to the latest in a series of dives for Lehman's shares and a threatened further downgrading of its credit rating from Standard & Poor's, the rating agency. Before the summer of 2007, Lehman was trading at nearly $70 a share. By 9 September, the shares were at less than $8 and there was worse to come. Meanwhile, the bank's other big capital-raising exercise, the sale of Neuberger-Berman, was getting nowhere. Time was running out. The bank's third-quarter results were due the following week and a new strategy was promised. In truth, Fuld had few options. The more his bank's woes were exposed, the less that potential investors were interested. The departures of a string of senior executives, of which Callan and Gregory were but two, told their own story.

On Wednesday, 10 September, in his final act of defiance, Fuld held an early morning conference call,[17] promising that Lehman would 'emerge clean' from the crisis. His proposals included a sale to investors of most of its commercial property assets and a slashing of the bank's dividend (despite the losses, it was still paying a dividend). He conceded that investment losses had 'clouded' Lehman's underlying strengths but insisted he could restore investor confidence. This was not the Dick Fuld of even a few weeks earlier. His tone was subdued. A lot of the old bounce, the aggression, had gone. The Gorilla had fought too many people for too long and he sounded tired. He knew that he had missed the boat and that by failing to sell all or part of his bank to investors, or to a more secure rival, he had let down Lehman, its investors and employees. A failure to conclude such a deal, or to sell off part of the bank, had left him at the mercy of the markets. It was an uncomfortable feeling for somebody who was used to beating the markets. At the height of his powers Fuld was formidable and feared, inside and outside Lehman. As the power visibly drained away from him as rapidly as Lehman's share price collapsed, there was nothing to fear any more. Neither was there much to respect. The only comfort he could draw on was that the US authorities could not possibly let Lehman fail. That had always been his fallback position. How wrong he was.

Fannie and Freddie

During the crisis of 2008/09, most of the important events happened at weekends, when financial markets were closed. Treasury and central bank officials got used to setting the alarm and heading off to the office in casual clothes, forgoing normal weekend activities. Sometimes they did not return home at night. The weekend of 6/7 September 2008, which preceded Lehman's last week, was one such occasion, and it was highly relevant to it. On Sunday, 7 September, James Lockhart, director of America's Federal Housing Finance Agency (FHFA), announced that he was taking the two government-sponsored enterprises that were the backbone of the US mortgage market into 'conservatorship', a form of public ownership. Fannie Mae (the Federal National Mortgage Association) and Freddie Mac (the Federal Home Loan Mortgage Association) were being bailed out by the government, a move which Ben Bernanke, chairman of the Federal Reserve, said he strongly endorsed. Hank Paulson, the US Treasury secretary, who authorised the move, blamed[18] the 'flawed business model' of the two enterprises and the 'ongoing housing correction' for the action, which critics described as government intervention on an unprecedented scale.

Fannie and Freddie between them had an 80 per cent share of the US mortgage market early in 2008 and $5.4 trillion of guaranteed mortgage-backed securities and outstanding debt, equivalent to the amount of all America's publicly held debt at that stage. As part of the terms of the bailout, the government required that the chief executives of the two bodies leave and that, from 2010, they reduce their risk by reducing the pool of mortgage-backed securities they guaranteed by 10 per cent a year.

Paulson had secured congressional approval two months earlier, in July, for government funding of Fannie and Freddie, whose problems were by that time becoming apparent. At the same time, they were given access to funds at the Federal Reserve's discount window, a sign of the liquidity strains they were coming under. The Securities and Exchange Commission announced a ban on 'naked' short selling of Fannie Mae and Freddie Mac in the markets. Paulson made clear that his tactics contained an element of bluff; in having the ability to make available unlimited government support, this might mean it would never have to be employed. 'I think that if you have a squirt gun in your pocket you may have to take it out,' he said.[19] 'If you have a bazooka in your pocket, and people know you have a bazooka, you may never have to take it out.' Paulson, however reluctantly, had to use his bazooka. The housing recession had left the two enterprises badly exposed, with combined losses of some $15 billion and the need for government guarantees, which Paulson, through the Federal Housing Finance Agency, provided.

There were three important consequences of this action in the days that followed. The first was that it revealed the extent of the difficulties faced by those with exposure to the US housing market and mortgage-backed securities. Nobody needed reminding that Lehman Brothers was among the most exposed. The second was that, intentionally or not, the deal done to bail out Fannie and Freddie acted as a disincentive to other potential investors. Because the US government's rights after the bailout became senior to those of other investors, and in particular the holders of $36 billion of 'safe' preferred stock, the message appeared clear. Anybody thinking of investing to prop up risky American institutions should do so at their peril. Anatole Kaletsky of *The Times* was one of the Treasury secretary's harshest critics on this. 'By deciding essentially to wipe out shareholders in Fannie Mae and Freddie Mac ...' he wrote,[20] 'Mr Paulson has sent the clearest possible message to investors around the world: do not buy shares in any bank or insurance company that could, under any conceivable circumstances, run short of capital and need to ask for government help; if this happens, the shareholders will be obliterated.'

The third consequence was that, by intervening to prop up Fannie Mae and Freddie Mac, Paulson found himself on the receiving end of some powerful criticism. As the former chief executive of Goldman Sachs, he may not have expected his free market credentials to be criticised. They were. Jim Bunning, a member of the Senate Banking Committee, accused him and Bernanke of acting like socialists. 'I sincerely believe that Henry Paulson and Ben Bernanke should resign,' he said.[21] 'They have taken the free market out of the free market. We no longer have a free market in the United States; we have a government controlled free market. Paulson is acting like the finance minister of China.' Even more forthright was Nouriel Roubini, the maverick economist who made his name during the financial crisis. Two days after the announcement, he gave it to the Bush administration and the Fed with both barrels. 'The US has performed the greatest nationalisation in the history of humanity,' he wrote on his blog.[22]

> By nationalising Fannie and Freddie the US has increased its public assets by almost $6 trillion and has increased its public debt/liabilities by another $6 trillion. The US has also undertaken the biggest and most levered LBO [leveraged buy-out] in human history that has a debt to equity ratio of 30 ($6,000 billion of debt against $200 billion of equity). So now Comrades Bush, Paulson and Bernanke ... have turned the USA into the USSRA (the United Socialist State Republic of America). Socialism is indeed alive and well in America; but this is socialism for the rich, the well connected and Wall Street. A socialism where profits are privatized and losses are socialized with the US tax-payer being charged the bill of $300 billion. This biggest bail-out and nationalisation in human history comes from the most fanatically and ideologically zealot free-market laissez-faire administration in US history ... so fanatically ideological about free markets that they did not realize that financial and other markets without proper rules, supervision and regulation are like a jungle where greed – untempered by fear of loss or of punishment – leads to credit bubbles and asset bubbles and manias and eventual bust and panics.

Politicians are used to criticism, even criticism as intense as this. What hurt most was that everything he was doing, Paulson insisted, was against his instincts. He did not like bailing out Fannie and Freddie, just as he was later to insist he hated bailing out the banks. The significance of this particular criticism was its timing. Paulson had just been through one tortured weekend and had been hammered for his response to it. He was about to face another.

'That kind of call is never good news'

The pressure on Lehman Brothers continued after Dick Fuld's conference call on Wednesday, 10 September, and newspapers began to openly speculate on the firm's bankruptcy, though few journalists believed it would be allowed to happen. Even if they did not share Fuld's confidence in his business, they assumed a deal would be cobbled together to prevent the disastrous impact of a Lehman failure on the markets. This was also very much what the US authorities were working to achieve. Lehman was running out of cash and it was running out of counterparties willing to provide it with funding. Confidence had turned violently against it. On Thursday, 11 September, Tim Geithner, then the president of the New York Federal Reserve, told Paulson that Lehman's situation was so grave that its ability to survive could be measured in days, even hours, not weeks. It was unlikely to be able to open for business the following Monday, 15 September, without a rescue deal. This was the worst possible news for Paulson, coming hard on the heels of the Fannie Mae and Freddie Mac bailout. 'We had been firefighting for over a year,' recalled Neel Kashkari, who was assistant secretary to the Treasury.[23] 'We were tired, numb to bad news, but still focused. We had just taken over Fannie Mae and Freddie Mac, and I had flown to Asia to explain our actions to foreign government officials. I returned ... to learn that Lehman was on the verge of bankruptcy. I was surprised the next emergency was already upon us. I thought our actions would buy us at least a few weeks of calm in the markets.' The Lehman share price, down nearly 95 per cent, told its own story.

Paulson was exasperated with Fuld, who he had been encouraging for months to find a buyer or a big investor. Paulson, perhaps, was not the ideal person to offer such advice. The two had been deadly Wall Street rivals. To be told what to do by somebody he would always associate with Goldman Sachs may have increased Fuld's resolve to stay independent. Paulson, 62 years old at the time of the crisis and with a personal fortune running into several hundred million dollars, may not have been the ideal Treasury secretary in the circumstances. His knowledge of the markets easily surpassed those of his two predecessors in the Bush administration, the industrialists Paul O'Neill and John Snow. But while they could reasonably be said to line up with Main Street rather than Wall Street, it was clear where Paulson's loyalties lay. It was easy for critics to say he was looking after his own. When it came to Lehman, he was clear that there had to be a private sector solution.

The first big meeting of what was to be a weekend of talks was at 6 p.m. on Friday afternoon, just after the markets closed. Federal Reserve officials had rung around at 5 p.m. to the private offices of Wall Street's top executives to tell them to turn up at the headquarters of the New York Federal Reserve, famous for its gold vaults containing billions of dollars of the precious metal dug deep into the rock of Manhattan Island. As one famously put it[24] when he got the summons: 'That kind of call is never good news.' Jamie Dimon of JP Morgan, who had struck the deal to rescue Bear Stearns, was there, as was Merrill Lynch's John Thain, for whom the weekend would be almost as momentous as it was for Fuld and Lehman. Others included Lloyd Blankfein of Goldman Sachs, Vikram Pandit of Citigroup, John Mack of Morgan Stanley and Brady Dougan of Credit Suisse. Paulson, who had breakfasted with Bernanke in Washington that morning before flying up to New York, was introduced by Geithner and told the bankers what he was looking for. He had every hope of a bidder for Lehman but, unlike the deal struck on Bear Stearns or the bailout of Fannie Mae and Freddie Mac, this rescue had to be accomplished without public money. Paulson was looking to Wall Street for a solution like that which had prevented severe contagion from the collapse of Long-Term Capital Management ten years earlier. That was a case of a single fund being in trouble and a temporary solution being needed to prevent its demise inflicting chaos. The problem in 2008 was that everybody was damaged by the crisis. Nor could anybody be sure that the rot would stop with Lehman.

Nobody left standing

The story of the 'Lehman weekend' of 13/14 September has entered legend, having been reconstructed, dramatised and analysed many times over. The BBC was first with a film, *The Last Days of Lehman Brothers*, screened twelve months after the collapse. The bald facts of the weekend are well known. The US authorities went into it believing that it had two potential saviours for Lehman, either of which would take a nasty problem off their hands. By Sunday, 14 September, both suitors had dropped out. Bank of America instead struck a deal to buy Merrill Lynch, one of Lehman Brothers' Wall Street rivals. Barclays, the final hope, dropped out of the bidding altogether. The result was that what should have been a collective effort to stave off disaster ended up with America's biggest corporate bankruptcy and, despite frenzied attempts to limit the damage, a catastrophic shock for the global financial system.

Bank of America, run by Ken Lewis, was not part of the Wall Street club. Lewis was born in Mississippi and Bank of America had its headquarters in Charlotte, North Carolina, more than six hundred miles from New York. Lewis once said that America's financial capital was a good place to visit, not to live in. Even so, it had long been his ambition to acquire a Wall Street investment bank. The bank had already been active in the crisis, buying Countrywide Financial in January 2008. When he was encouraged by Hank Paulson to talk to Dick Fuld about acquiring Lehman he was happy to do so.

Four things happened in the 36 hours between the Friday evening of 12 September and the Sunday morning of 14 September to switch his attentions instead to Merrill Lynch. The first was that, under pressure from Gregory Fleming, one of his senior colleagues, John Thain, Merrill's chairman and chief executive, contacted Lewis directly[25] about what he described as 'strategic options'. Thain, initially sceptical about any arrangement with Bank of America, was prepared to offer a 9.9 per cent stake in Merrill Lynch to Lewis, a condition of which was that Merrill would be provided with a $10 billion credit facility. The second was that Thain's scepticism evaporated during the Saturday discussions with his Wall Street rivals and officials at the New York Fed. Even if Lehman could be saved, others were directly in line. AIG, the giant insurance company, was one. Merrill, America's biggest brokerage, was the next-most vulnerable. It had sustained losses of more than $50 billion on subprime securities and its shares had slumped by 36 per cent the previous week, so it needed support.

The third factor was that Lewis, his appetite whetted by Thain's call, lost interest in Lehman, preferring Merrill. When he flew to New York on the Saturday, he made clear to Thain he was not interested in a 9.9 per cent stake and a credit line. He wanted to buy the firm and the two eventually shook hands on a price of $29 a share, or $50 billion in total. Even at the time it looked like a good deal for Merrill (not least because the scale of its losses was to prove problematical for Bank of America), though Thain was later to claim that had he not signed up, Lewis would have withdrawn its credit lines. He had, as he put it, his foot on Merrill's windpipe. The weekend that saw the demise of Lehman was the saving of Merrill, though Thain and Lewis did not work together for long, Lewis forcing Thain's resignation in January 2009 when Merrill's losses turned out to be larger than expected, and there was controversy over bonus payments by the bank and Thain's personal excesses, notably a $1 million-plus office refit, which included a $1,400 waste bin, which were mercilessly exposed in the press. That was for later. For the moment, Thain could congratulate himself on having snatched Lewis from Lehman at the altar. The final piece in the jigsaw was the approval of the US authorities. Paulson gave his blessing to the deal, seeing it as removing a potential headache. After all, he still had Barclays for Lehman.

Barclays was a British bank with big global ambitions. In the summer of 2007 it had been frustrated in those ambitions when it failed to win a bidding war for ABN-Amro, the Dutch bank, losing out to its rival, Royal Bank of Scotland. Barclays had a presence on Wall Street but it was not in the big league, to the frustration of Bob Diamond, its Massachusetts-born president, chief executive of Barclays Capital, its investment banking arm. He and Rich Ricci, the chief operating officer of Barclays' investment banking and wealth management arms, had seen that a weakened Lehman was a potential target during the summer and had made a presentation to that effect to the Barclays board in July. 'We were interested in Lehman at a price but not at any price,' Ricci recalled later.[26] On Friday, 12 September, after a call from Paulson, he and Diamond flew to New York to take part in the discussions over Lehman. At first it was made clear to them that Bank of America was in the driving seat but that should anything happen to its effort to take over Lehman, Barclays was next in the queue. Diamond and Ricci had a novel plan for Lehman. What it described as Lehman's 'big immovable illiquid assets', in other words much of the toxic debt, would be placed into a so-called bad bank, called Newco, underwritten by the rest of Wall Street on the model of the Long-Term Capital Management bailout a decade earlier. The viable parts of Lehman would carry on trading under Barclays' ownership, minimising market disruption. For it to work, however, somebody would have to guarantee Lehman's trades, estimated at some $15 billion, due the following Monday.

Barclays could not guarantee those trades itself, and certainly not without the approval of its shareholders, which would take time. Diamond contacted Warren Buffett, the legendary investor, who said he would guarantee $5 billion, but no more. On the morning of Saturday, 13 September, back in England, John Varley, Barclays' chief executive, and Hector Sants, chief executive of the Financial Services Authority, spoke on the phone and agreed that no deal was possible unless the US authorities were prepared to offer a guarantee. Alistair Darling, the chancellor, was attending an informal meeting of European finance ministers and central bankers near Nice on the Friday and Saturday, along with Sir John Gieve, deputy governor of the Bank of England. Both agreed that it was unthinkable for Barclays to proceed without a guarantee. 'I thought the idea was crackers,' said Gieve.[27] Quite why Barclays stayed in the talks for another day is not clear. One suggestion is that Sir Callum McCarthy, the FSA's chairman, was not sufficiently clear in his conversations with his US counterpart, Christopher Cox, chairman of the Securities and Exchange Commission (SEC), and Tim Geithner of the New York Fed, who was leading the rescue. Another is that Diamond thought he was playing an elaborate game of bluff with Paulson, and that the US Treasury secretary was keeping back the government guarantee as his last card. Either way, the prospect of a Barclays takeover merely prolonged the agony. When it was taken off the table during Sunday morning, New York time, Lehman was on its own. Fuld had always wanted his bank to remain independent. Now, unfortunately for him, he had got his wish. The ship was going down and he would go down with it.

The world's biggest bankruptcy

On Sunday afternoon, 14 September, the board of Lehman Brothers met on the 31st floor of the bank's Seventh Avenue headquarters in New York. The 31st floor, which included Fuld's huge executive office suite, was blamed by insiders for many of the bank's problems. In that rarefied atmosphere, cut off from the trading floors, senior management had little idea of what was really going on within the bank. Most of the board were shell-shocked, particularly Fuld. 'I don't know how this happened,' he said.[28] His last throw of the dice had been to get George Walker, a non-executive director of Lehman and a cousin of George W. Bush, to try to get through to the president to persuade him to intervene. Bush refused to come to the phone. On the 31st floor, a call came through on speakerphone from Christopher Cox, chairman of the SEC. He made clear he had no power to direct the board to put Lehman into bankruptcy but he also reminded those listening of their wider responsibilities. After an hour's discussion, the board agreed. 'I guess this is goodbye,' said Fuld.[29] Lehman's lawyers got to work and within hours the filing for Chapter 11 bankruptcy was ready, citing debts of almost $800 billion, against core capital of $18 billion, a leverage ratio of 44. Some firms come back from Chapter 11 bankruptcy but Lehman never would. Bits of the business were quickly sold, including most of the US investment banking operation to Barclays for $1.75 billion. It quickly got to work in the following weeks rebranding the firm, ripping up the green carpets and Lehman signs and replacing them with Barclays' blue. Neuberger Berman was sold for $2.15 billion, a fraction of what it was thought to be worth in the summer. It was a fire sale. By then, such decisions were out of Fuld's hands, and out of the hands of the Lehman board.

On the encouragement of Geithner, dealers were called in from their weekend breaks for an emergency trading session under the auspices of the International Swaps and Derivatives Association (ISDA). The aim was to encourage firms to 'net out' their Lehman positions, and thus minimise the amount of market disruption the following day, on the assumption that Lehman would file for bankruptcy before midnight. In the event Lehman missed the deadline, filing at 1 a.m. on the morning of Monday, 15 September. The difference was not important. The fact was that, as trading began in the Far East at the beginning of the working week, everybody knew that Lehman had gone. Though some Asian markets were closed for holidays, those that were trading slumped. Most in the markets were also aware that, despite the netting-out session, and measures by the Federal Reserve and market participants to ensure an orderly run-down of Lehman's positions, it would be bloody. Paulson tried to offer some reassurance. Applauding the efforts of the Federal Reserve and the SEC, he also praised the markets. 'I particularly appreciate the efforts of market participants who came together this weekend and initiated a set of steps to facilitate orderliness and stability in our financial markets as we work through this extraordinary environment,' he said.[30] 'Today we are looking forward. This weekend's discussions made clear that both market participants and regulators in this country and abroad recognize the need to support market stability and remove uncertainty as they address current challenges.' It was an attempt, and not a very convincing one, to make the best of a bad job. For a few hours, the US authorities tried to convince people that the effects of the Lehman collapse were containable. 'For several days, we have worked closely with regulators around the world … to coordinate our actions in the interest of orderly markets,' said Christopher Cox of the SEC.[31] 'In doing so we have also worked closely with the Treasury and the Federal Reserve and market participants. We are committed to using our regulatory and supervisory authorities to reduce the potential for dislocations from recent events, and to maintain the smooth functioning of the financial markets.' It was a vain hope. The functioning of the markets for the next few weeks was going to be anything but smooth, as everybody probably knew.

Getting to the truth about Lehman

There remain important questions about the Lehman weekend that go beyond the straightforward 'how was it allowed to happen?' It is worth going into some of them in a little more detail.

1. Was public money on offer for Lehman?

One of the puzzles about Lehman Brothers and the failed attempt to secure a rescue for it is whether, contrary to the apparently hard line taken by the authorities, there was in fact taxpayer money on hand to help out. Would the Bear Stearns solution, apparently ruled out by

Paulson at the start of the weekend, have been possible? The answer to this, despite the outcry that it would have created, seems to be yes. Paulson, who after George W. Bush was voted out of office embarked on his own account of the crisis, appeared to confirm it in an interview with the *New Yorker*. 'We said, "No public money",' Paulson told its reporter.[32] 'We said this publicly. We repeated it when these guys came in. But to ourselves we said, "If there's a chance to put in public money and avert a disaster, we're open to it."'

Tim Geithner, who on the face of it took a firmer line against any form of public intervention, insisted that the authorities were severely constrained in their ability to use public money. As Treasury secretary in the Obama administration, he could have chosen to blame his predecessor had he wished, but chose not to. 'People got the impression that we were trying to make a point,' he said in an interview with *Fortune* in September 2009.[33]

> There's zero truth in that. Understandably, there was a deep public antipathy to putting public money at risk, to rewarding firms for taking too much risk. But that was not relevant. What was relevant in the end was that the government of the US did not have the ability to help rescue Lehman in the absence of a willing buyer. In a crisis you need to make a choice. You can choose to solve the problem and protect the innocent from the results of a firestorm. Or you can try to teach a lesson. You can't solve the problem by teaching people a lesson. That's not a strategy for solving a crisis. It's a strategy for inflicting a lot of damage.

The key point was that the government could not help out 'in the absence of a willing buyer', not that it could not help out at all.

2. Did Britain wreck a Lehman rescue?

If there was uncertainty in the discussions in New York, there was even more when it came to transatlantic conversations over the Lehman rescue. To this day, some American policymakers blame British caution and an insistence on the letter of the law for the failure of Barclays to complete its bid for Lehman Brothers. What is the truth of this? While the Financial Services Authority, as Barclays' regulator, took the lead, both the Bank of England and the Treasury were opposed to a deal that would leave one of Britain's biggest banks dangerously exposed. Even before the Lehman crisis, the tripartite grouping was coming to the conclusion that most UK banks, including Barclays, were undercapitalised. For Barclays to take on a substantial amount of additional debt, and risk, was seen in London as extreme folly. 'We were horrified by the idea,' said one senior Bank of England official.[34] Thus, what came over to the Americans as pettifogging bureaucracy – the FSA insisting that any takeover had to be preceded by a shareholder vote – was a device by the British authorities to put on the brakes. Paulson and Darling appear to have achieved a better understanding in their telephone calls. When the Treasury secretary complained to the chancellor that the FSA was being obstructive, Darling replied that he had to take into account the wider British interest and that of the taxpayer. He may already have been looking forward to the time, just weeks away, when the taxpayer would be required to step in and rescue British banks in a big way. Paulson interpreted Darling's response to mean that Britain did not want to import America's banking 'cancer'.

What is not clear is what would have happened if the Barclays deal had been available with US government guarantees. The British authorities insist that no such plan was put to them, even though they thought it was implicit in earlier conversations that some such guarantee would be needed. The Americans appear to have taken Britain's objections at face value, concluding that the FSA was prepared to block any deal. Barclays walked away from the talks (though it subsequently acquired Lehman's American business for a knockdown price), insisting it had decided without pressure from the authorities that it could not guarantee the billions of Lehman debt about to be rolled over in the markets. It was a three-way misunderstanding. Had there been a few more days to work with, perhaps it could all have been resolved. There was not. A failure of communication compounded an already difficult situation.

3. Was Lehman's failure a good thing?

It took a long time for the dust to settle on the collapse of Lehman

Brothers and its impact on financial markets, the international banking system and the world economy. The question was whether it should have been prevented, or whether it was the shock needed to provoke policymakers into the kind of extreme action required to prevent a drift into a second Great Depression. It is possible to envisage a situation in which Lehman would have been bought by another bank, in an officially brokered and supported deal similar to that for JP Morgan and Bear Stearns, but, six months later, another crisis would have erupted and valuable time lost in the fight against depression. It was only after Lehman, after all, that central banks outside the United States stopped worrying about inflation and started worrying about the slump. On this view, Lehman's collapse was the essential wake-up call. Suddenly, policymakers could do things that they could not do before – secure public support for unprecedented and costly measures to support the banking system with taxpayers' money. The world, in other words, had to stare into the abyss before such action was possible. Lehman was the catalyst.

As well as that, it could be seen as the end of Wall Street's age of arrogance, a dramatic demonstration that nobody was too big to fail. Niall Ferguson, the historian, pointed out[35] that to take the argument about saving Lehman to its absurd conclusion, people might argue that had it not failed, the singer Michael Jackson might still be alive, as he would not have had to rehearse a gruelling schedule of concerts to compensate for the plunge in the value of his investments. 'The real tragedy is that the failure of Lehman has left Wall Street's survivors both bigger in relative terms and more secure politically,' wrote Ferguson.[36] 'As long as the big banks feel confident that they can count on the government to bail them out – for who would now risk "another Lehman"? – they can more or less ignore calls for lower leverage and saner compensation. If only we had learnt from Lehman that no bank should be "too big to fail", we might still have a real capitalist system, instead of the state-guaranteed monstrosity that is the real legacy of the crisis.'

4. Was it an unnecessary panic?
Why was Lehman's collapse so devastating? One Bank of England

official, its executive director for financial stability Andy Haldane, likened it to a global health scare such as the SARS (severe acute respiratory syndrome) outbreak of 2002/03. The fear of SARS spread around the world much more than the disease did. It dealt a serious blow to many Asian economies, cutting between one and four percentage points off their growth rates. Travel was cut back sharply and hotel occupancy rates in cities such as Hong Kong plummeted. Chinese restaurants were boycotted in America. Yet the direct health effects of the crisis were, on a global scale, tiny. Only 8,000 people contracted SARS and fewer than 1,000 died. The impact, in other words, was out of proportion to the underlying problem. That was also true in the case of Lehman's failure, Haldane argued. When it went bankrupt, the fear was of defaults on a scale never before seen. The fear of falling victim to the Lehman contagion, or being on the wrong side of the $5 trillion of credit default swaps it was counterparty to, froze activity.

'Media and modern communications fed this frenzy and transmitted it across markets,' said Haldane.[37]

> Banks hoarded liquidity for fear of lending to infected banks, causing gridlock in term money markets, spreads on lower-rated companies' bonds spiked and there was an effective boycott of the remaining large US investment banks. Professor Paul Krugman, Nobel Prize winner in economics, commented: 'Letting Lehman fail basically brought the entire world capital market down.' The macroeconomic impact of Lehman Brothers' failure will never be known with any certainty … Yet in the final reckoning, the direct losses from Lehman's failure seem likely to be relatively modest. Net payouts on Lehman's CDS contracts amounted to only around $5 billion.

The paralysing fear that magnified the crisis, in other words, was hugely out of proportion to the underlying event.

Some say the failure to prevent Lehman from collapsing changed little. The world was hurtling towards an economic and financial disaster in any event and policymakers were aware of it. Saving Lehman might have shifted the focus to another weekend, another bank, but no more. 'The dominant reality was that a solution for Lehman would not be sufficient to contain the intensifying storm,' said Geithner later.[38] 'Remember, Lehman was the symptom of how powerful this crisis was, not the cause or the precipitator. Going into that weekend, we were already in the midst of a run on other institutions. You really did have – for the first time in 80 years – the initial signs of a classic panic. Everybody knew we were looking at the abyss.' There may be an element of self-justification in this from an official who worked hard to save Lehman but failed. The fact is that we can never know for certain what would have happened to the financial system if Lehman had been rescued. It is hard to imagine that a rescue would have resulted in a worse outcome in the few months that followed its collapse. It is hard to imagine, too, that the cost to governments around the world of bailing out their banks would have been any more. It was the weekend that changed the world and, for a while at least, changed it in a very frightening way. The consequences were to be very dramatic, and in some cases verged on the tragic.

Every financial crisis throws up huge frauds – scams and schemes that would never have been discovered had things not turned sour. In the 1930s it was Ivar Kreuger, 'the Match King', who shot himself in a Paris hotel room in 1932 after his fraud was discovered. Kreuger was running a Ponzi scheme, named after Charles Ponzi, who defrauded US investors in the early 1900s by the simple but ultimately unsustainable method of paying existing investors out of the money flowing in from new ones. Bernard 'Bernie' Madoff was a natural successor to Ponzi and Kreuger, and the extraordinary thing was how long he managed to pull off his deception. Madoff had set up in business in 1960, though in court testimony he said his Ponzi scheme had begun only in 1991. The funds on which he apparently achieved market-beating returns for investors were simply put in the bank, the returns either coming from new investors, who Madoff screened carefully, or from the capital of existing investors. It came to an abrupt end in December 2008, when investors, hit by the Lehman collapse, sought to withdraw $7 billion that Madoff did not have at his disposal. He confessed to his sons, who worked in the firm, that his scheme had been 'one big lie' from the start.[39]

The financial collapse brought widespread misery. Somehow, however, the story, of Bernie Madoff himself as a pillar of Wall Street and the New York and Florida Jewish communities while secretly defrauding his clients, seemed unusually cruel. Madoff's philanthropy, and his investment record, attracted him to Jewish charities, some of which were bankrupted by the fraud. Elie Wiesel, the Nazi concentration camp survivor and Nobel peace prize winner, lost most of his own money and the $15.2 million his foundation had accumulated. The film-maker Steven Spielberg's Wunderkind charity had 70 per cent of its money invested with Madoff. There were many more such victims. Madoff's fraud was originally put at $50 billion, though losses were eventually estimated to be just under $20 billion. The Securities and Exchange Commission, the regulator, had failed to uncover the fraud despite eight investigations over sixteen years and frequent tip-offs that the returns Madoff was claiming were impossible. Madoff pleaded guilty in March 2009 to eleven counts of fraud and in June was sentenced to 150 years in jail, with a target release date of 2039 for good behaviour, by which time he would be 101. By the time of his sentencing, more than 15,000 claims for compensation had been received, some aimed at securing the return of funds withdrawn by investors just before the collapse. Most of the claimants would see little of their money again.

10

Battling the Meltdown

The collapse of Lehman Brothers was followed by six weeks of extreme turmoil on financial markets. Wave after wave of alarming news washed over the financial wires, threatening to engulf policymakers. The 24-hour news channels became required viewing. For journalists it was both exhilarating and frustrating. The excitement and drama of a global financial system in acute crisis were tinged by the fact that once-in-a-decade stories were coming along almost daily. How bad was it? George W. Bush, in one memorable phrase, when he was pleading with congressional leaders to back the White House's banking bailout package, two weeks after Lehman, put it bluntly:[1] 'If money isn't loosened up, this sucker could go down.' Mervyn King, the governor of the Bank of England, was more elegant in his language but his message was similar. The global banking system had nearly shut down, with devastating consequences. 'Following the failure of Lehman Brothers on 15 September, an extraordinary, almost unimaginable, sequence of events began ...' King said.[2]

It is difficult to exaggerate the severity and importance of those events. Not since the beginning of the First World War has our banking system been so close to collapse. In the second half of September, companies and non-bank financial institutions accelerated their withdrawal from even short-term funding of banks, and banks increasingly lost confidence in the safety of lending to each other. Funding costs rose sharply and for many institutions it was possible to borrow only overnight. Credit to the real economy almost stopped flowing.

American international disaster

The sequence of events King was referring to began on Monday, 15 September with a slump on world markets as dealers digested the implications of the Lehman collapse. Next day came an announcement that was even more shocking, in its way. Throughout the 'Lehman weekend' of 13/14 September, Hank Paulson, the Treasury secretary, and Tim Geithner, head of the New York Fed, gradually became aware that saving Lehman was not their only priority. AIG, American International Group, at one time the world's biggest insurance company, was looming as an even bigger headache. Why was a company that sold motor and home insurance and sponsored sports teams such as Manchester United in such deep trouble? The answer was that, mainly through its financial products division in London, it had become a global leader in credit default swaps (CDS). In the good times issuing CDS – effectively an insurance against borrowers defaulting on their debts – was a hugely profitable business for AIG, much more so than conventional insurance. The firm's earnings on CDS, at a time when nobody was defaulting, were the equivalent of taking candy from a baby. This may have been AIG's problem. It failed to hedge its own risks, not believing that it would ever need to. The design of CDS contracts landed AIG with a huge problem when the market in subprime and other asset-backed securities froze and prices slumped in the summer of 2007. It had to post increasing amounts of collateral to cover the weakness in these securities. Meanwhile, AIG's holdings of risky assets would have made even a red-blooded investment bank blush. On one estimate, it was carrying $560 billion of so-called super-senior risk as the credit crisis broke.

AIG's road to crisis during 2008 was almost as well signposted as that of Lehman, but when it came it was still shocking. Even as Paulson and Ben Bernanke were issuing calming statements on the evening of 14 September, they knew another potential disaster was looming. AIG had tens of billions of dollars of payments coming due over the next two to three weeks and it did not have the money. An initial offer of $20 billion to AIG on Monday, 15 September was withdrawn because it would have done little. The following day the Federal Reserve announced, 'with the full support of the Treasury department', that it was providing AIG with an $85 billion loan facility, for two years, in return for a 79.9 per cent equity stake in the business. If the 'conservatorship' of Fannie Mae and Freddie Mac had brought accusations of socialism, this was Karl Marx red in tooth and claw, and it stuck in the craw. 'I think if there's a single episode in this entire 18 months that has made me more angry, I can't think of one, than AIG,' Bernanke told Congress six months later.[3] 'AIG exploited a huge gap in the regulatory system. There was no oversight of the Financial Products division. This was a hedge fund, basically, that was attached to a large and stable insurance company, made huge numbers of irresponsible bets – took huge losses. There was no regulatory oversight because there was a gap in the system.'

He had a right to be angry. Like Lehman, this was a freebooting capitalist company, built up aggressively by Maurice 'Hank' Greenberg, who was forced to step down in 2005 after huge accounting irregularities were uncovered. That did not stop AIG's reckless expansion, as Bernanke had found out. The initial $85 billion was a down payment, the US authorities eventually injecting roughly double that amount into AIG. It looked for all the world as if the US authorities were picking up the pieces from their reluctance to bail out Lehman. Why let Lehman fail and then expensively rescue AIG? Because, insisted those involved in the rescue, the threat of an AIG collapse was even more serious. 'We had no choice but to try to stabilize the system because of the implications that the failure would have had for the broad economic system,' said Bernanke.[4] Geithner agreed. 'Your government made the judgment back in the fall that there was no way that you could allow default to happen without catastrophic damage to the American people,' he said.[5]

The US authorities were fighting fires on all fronts. Bruce Bent was the founder of the money market fund industry. On Monday, 15 September, in Rome to celebrate his 50th wedding anniversary, he received a call from his son, also Bruce, in his New York office. As a result of Lehman, he said, they had problems. The following day, their prominent money market fund, the Reserve Primary Fund, announced that as a result of Lehman debt securities it held, which had been valued at $785 million but were now deemed to be worth nothing, its net asset value had fallen to $0.97 a share. The significance of this was huge. Money market funds were popular among retail investors in America and were regarded as being as safe as cash in the bank. The drop in Reserve Primary's net asset value to less than a dollar, otherwise known as 'breaking the buck', was not supposed to happen. Investors were allowed to redeem their investments at a dollar and plenty chose to do so. On Monday, as rumours of its Lehman exposure spread, Reserve Primary had $20 billion of redemption requests. The next day, as the panic spread to other funds, more than $33 billion of redemption requests were lodged by the industry. Statements reassuring investors that there was no cause for concern merely succeeded in adding to the sense of crisis. It was an American banking run in all but name. Only on Friday, 19 September, when the US Treasury resurrected an old tool, the Exchange Stabilisation Fund established in the Depression era, did the panic subside. It provided $50 billion of guarantees to the money market funds, saying:[6] 'Maintenance of the standard $1 net asset value for money market mutual funds is important to investors. If the net asset value for a fund falls below $1, this undermines investor confidence. The program provides support to investors in funds that participate in the program and those funds will not "break the buck".'

'We will deal with the competition issues'

Across the Atlantic, the Lehman effect was also evident. Monday, 15 September was a terrible day for banking shares and, in particular, for HBOS (Halifax Bank of Scotland), which saw its shares immediately marked down by 34 per cent. HBOS should have been one of Britain's most solid and reliable banks. It was formed in 2001 by a merger of two respected institutions. Halifax, which had been Britain's biggest building society until its demutualisation in 1997, was Britain's biggest lender, having swallowed up a number of its smaller rivals over the years. Bank of Scotland was Britain's oldest clearing bank, created by an Act of Parliament in 1686. They were a good fit. Halifax was strong in retail banking and in particular in the mortgage market. Bank of Scotland's strength was business banking, both north of the border and, increasingly, across Britain. Eyebrows were raised in 2006 when Andy Hornby, an undoubted high-flyer, was made chief executive at the age of 38. Old banking hands grumbled, not just about his age but about his limited banking experience. Though he had been with the bank for a few years before his elevation, his early career was with Asda, the supermarket chain.

HBOS did well during the good times but by 2008 it was in trouble. Its mortgage business was threatened by similar funding problems to those that had afflicted Northern Rock. Its reliance on wholesale funding was not as acute as Northern Rock's but the freezing of credit markets exposed weaknesses in its funding model. Halifax, as the country's biggest mortgage lender, was also threatened by Britain's falling housing market. Its own house price index showed housing values down by 10.9 per cent on a year earlier, with the pace of decline accelerating fast. Meanwhile, its corporate banking division, run by Peter Cummings, had expanded into areas where other banks feared to tread. Entrepreneurs wanting to launch audacious bids came to Cummings first. He was the man Sir Philip Green turned to when he tried to acquire Marks & Spencer in 2004, and he bankrolled Baugur, the Icelandic group which took over much of Britain's high street. Though the full extent was not to become known for some time, it was already clear that many of Cummings's loans were turning sour.

Lloyds Bank, in contrast, was regarded as safe to the point of being staid. Under Eric Daniels, its American chief executive, it had avoided being drawn into many of the risky areas that were proving so problematical for its rivals. Even so, it had ambitions, and it saw the crisis as the opportunity for realising those ambitions. In August 2008, before the Lehman collapse, Daniels met Hornby for a drink. They agreed that a link up between the two banks would be beneficial but there was an obvious problem. Even in these unusual circumstances, there would be no chance of getting a merger past the competition authorities. Seven years earlier Lloyds had attempted to buy Abbey, another former building society turned bank, and had been prevented from doing so by the Competition Commission. Lloyds and HBOS would be an even more powerful force in UK banking, with nearly 30 per cent of the mortgage market. Lloyds, however, still sensed an opportunity. By chance its chairman, Sir Victor Blank, had been part of a business delegation visiting Israel and Palestine with Gordon Brown in July. In conversation with the prime minister he had suggested that if a British bank got into trouble and needed rescuing it would be no use waiting around for many months while the competition authorities assessed whether a takeover should be permitted. Brown was receptive to the idea, having no desire for a repeat of the long uncertainty of Northern Rock, though he did not know at that stage that other banks would need rescuing. That all changed after Lehman. Blank and Brown were together at a dinner on the evening of 15 September, after a torrid day for bank shares, particularly HBOS, and the prime minister reminded the Lloyds chairman of their earlier conversation. 'If you think you want to advance on this, we will deal with the competition issues,' Brown said, according to Blank's account.[7]

Events moved quickly. Blank was contacted first thing the following morning by Sir Callum McCarthy, chairman of the Financial Services Authority, and detailed negotiations began on a merger that would see Lloyds as the senior partner in a merged business, with a 56 per cent share. Still HBOS shares hurtled downwards, however. Daniels and Hornby knew they had to get an announcement out quickly to stop the rot. They did, on Wednesday, 17 September, but not before Robert Peston, the BBC's business editor, had broken the story. It was, said some banking experts, a once-in-a-lifetime opportunity for Lloyds, which it had to grab with both hands, though unions were concerned about the loss of tens of thousands of jobs among the 140,000 workforce. The heady deal-making days of September had an unhappy ending, however, at least for some of those involved. As news emerged in the following weeks about the scale of HBOS's problems, prompting a renegotiation of the terms of the original deal, Lloyds was accused of failing to carry out due diligence. Shareholders complained that their safe bank had been contaminated by HBOS and fatally weakened. Neither Hornby nor Blank stayed long with the bank.

Scaring Congress

Back in Washington, the situation was not improving either. The AIG bailout on Tuesday, 16 September had merely added to the sense of panic on the New York markets. On the evening of 17 September, Bernanke, Paulson and Geithner held a conference call. 'We can't do this anymore,' said Bernanke.[8] 'We have to go to Congress.' The following day, Bernanke and Paulson went to Capitol Hill to talk to congressional leaders. The Federal Reserve Board chairman, who had almost failed to get the job in 2006 because of his 'gentle' understated manner, was forthright. History had taught us that severe banking crises and financial meltdowns were followed by major recessions, he warned. Without action by Congress, the recession America was facing would be unusually deep and prolonged. Banks had stopped lending to one another. The credit lines in the US economy were frozen, and they were the lifeblood of the economy. Banking failures would just be the start. Within days, big brand-name firms could go down. The congressional leaders were impressed and more than a little frightened. 'I kind of scared them,' Bernanke said later.[9] 'I kind of scared myself.' Plenty of other people were scared. PIMCO (the Pacific Investment Management Company) is the world's biggest bond fund manager and Mohamed El-Erian, its chief executive, a former senior official at the International Monetary Fund, was used to financial scares. This one was different. 'On the Wednesday and Thursday after Lehman filed for Chapter 11, I asked my wife to please go to the ATM and take as much cash as she could,' he said.[10] 'When she asked why, I said it was because I didn't know whether there was a chance banks might not open. I remember my wife sort of pausing and saying: "Are you serious?" And I said: "Yes I am."'

Perhaps Bernanke should have addressed the whole Congress. Two days after the meeting with congressional leaders, Paulson submitted a three-page document to Capital Hill. The Troubled Asset Relief Program (TARP) was a $700 billion plan to get the banking system through the crisis, initially at least, by taking toxic assets off their books. It was an extraordinary document, not just because of the scale of the intervention it implied. It also gave the Treasury secretary apparently unlimited powers. 'Decisions by the Secretary pursuant to the authority of this Act are non-reviewable and committed to agency discretion, and may not be reviewed by any court of law or any administrative agency,' it said.[11] The aim was to promote market stability (and help protect American families) by comprehensively addressing the root cause of the stresses in the financial system. Take away the toxic assets blocking the banking system and clogging financial markets and normality would begin to return. In time, those assets, which would be managed on the government's behalf by private managers, would be sold and the proceeds handed back to taxpayers. It sounded like a cure-all and, for many in Congress, it sounded too good to be true, as Paulson quickly discovered. Days of wrangling followed, during which President Bush broadcast to the nation on the vital importance of Congress approving the plan. 'At first I thought we could deal with the problem one issue at a time,' Bush said.[12] 'The house of cards was much bigger and started to stretch beyond Wall Street. When one card started to go, we worried about the whole deck going down.' One such card was Washington Mutual, a mortgage lender, which was taken over by regulators. Though most of it was quickly sold on to JP Morgan Chase, it counted as the biggest failure of a conventional bank in American history, though it almost passed in a blur.

Raw politics rubbed against unstable finance. Many in Congress hated the original TARP, both because of the sweeping powers it gave the Treasury secretary and because it was seen as benefiting Wall Street and ignoring Main Street. This was Paulson's weak spot; because of his background he was seen as too close to the investment banks he was trying to bail out. Despite presidential pleas, behind-the-scenes arm-twisting and a temporary suspension of the election campaign being fought between John McCain and Barack Obama (who attended emergency meetings in Washington), the House of Representatives rejected the TARP by 228 votes to 205 on Monday, 29 September, sending the Dow Jones industrial average down by nearly 800 points. Bush returned to the nation's television screens the following day to implore Congress to pass the plan. The TARP was amended to provide more direct help to homeowners and businesses, and funding for disaster emergency relief, which proved to be enough to get it through the Senate on 1 October and the more sceptical House of Representatives two days later. The TARP was to change many times in the following months, becoming a catch-all economic rescue fund. A political hurdle had been passed but the economic hurdles were getting taller. The day the House of Representatives passed the plan, figures showed a 159,000 drop in American employment, the biggest for five years. There would be much worse to come. That day too, Arnold Schwarzenegger, the governor of California, wrote to Paulson warning him that the state could require an emergency bailout. From embattled New York to the 'Golden State', the crisis was deepening.

Financial contagion

Other political leaders were coming to the same conclusion as Bush; that piecemeal rescues of troubled financial institutions were not going to do the trick. The problem was a familiar one. If one bank failed, or had to be bailed out by its government, the markets moved on to the next victim. Few banks were safe from speculative attack. Governments and regulators were forced into more rescues in the weeks after Lehman's bankruptcy than in the several decades that preceded it. In Europe, the weekend of 27/28 September saw the 'Benelux' countries, Belgium, the Netherlands and Luxembourg, joining forces to rescue Fortis, a banking, insurance and investment management conglomerate which had its main activities split between the three countries. The three governments injected more than €11 billion to partly nationalise the firm. A few days later the Dutch government announced plans to take over the parts of the business based in the Netherlands, while most of the rest was sold to BNP Paribas, the French bank. European governments and regulators, like their US counterparts, were fighting fires everywhere. Two days after Fortis, Dexia, the Belgian-French specialist lender, had to be bailed out. The German government, acting in concert with leading banks, launched a €35 billion lifeboat to save Hypo Real Estate, the country's second largest commercial property lender.

In Britain, just over a year after the authorities had struggled and stumbled over what to do about the plight of Northern Rock, an opportunity to redeem themselves cropped up. Bradford & Bingley, yet another former building society turned bank, had suffered the now familiar prelude to disaster, a collapse in its share price. The former building societies, many of which used their new status as banks to expand into riskier areas of commercial and buy-to-let lending, and which had left their traditional deposit base in favour of reliance on wholesale funding, had become a dying breed. Over the weekend of 27/28 September, after another weekend of tense negotiations, Bradford & Bingley became Britain's second big nationalisation of the crisis. Banco Santander of Spain (which already owned Abbey) stepped in to buy the bank's 200 branches and its savings accounts of just over £20 billion, but UK tax-payers were left with the rump of the business, a £50 billion mortgage book, some of it risky and prone to default.

Financial contagion and chaos describe the events of September and October 2008 well. Wachovia, an American bank, first struck a deal to be rescued by Citigroup, then Wells Fargo. Switzerland, apparently the home of safe banks, suffered more reputational damage than most. UBS (Union Bank of Switzerland), a pillar of the country's banking establish-ment, was knee deep in toxic assets. In mid-October the Swiss govern-ment agreed to inject $5 billion into the bank, alongside an officially backed fund to take up to $60 billion of its toxic assets. In 2008 UBS lost more than $17 billion, the largest corporate loss in Swiss history. ING, the big Dutch bank, had to be helped out at the same time by a €10 billion capital injection from its government. The crisis was spreading fast, and nowhere was worse affected than one particular country.

The melting of Iceland

On 5 October 2008, Geir Haarde, Iceland's prime minister, gave reas-surances that the country's banking system, with assets and liabilities equivalent to many times the nation's gross domestic product, could get through without special measures. A day later, a freezing of all the banks' credit lines, a collapse in their share prices and a 30 per cent fall in the value of the Icelandic krona had destroyed that hope in the space of 24 hours. Iceland's financial regulator had suspended the shares of the banks and savings funds, while the government guaranteed the deposits of Iceland's savers. Financial meltdown had come to Iceland and the prime minister addressed the nation again, trying to invoke the wartime spirit. 'If there was ever a time when the Icelandic nation needed to stand together and show fortitude in the face of adversity, then this is the moment,' he said.[13]

> I urge you all to guard that which is most important in the life of every-one of us, protect those values which will survive the storm now begin-ning. What is most important is that the foundations of our society and the economy are solid, even though the superstructure has given way in the face of the present disaster. We have natural resources, both on sea and land, which will ensure us a good living whatever happens. Our level of education and the human resources which we have here are no less enviable in the eyes of other nations than our natural resources. Fellow Icelanders, the task of the authorities over the coming days is clear: to make sure that chaos does not ensue if the Icelandic banks become to some extent non-operational. It is very important that we display both calm and consideration during the difficult days ahead, that we do not lose courage and support each other as well as we can. Thus with Icelan-dic optimism, fortitude and solidarity as weapons, we will ride out the storm. God bless Iceland.

How had Iceland, a country with a population of just over 304,000 people, come to be battered to the point of surrender by the global finan-cial crisis? How did a country previously known for its fishing indus-try and its geysers come to be at the centre of the banking storm? The answer, as it does to many such questions arising from the crisis, lies with reckless expansion of banking. Nor was this unnoticed. For years, doubts had been raised about Iceland, and the ability of such a tiny economy to provide the springboard for so much international activity. Other aspects of the global financial crisis emerged from beneath the surface. This was not the case for Iceland. Iceland's major banks had been state owned until the early 2000s, their privatisation being com-pleted only in 2003. At the time, Iceland's banking assets were equiva-lent to slightly less than twice the country's GDP; high but not unusual. Five years later, they had risen to at least eight times GDP. If anything went wrong with Iceland's banks, it had the potential to bankrupt the host country several times over.

Iceland's banks, principally Kaupthing, Landsbanki and Glitnir, had expanded beyond their tiny national deposit bases in the conventional way, by accessing wholesale funding on the international markets. Then in 2006 Landsbanki hit on the idea of tapping into the retail deposits of other countries, by launching Icesave, its online savings bank. Landsbanki, with limited costs because of its small number of branches, was used to paying high interest rates to savers at home. By offering attractive rates to savers in other countries, regularly topping 'best buy' tables in Britain and elsewhere, Icesave was able to fund a large part of its activities. Kaupthing followed a similar approach, launching Kaupthing Edge. There was an added bonus for the customers of the banks in Iceland, or so it seemed. They could borrow in foreign currencies to buy homes or prestige cars (Range Rovers were very popular in Iceland), at much lower interest rates than if borrowing in domestic currency. The business customers of the Icelandic banks, meanwhile, could expand aggressively on the back of this international funding. One such company, Baugur, founded in 1989 with a single supermarket in Reykjavik, had a spectacular 20-year arc, cutting a swathe through Britain's high streets with the acquisition of Hamleys, Oasis, Karen Millen, Coast, Goldsmiths, Julian Graves and others, as well as a substantial stake in House of Fraser. It sought bankruptcy in February 2009.

By then, Iceland's prime minister, Geir Haarde, had been forced out of office, in January 2009, and there had been riots outside the country's parliament, the building splattered with paint and yogurt, fireworks aimed at the windows and fires lit outside doors. A 'hate list' of the ten people responsible for the mess had been drawn up. The crisis had come to a head on the day of Haarde's October address. A few days earlier Glitnir, one of the three big banks, had been effectively nationalised, a move that, far from calming nerves, merely pointed to the impending failure of Landsbanki and Kaupthing, both of which were taken over by the financial regulator. Iceland's finance minister later revealed that when he attended the annual meetings of the IMF and the World Bank in autumn 2008, he had taken more cash than he had ever carried before, because he did not expect any of his credit cards to work. There was the huge issue of the banks' big overseas deposit base. Retail customers rushed to get their money out of Icesave and Kaupthing Edge. To stem the panic, other governments, including Britain's, were forced to guarantee the deposits of the Icelandic banks. They failed to extend these guarantees to local authorities and charities, however, which had also been attracted by the interest rates on offer. In November 2008, Iceland was given a two-year loan of $2.1 billion from the IMF, together with pledges from Poland, Britain, the Netherlands and Germany, which would take its stand-by facility to more than $10 billion, half the country's GDP. On one estimate, bailing out the country's banks and paying off international creditors would cost 90 per cent of Iceland's GDP. In early 2010, Icelanders baulked at compensating Britain and The Netherlands for Icesave's losses, forcing a referendum. The failure of Iceland's three banks was, according to the IMF, the biggest in relation to the size of the economy anywhere, at any time. The puzzle was why, with the country effectively bankrupt, the economic pain was not even greater. Against predictions of a 10 per cent slump in GDP in 2009, Iceland had a decline of closer to 6.5 per cent. Perhaps it was just that the pain was going to be extended. It certainly felt that way in Iceland.

From a shotgun wedding to a drive-by shooting

For the authorities in London, it was becoming increasingly clear that the only solution to the deepening banking crisis was a taxpayer rescue for all the UK banks. The government had to stand ready to support everybody who needed it. Action had been taken to reassure depositors by increasing the level of savings guaranteed against failure to £50,000 for each customer in every bank. The 'shotgun wedding' between Lloyds Bank and HBOS had averted one immediate crisis but failed to calm the situation. Now the task was to provide system-wide reassurance which would end the battering for bank shares, prevent corporate customers shifting their deposits and bring confidence back to the wholesale markets. On Sunday, 5 October, Gordon Brown contacted Paul Myners, a long-time Labour Party supporter and chairman of the Guardian Media Group, Land Securities, the Tate Gallery and the Low Pay Commission, the body that set Britain's national minimum wage. The prime minister told him that he needed somebody to negotiate with the banks about an unprecedented programme that would involve injections of taxpayer-provided capital, liquidity and lending guarantees, potentially to all Britain's banks. Myners's ennoblement was set in train to allow him to become a minister. On arriving at the Treasury, he was made aware of the urgency of the situation.

Royal Bank of Scotland (RBS), Britain's second-largest bank, was about to suffer the fate of Lehman Brothers. It was running out of money, had lost the confidence of its counterparties in the wholesale markets and, even more so than its competitors, was finding its shares being battered on the stock market. More than any other British bank, including Northern Rock, RBS had ridden the wave of the global credit boom. Sir Fred Goodwin, its chief executive, was the Icarus of Britain's banking sector, driving what had been a regional UK bank in search first of domination of the national banking scene and then a major world role. The moment when he flew too close to the sun was on the eve of the financial crisis in 2007 when, as part of a consortium, he beat off Barclays for the acquisition of the Dutch bank ABN-Amro, a £10 billion purchase that was eventually to cost RBS a further £20 billion in goodwill write-downs alone.

It was just the latest in a series of bold purchases by the man known as 'Fred the Shred' for his ability, perhaps due to his training as an accountant, to cut costs, even if it meant slashing jobs. Goodwin's most audacious purchase was in 2000 when he won a battle with his Edinburgh rival Bank of Scotland (later part of HBOS) to buy National Westminster bank. NatWest, as it was known, was significantly bigger in size than RBS but, largely as a result of weak management, had made itself a takeover candidate. Suddenly, after taking over NatWest, RBS was an important national player. Goodwin's expansion drive resulted in a financial services empire, including Coutts (the Queen's bank), Adam & Co., Direct Line and Churchill, the insurance groups, Ulster Bank and, in America, Citizens' Bank. When the crisis broke, RBS was fast expanding into China, including a minority stake in Bank of China. Now all that expansion looked like a spectacular example of hubris. In the spring of 2008 RBS had raised £12 billion from shareholders in Britain's biggest-ever rights issue: persuading existing owners of the bank to put in more funds. It was not enough and, indeed, shareholders were angry about having been persuaded to part with their cash.

The 'make or break' week for Britain's banking system began on Monday, 6 October 2008 and lasted until the following Monday. The week began badly, with talk of banking rescues or outright nation-alisation. For bank investors and for hedge funds and others driving share price movements, the uncertainty was a reason to sell. Nor was this an irrational response. RBS and HBOS, which had still not been absorbed into Lloyds, were under extreme pressure, and not just in the stock market. A 'silent run' was taking place in which corporate and other customers were moving their money out. Only official support kept them going. 'On that Monday and Tuesday, it was not possible for those two banks to be confident they could get to the end of the day,' recalled Mervyn King later.[14] More than a year later, the Bank revealed that it had secretly lent £61.6 billion to the two banks, RBS and HBOS, to get them through the crisis. After a series of crisis meetings involv-ing Treasury, Bank of England and FSA officials, together with their City advisers, the crunch came on the evening of Tuesday, 7 October. A meeting at 11 Downing Street chaired by Alistair Darling the previous evening had been reported by the BBC's Robert Peston as a demand by the heads of RBS, Lloyds and Barclays for an immediate injection of taxpayer capital. If these banks were so desperate to be bailed out by the taxpayer, the markets decided something must indeed be badly wrong.

In fact, when Sir Fred Goodwin turned up at the Treasury at 5 p.m. on Tuesday, 7 October, for a meeting with Lord Myners and officials, to be told he was to get an injection of capital whether he wanted it or not, he was furious. 'No business ever dies because it runs out of capital,' he said.[15] 'Businesses die because they run out of cash.' Myners was adamant and Goodwin was in no position to resist. Eric Daniels, the chief executive of Lloyds, was next to be called in. He accepted that the banking system was short of capital and that taxpayers represented one of the few sources of it available. He thought, however, that while HBOS clearly needed the money, Lloyds did not. Later that evening, the heads of the seven leading banks, together with the Nationwide Building Society, were told by Darling what was to be announced the following morning. All of them would be named in the government's rescue plan, whether they needed help or not, to avoid stigma being attached to the weaker banks. Which of them would actually need assistance could be worked out later. The important thing was to get out a market-calming statement as quickly as possible. So the following morning, 8 October, Abbey, Barclays, HBOS, HSBC, Lloyds, Nationwide, RBS and Standard Chartered were named in a package that would provide up to £50 billion of capital, and hundreds of billions of taxpayer-provided liquidity and credit guarantees. It would, said Gordon Brown 'put the British banking system on a sounder footing'.[16] The question was whether it would be enough, and who would need the bailout most.

The announcement of the broad outlines of the government's rescue and recapitalisation package was a major step forward. Most of the hard work still had to be done, however. The banking system had not yet been rescued, and banks like RBS were still clinging on for dear life, as Iain Dey later reported following a key meeting at the Treasury on Thursday, 9 October. 'John Kingman, one of the top civil servants in the Treasury, strode into the meeting room,' he wrote.[17]

He sat down, knitted his hands together on the table and started to talk. As he spoke clearly, and calmly, the five investment bankers sitting across from him could hardly believe what they were hearing. Royal Bank of Scotland was bust, Kingman said. It was in the grip of the most astonishing bank run the UK had known. Although the public didn't know, a torrent of money was flooding out, withdrawn by big companies, central banks and wealthy individuals. Even on the Bank of England's most optimistic forecasts, RBS would be dead by Tuesday. Unless a government bail-out could be agreed that weekend, RBS would be shut down first thing on Monday ... RBS wasn't only the biggest bank in Britain – it had a bigger loan book than any bank in the world, with assets worth more than £1 trillion. Britain's financial system was on the brink of disaster – with one weekend to save it. A day earlier, the government had unveiled a draft plan to recapitalise the banking system, revealing that it would be willing to pump up to £50 billion of taxpayers' money into the banks and building societies over the coming weeks. The Credit

Suisse team had won the brief to implement that plan. Now that they had been brought into the government's confidence, it became apparent the bail-out had to be put into action immediately. If RBS collapsed, Kingman continued, one third of payments made every day would stop. Wages would go missing, bills go unpaid, savings disappear overnight. The bankers knew it would be a disaster that would make the fall of Northern Rock a year earlier seem an irrelevance. It could even have a more far-reaching impact than Lehman – RBS was about three times the size, with outposts all over the world.

The experts got to work, and carried on over the weekend of 11/12 October. It was imperative that the announcement be made on Monday. Goodwin, who described the deal imposed on RBS as 'more of a drive-by shooting than a negotiation',[18] was out, to be replaced by Stephen Hester, leaving the issue of his £700,000 a year pension (later reduced) as a ticking time bomb to embarrass the government. Lloyds was the biggest hurdle, its chief executive angry and humiliated by the imposition of taxpayer capital on his bank at the insistence of the FSA. He had done the government a favour by rescuing HBOS, he reasoned, and now it was being thrown back in his face. All weekend, over pizzas and takeaway curries, the bankers and officials hammered out the details. By Sunday evening, the Treasury's headquarters, redesigned by Sir Norman Foster and overlooking St James's Park, was looking distinctly squalid. Four of the eight named in the announcement on Wednesday, Abbey, HSBC, Nationwide and Standard Chartered, had convinced the regulators that they did not need more capital. That left Barclays, HBOS, Lloyds and RBS. Barclays was determined to avoid taxpayer capital and John Varley, its chief executive, refused to get involved in the horse-trading at the Treasury, remaining at the bank's Canary Wharf headquarters. By the end of the weekend he had convinced the authorities that he could raise capital from elsewhere. This Barclays did, announcing later in the month that it was raising up to £7.3 billion, mainly from the royal families of Abu Dhabi and Qatar.

Negotiations with the three remaining banks went on until the early hours of Monday morning. Darling, who had flown to Washington after the Wednesday announcement for the annual meetings of the IMF and the World Bank, returned on Sunday. He went to bed at 12.30 a.m. on the Sunday night, waking the following morning at 5 a.m., to find that one bank was still pressing for changes in the terms of the deal. But the time for talking was over. At 6.25 a.m. an announcement from the Treasury gave brief details of a £37 billion recapitalisation plan for RBS, Lloyds and HBOS, £20 billion of it for RBS. In return, the taxpayer would take stakes in the banks, roughly 57 per cent in RBS and 43 per cent in Lloyds-HBOS, and the rescued banks would sign binding agreements to lend into the economy and limit their bonus payments. Northern Rock and Bradford & Bingley had been the hors d'oeuvre; this was the big one, state ownership of the banks on an unimagined scale. It was accompanied by the provision of liquidity to all banks, some £200 billion, to ensure that the problem that had dogged them since August 2007, periodic shortages of liquidity, would not recur. The third element was an officially backed Credit Guarantee Scheme (CGS), again available to all UK banks and subsidiaries of foreign banks operating in Britain to guarantee up to £250 billion of lending. It did not mark the end – another banking package to take toxic assets off the banks' books was unveiled the following January, but it was the beginning of the end, appropriately enough when most of the negotiations had taken place in a building used by Churchill during the war. Britain had established the template for banking rescues in other countries. 'Has Gordon Brown, the British prime minister, saved the world financial system?' asked Paul Krugman in the *New York Times*.[19]

> O.K., the question is premature – we still don't know the exact shape of the planned financial rescues in Europe or for that matter the United States, let alone whether they'll really work. What we do know, however, is that Mr. Brown and Alistair Darling, the Chancellor of the Exchequer (equivalent to our Treasury secretary), have defined the character of the worldwide rescue effort, with other wealthy nations playing catch-up ... The Brown government has shown itself willing to think clearly about the financial crisis, and act quickly on its conclusions. And this combination of clarity and decisiveness hasn't been matched by any other Western government, least of all our own.

Some were rather less charitable, certainly later, but the UK authorities had shown themselves prepared to act boldly. Perhaps a little praise was deserved.

Shooting the Celtic Tiger

Ireland and Iceland are separated by a single letter and a large expanse of sea. Their shared experience during the financial crisis was, however, far too close for comfort. Ireland's economic success had always appeared to be soundly based, based on a skilled and well-educated workforce, relatively low tax rates, particularly for business, and an ability, dating back to the 1980s, to attract high-quality inward investment. Ireland, which had been good at exporting people, suddenly became good at exporting high-quality goods and services. The Celtic Tiger, as it was christened in 1994 by Kevin Gardiner, then an economist with Morgan Stanley, was achieving growth rates previously known only in the fast-expanding economies of East Asia; the Asian tigers. Growth rates of 8 or 9 per cent a year were not unusual. Between 1990 and 2005, Irish employment virtually doubled, from 1.1 million to 1.9 million. Along the way, and against the odds, Ireland's per capita GDP rose to become the second highest in the European Union, behind only Luxembourg's. So why did Ireland, having apparently achieved a prolonged period of virtuous economic growth, get into trouble? The most convincing analysis was provided by Professor Patrick Honohan of Trinity College, Dublin, who, in September 2009, was appointed governor of the central bank and head of Ireland's Financial Services Authority. Before his appointment, Honohan published a series of articles on his country's plight.

'To understand what went wrong it is essential to distinguish between two different growth phases,' he wrote.[20]

Up to 2000 there was the true 'Celtic Tiger' period of exceptional export-led growth with moderate wage and price inflation and healthy public finances ... By 2000, the convergence phase was over, but rapid growth continued in Ireland – though now the sources of growth shifted sharply. An unsustainable decade-long property price and construction boom, which began before that of the US and UK and went further than these both in price and quantity, had taken over from exports as the main driver of Irish growth. Initially prompted by the increased household formation (related to unprecedented levels of net immigration) and by the sharp fall in interest rates that accompanied the transition to EMU [European monetary union] membership, the property boom was increasingly financed after 2003 with foreign borrowing by the banks.

Ireland's good and sustainable growth had been succeeded by a bad and unsustainable expansion. The bad phase of that expansion saw not only an enormous boom in both residential and commercial property but also unhealthy competition among banks. One, Anglo Irish, increased its share of the retail banking market from 3 to 18 per cent in the space of a decade, prompting other banks, including the subsidiaries of British banks such as HBOS, which did not want to miss out on the boom, to respond. This intense competition drove down lending standards and the regulators either could not do anything about it or did not want to. More than two-thirds of mortgage loans to first-time buyers were for more than 90 per cent of the property's (inflated) value. A third of loans were at 100 per cent. Most dramatically of all, in the five years from 2003 to 2008, the net foreign borrowing of Irish banks increased from 10 to 60 per cent of GDP.

Ireland's banks were closely linked to the fortunes of the property market, both directly through mortgage lending and through their close links to the developers who drove the latter phase of the Irish expansion. The crisis also revealed much murky behaviour, particularly at Anglo Irish. In December 2008 Sean Fitzpatrick, chairman of Anglo Irish, resigned over the so-called 'hidden loans' scandal, the concealment of €87 million of loans. There was also huge controversy when it emerged that Anglo Irish had lent hundreds of millions to what became known as the 'golden circle' of ten businessmen, for the purposes of buying shares in the bank. Investments and deposits, some of which verged on the illegal, were uncovered. A string of resignations followed, both from Anglo Irish and other banks and financial institutions, including the chief executives of Irish Life and Permanent and the Irish Nationwide Building Society. The Irish financial regulator, Patrick Neary, resigned in January 2009, mainly over Anglo Irish. That month the bank was nationalised. A few months later it revealed the biggest loss in Irish corporate history, as its portfolio of property loans turned sour.

At the height of the crisis in the autumn of 2008, with the country's banks under enormous pressure and after warnings from senior bankers that the entire system was on the brink of collapse, Ireland's finance minister, Brian Lenihan, shocked his international counterparts by agreeing to guarantee all debt and deposits in the six main Irish banks and financial institutions. The effect, paradoxically, was to encourage depositors, particularly from the UK, to put their funds in these government-backed Irish banks, thus increasing the pressure on British banks. Alistair Darling was critical of the move and its unintended consequences. 'You can't do these things on your own – you've got to talk,' he said later.[21] When Lenihan told Christine Lagarde, the French finance minister and the then head of the euro group of finance ministers, her response was 'Oh gosh'.[22] Ireland could do this, it seemed, because of the implicit guarantee provided by membership of the euro. There was no devaluation option.

The markets feared a default on Irish government debt. In the event of the guarantee on Irish bank debt and deposits being called, Ireland would not have been able to meet her obligations. This fear was reflected in a sharp widening of the spread between Irish government bonds and those in Germany, regarded as the safe benchmark in Europe. In September 2008, that spread was just 30 basis points, three-tenths of a percentage point. By the following March it had risen to 284 basis points and analysts were talking seriously, though as it turned out wrongly, about an Irish government default. Two of the leading credit rating agencies, Standard & Poor's and Fitch, cut Ireland's AAA sovereign debt rating. The banking crisis and the bursting of the property bubble brought the second phase of Ireland's Celtic Tiger expansion to an abrupt halt, pushing the economy into sharp reverse, with a drop in gross national product of nearly 3 per cent in 2008, followed by a slump of roughly 10 per cent in 2009. Ireland would bounce back, and many of its newer industries, including pharmaceuticals and chemicals, held up well, but it had been a sobering lesson. An unemployment rate of 13 per cent told its own story and revived emigration from Ireland. The debt hangover, public and private, would be around for years.

Every government had to design its own approach to deal with the banking crisis, taking into account local circumstances. In Ireland's case, as well as a significant injection of taxpayer capital, it involved the establishment of a 'bad bank', to take over the banks' toxic assets, which in Ireland's case mainly involved bad property loans. The bad bank, the National Asset Management Agency, was the cause of fierce debate for months before Brian Lenihan set out the details in an address to the Irish parliament in September 2009. NAMA, he said, would acquire €77 billion of toxic loans from five institutions, Allied Irish Bank, Anglo Irish, Bank of Ireland, the Educational Building Society and the Irish Nationwide Building Society, paying €54 billion, a 30 per cent discount. 'NAMA will facilitate the speedy removal of higher risk property related assets which are clogging up the banks' balance sheets and greatly hampering their ability to lend to credit-worthy individuals and households and thereby support economic activity,' said Lenihan.[23]

> This general approach to dealing with distressed assets has been supported and recommended by banking experts across the globe. The model has been successfully implemented in a number of countries in the past where similar issues with problem loans have arisen. Countries such as Germany and the UK are also introducing asset relief schemes … International agencies such as the IMF and the ECB have commented favourably on the approach. In other words, this is a proven policy response that has been successful elsewhere and will be successful in Ireland.

That, at least, was the hope.

There was more to be done. Banking rescues in all countries evolved and changed as circumstances did. In America there was a scramble by those banks that could afford to do so to pay back official assistance and get themselves off the government hook. In Britain, a second major banking package was announced in January 2009, in response to what the Treasury described as an intensification of the global economic downturn. It included a further injection of taxpayer capital into RBS and an Asset Protection Scheme, designed to provide government guarantees, initially of up to £600 billion, against the bad loans and other toxic assets of the banks, mainly RBS and Lloyds-HBOS, in return for fees. Later, the banks were to seek ways of not participating in the scheme, for fear it was too expensive, and Lloyds managed to remain outside it, raising capital from investors (including the British government) instead, and cutting the scheme's scope to under £300 billion. Northern Rock, the nationalised bank, was told to stop running down its mortgage book and start lending again. For months after the October rescues, it looked as though the banking system was still on the brink. Gradually, however, confidence began to creep back into the money markets, and into the banks.

11

Keynes Makes a Comeback

Rescuing the banks was the key element in dragging the global economy back from the brink, but there were others. Confidence was shattered, trade collapsing and economic activity falling sharply. For years, policymakers had used monetary policy – interest rates – as the main lever for influencing short-term economic activity. That, as we shall see, was still to be an important weapon. There were also, however, worrying parallels with the Depression years, and Keynes's famous observation that reducing interest rates could be as ineffective as pushing on a piece of string. With the banking system hobbled by toxic debts and huge write-downs, this seemed more pertinent than at any time since the 1930s. Lord Skidelsky, Keynes's biographer, who has made the study of Keynes his life work, in a book written in the light of the crisis, *Keynes: The Return of the Master*, observed:[1]

> Even though money was cheaper, people weren't borrowing. Keynes put this in a nutshell near the bottom of the Great Depression: 'Cheap money means the riskless, or supposedly riskless, rate of interest will be low. But actual enterprise always involves some degree of risk. It may still be the case that the lender, with his confidence shattered by his experience, will continue to ask for new enterprise rates of interest which the borrower cannot be expected to earn ... If this proves to be so, there will be no means of escape from prolonged and perhaps interminable depression except by state intervention to promote and subsidize new investment.' So the scene was set for a new stimulus. The theory behind the stimulus is one of the bequests of the Keynesian revolution. The

authorities forecast the 'output gap' over, say, the next twelve months – the amount by which, because of the decline in total spending, actual output in the economy is expected to fall short of potential output. This gives a number for the extra spending which is required to fill the gap. Very crudely, if, starting at full employment, GDP is expected to fall by 5 per cent, the government should inject 5 per cent of extra spending into the economy.

Policymakers had got the message. In November 2008, the IMF called for a global fiscal stimulus equivalent to around 2 per cent of GDP, some $1.3 trillion, though that was based on a prediction that the world economy would merely slow to 2 per cent growth in 2009. The Washington-based body later revised its prediction for the global economy in 2009 to a fall of nearly 2 per cent. Before the crisis, the key policymaking forums for the world were the G7, on financial and economic matters, and the G8 for broader global political issues. The G7 consisted of the old advanced economies – America, Japan, Germany, Britain, France, Italy and Canada – while the G8 was made up of the seven plus Russia. The crisis changed all that. Suddenly the G20, a body that had held its first meeting late in 1999 but had not made a big impact, came to the fore. This was because the G20 included the big emerging economies, notably China, India, Brazil, Indonesia, Mexico and Turkey, as well as Saudi Arabia, among its membership. One striking feature of the 2008/09 world recession was the much more serious impact on advanced economies than on the emerging world. The first meeting of the G20 during the crisis took place on 15 November 2008 in Washington. It was a slightly odd gathering, hosted by George W. Bush days after Barack Obama had won the presidential election. Obama stayed away. Even so, the G20 endorsed fiscal measures to stimulate demand 'with rapid effect', while pledging to also take steps to ensure that 'fiscal sustainability' would be achieved again when the crisis was over. Bigger budget deficits, in other words, would be temporary, though for many countries, including America and Britain, temporary meant very many years.

Stimulating the economy

Around the world, governments introduced stimulus packages, including $586 billion in China, €50 billion in Germany (despite the apparent scepticism of Angela Merkel, the country's Chancellor), €26 billion in France, ¥12 trillion in Japan and £20 billion in Britain. The latter, necessarily small because of the poor state of the country's public finances, was mainly centred on a temporary reduction in VAT from 17.5 to 15 per cent, to run from 1 December 2008 to the end of 2009. It created a political divide between the Labour Party and its opponents. The Conservatives, under David Cameron, argued that Britain's public finances were too fragile to justify any largesse, and that the VAT cut was ineffective. The Liberal Democrats said that a stimulus was justified but that cutting VAT was a wasteful way of doing it. The evidence on the effectiveness of the VAT reduction was hard to pin down, though retail sales held up better during the recession than expected. Though some retailers had pushed hard for the cut, many argued that such a small change in prices (the reduction was worth 2.17 per cent off the price of goods) was too small to make any difference. Economists pointed out that the effect had to be looked at more broadly, in that price reductions across the entire household budget would free up income to be spent elsewhere. 'Scrappage' schemes, called 'cash for clunkers' in America, were introduced in many countries, including Britain, in which governments offered a subsidy on old cars being traded in for new ones, and were generally very effective.

The revival of Keynes was genuine. 'I guess everyone is a Keynesian in a foxhole,' said Robert Lucas,[2] the University of Chicago's new classical economist, only half joking. It also provided a reminder, though, why proactive fiscal policy had fallen into disrepute. In February 2008, in response to the pre-Lehman downturn, Congress had passed a $168 billion package of tax cuts and rebates. A year later, as one of Obama's first acts as president, his $789 billion stimulus passed in the face of Republican opposition. The White House later estimated that approval had been given for $158 billion of the spending under the stimulus but that only a third had been spent. Tax cuts had been introduced but at $43 billion were relatively modest. It would be unfair to say that the stimulus measures had no effect but it would also be going too far to argue that they were the lifesaver of the global economy. Not that countries sought to understate the effect. In April 2009, Gordon Brown hosted another G20 summit, this time in London's Docklands, in a vast exhibition centre well away from potential protesters. There they boasted[3] of 'a concerted and unprecedented fiscal expansion' amounting to $5 trillion, which would boost the global economy by 4 per cent. The $5 trillion, it turned out, mainly consisted of the combined deterioration in fiscal balances in the global economy, most of it due to the recession's impact on tax revenues and government spending. Despite this caveat, there was more than a bit of Keynes in the policy response.

Monetary policy: unusual and unconventional

There was another vital leg to the policy response to the crisis, and this was monetary policy. Since August 2007 central banks had, to a greater or lesser extent, supplied the markets with liquidity, with the Federal Reserve leading an international operation to ensure markets were adequately supplied with dollars. Until the collapse of Lehman, however, there was little evidence of coordination when it came to the main weapon at the disposal of central banks, interest rates. The Federal Reserve began cutting interest rates in September 2007, soon after the crisis broke. By the end of 2007, the Fed Funds rate was down from 5.25 to 4.25 per cent. By the end of April 2008, the bailout of Bear Stearns having occurred in the meantime, this key policy rate had been reduced to just 2 per cent. The Fed, under Ben Bernanke, was doing its best to counter the crisis with a conventional monetary policy response, cutting interest rates as quickly as it could. There was a very different response on the other side of the Atlantic, however.

The prevailing view in Frankfurt, home of the European Central Bank (ECB), was that the crisis's impact would be most severe on the US economy and that there was still an inflation battle to be fought in Europe. The oil price was rising alarmingly, as were prices for food and other commodities, pushing euro zone inflation up to 4 per cent, well outside the ECB's comfort zone. While the Fed was busy reducing rates to try to offset the effects of the crisis, the ECB held steady at

4 per cent. In July 2008, in what must rank as the most bizarre move in its short history, it announced an increase to 4.25 per cent. Even a hint from Jean-Claude Trichet, its president, that the move was likely to be a one-off, failed to calm the criticism the ECB faced from European politicians, concerned that the central bank was prepared to sacrifice the European economy on the altar of inflation. The Bank of England, as so often, was somewhere in between. It reduced Bank rate three times, in December 2007, and February and April 2008, taking it from 5.75 to 5 per cent. Then it too put worries about inflation ahead of concerns about recession. Under the framework established for independence, the Bank governor has to write an open letter to the chancellor when inflation moves a percentage point either side of the official target (2 per cent). When it did, in May 2008, rising above 3 per cent, the Bank stopped cutting rates.

All that changed after the collapse of Lehman Brothers. On 8 October 2008, in a move designed to shore up confidence in the markets by demonstrating that central banks were acting together, the Federal Reserve, the European Central Bank, the Bank of England, the Bank of Canada and the central banks of Sweden and Switzerland simultaneously announced a half-point reduction in interest rates. The move followed days of telephone discussions between central bankers, initiated by Bernanke. It surprised the markets because, in most cases, it was outside the normal schedule of decisions. Mervyn King had to get the Bank of England's monetary policy committee to come into the Bank a day earlier than usual, on a pretext, to get its agreement on the decision. The People's Bank of China, while not part of the agreement, also announced a small cut in interest rates. Further big cuts were to come. The October move left the Fed Funds rate at just 1.5 per cent but another cut followed at the end of the month, and by 16 December American interest rates were effectively at zero; the actual rate was 0 to 0.25 per cent. The ECB, always a reluctant cutter, took longer, but by May 2009 had cut to 1 per cent. Most dramatic of all, perhaps, was the Bank of England. It could boast a longer history than its rivals, having been founded as long ago as 1694 by a Scotsman, William Paterson. In that time, even in times of war and depression, Bank rate had never been lower than 2 per cent.

That changed on 8 January 2009, when it was reduced to 1.5 per cent. Two months later, it was cut to only 0.5 per cent. Britain, like America, had to all intents and purposes entered the era of zero-interest rates.

The reductions in interest rates took monetary policy out of its comfort zone. Central bankers had come to regard the interest-rate weapon as not only highly effective in managing economic activity but also to be used in a cautious way. The norm for interest-rate changes had been for movements of a quarter of a percentage point at a time, separated by weeks. That was appropriate to a time when the economy required occasional small nudges. What happened, however, when the task was to prevent it sliding into the abyss? The answer was bigger and bolder changes, and ones that took interest rates into new territory. What if, however, even that was not enough? Such thinking took central banks into even more unfamiliar territory, the area of unconventional monetary policy.

Creating money

Until 2008/09, the only central bank in modern times that had faced the dilemma of what to do when even zero-interest rates were not enough was the Bank of Japan. In February 2001, when Japan's first 'lost decade' after the bursting of the bubble economy of the late 1980s was threatening to turn into a second one, the Bank of Japan cut interest rates to zero, and the following month embarked on a strategy of 'quantitative easing'. This strategy involved buying Japanese government bonds in the markets, the so-called Rinban policy, and expanding bank reserves. Though the strategy, which lasted until 2006, was followed by a period of economic growth in Japan, most economists were sceptical of the contribution of quantitative easing (QE) to that recovery. Japan's QE was a policy curiosity. Suddenly, however, it became a curiosity that everybody wanted to learn a lot more about.

In January 2009, Ben Bernanke visited the London School of Economics to deliver the annual Stamp Lecture. There, in his typically dry and understated manner, he explained that, while US interest rates were effectively zero, the Federal Reserve still had plenty of scope for action. Its 'policy toolkit', as he described it, still had plenty of tools in it, and they were being deployed. The Fed had studied the Japanese experience and adapted it to suit the particular circumstances of the credit crunch. 'The Federal Reserve's approach to supporting credit markets is conceptually distinct from quantitative easing (QE), the policy approach used by the Bank of Japan from 2001 to 2006,' he said.[4]

> Our approach, which could be described as 'credit easing' ... focuses on the mix of loans and securities that it holds and on how this composition of assets affects credit conditions for households and businesses. This difference does not reflect any doctrinal disagreement with the Japanese approach, but rather the differences in financial and economic conditions between the two episodes. In particular, credit spreads are much wider and credit markets more dysfunctional in the United States today than was the case during the Japanese experiment with quantitative easing. To stimulate aggregate demand in the current environment, the Federal Reserve must focus its policies on reducing those spreads and improving the functioning of private credit markets more generally.

In Britain, the Bank of England did not mind calling what it was doing quantitative easing. It was an unconventional approach and, to some, rather worrying. By November 2009, the Bank's monetary policy committee had committed to purchasing £200 billion of assets, mainly UK government bonds – gilt-edged securities. Such securities, so called because their certificates used to be gold-edged, are used by the British government to fund its budget deficit by borrowing over the medium and long term from the markets. Critics said there was something disturbing about the government issuing large quantities of debt into the markets on one side, as a result of a budget deficit predicted to be £178 billion in 2009/10, and the Bank purchasing such gilt-edged securities on the other. Even the numbers were similar, a £178 billion budget deficit requiring around £200 billion of gilt issuance. Was not this the kind of thing that hyperinflation economies such as Zimbabwe did? The Bank, however, insisted it was doing the right thing and that there was no question of government debt being magicked away by being 'monetised'. Though there was scepticism about the policy, most notably from businesses and households, which said it was not freeing up the supply of credit, the Bank insisted that it was working. 'I believe the evidence is that QE is having an impact and that it is relevant to economic conditions right across the country,' said Professor David Miles, a member of its monetary policy committee, in September 2009.[5] 'And not just in financial markets in London but in high streets and factories and homes throughout the UK.' Most economists agreed.

Different central banks used different unconventional approaches. The European Central Bank's low point for its main interest, 1 per cent, was reached in May 2009 (though another rate, more directly comparable with those in America and Britain, was just 0.25 per cent), at which time it embarked on its version of the unconventional, which it described as 'enhanced credit support', including the purchase of an initial €60 billion of covered bonds (financial instruments similar to mortgage-backed securities), providing liquidity to the banking system for twelve months and allowing the European Investment Bank access to ECB facilities to enable it to channel lending into the European economy. The common theme was that central banks were responding to the threat, and the emerging reality, of a collapse in the money supply and a dramatic reduction in credit growth. The quantity theory of money told you that, other things being equal, a collapse in the money supply meant a plunge into depression and deflation – falling prices. This had happened in the 1930s, and the Great Depression was the result. Bernanke, as a student of the era, knew this had to be avoided at all costs, and so did most of his counterparts elsewhere. The balance sheets of both the Federal Reserve and the Bank of England more than doubled in size, that of the European Central Bank by over 50 per cent. Unusual times required unconventional responses. At some stage exit strategies from these policies would be implemented, typically involving the sale of the assets purchased back into the markets, the effect of which would be equivalent, in policy terms, to raising interest rates. That, however, was for later.

The mood lifted. Though the economic numbers in the early months of 2009 showed a plunge into recession as precipitous as anybody could remember, by Easter things were beginning to stabilise. Japan, Germany and France all recorded small increases in gross domestic product in the second quarter of the year, with other economies following not far behind. Economies were being supported by a huge monetary and fiscal stimulus and banking systems were on life support. The fall, however, had been arrested by these exceptional measures. The nightmare was not over but the memories of its worst phase were beginning to fade. G20 leaders met for their third meeting of the crisis in Pittsburgh – a steel city that had come impressively through more than its share of economic adversity – on 24/25 September, in a summit hosted by Barack Obama. While desperate not to sound complacent and self-satisfied, they did allow themselves a small note of self-congratulation. 'Our forceful response helped stop the dangerous, sharp decline in global activity and stabilize financial markets,' they declared.[6] The first battle had been won, though at a huge cost in terms of the burden on current and future taxpayers. There would be many more challenges ahead.

12

If These Things Were so Large, How Come Everyone Missed Them?

For economists, the macroeconomic crisis unleashed by the credit crunch was a time of enormous excitement, interest and activity. It was also tinged with guilt. How could things turn nasty so quickly, and how come they, with their sophisticated economic models and tools, and close monitoring of all the indicators, did not see it coming?

The Queen's question

In November 2008, the Queen visited the London School of Economics to open a new £71 million building. The eight-floor New Academic Building, to house the management and law departments and a new research institute on climate change, is in sharp contrast to the LSE's famously scruffy premises. As she and the Duke of Edinburgh toured the building, they engaged in conversation with academics and students, as well as those responsible for designing and constructing the new building. Protocol normally dictates that any discussions she has on these occasions, even small talk, remain private. This time, however, was different. In conversation with Professor Luis Garicano, director of research at the LSE's management department, she described the global financial crisis as 'awful' and asked the kind of question economists dread: 'If these things were so large how come everyone missed them?' Garicano, who was accused in the following day's newspapers of stammering a response to her searching question, subsequently insisted that he had provided a full explanation related to declining lending standards, particularly in the US housing market, and the herd instinct in financial markets. But he also conceded: 'We economists and academics should have been louder in our warnings and more proactive in suggesting solutions ... The public is right to be outraged.'[1]

A further response was provided a few months later, following a forum convened by the British Academy on 17 June 2009. Participants included three members of the Bank of England's monetary policy committee (MPC), four former members, and the current and two previous permanent secretaries to the Treasury. Tim Besley and Peter Hennessy, both professors and fellows of the British Academy, summed up the forum's conclusions in a letter to the Queen. Though the tone verged on the obsequious, it summed up well consensus thinking about the crisis and the inability of experts to foresee it. Though some had foreseen a crisis of some sort, it said, 'the exact form it would take and the timing of its onset and ferocity were foreseen by nobody'.[2] On the important question of risk, and the pricing of it in financial markets, the letter noted that plenty of people had engaged in the assessment of risk, including 4,000 risk managers in one of Britain's big banks alone. 'But the difficulty was seeing the risk to the system as a whole rather than to any specific financial instrument or loan,' Besley and Hennessy wrote. 'Risk calculations were most often confined to slices of financial activity, using some of the best mathematical models in our country and abroad. But they frequently lost sight of the bigger picture.'

They probably got closest to the nub of the problem when talking about the banks. To the extent that economists thought about the banking system it was as an intermediary, a utility. Lending could be influenced by the Bank of England and the level of interest rates it set but the banks would always be there and ready to lend, at a price. As for their more exotic and hugely profitable activities, most outside the banking sector (and plenty within it)

> believed that the financial wizards had found new and clever ways of managing risks. Indeed, some claimed to have so dispersed them through

an array of novel financial instruments that they had virtually removed them. It is difficult to recall a greater example of wishful thinking combined with hubris. There was a firm belief, too, that financial markets had changed. And politicians of all types were charmed by the market. These views were abetted by financial and economic models that were good at predicting the short-term and small risks, but few were equipped to say what would happen when things went as wrong as they have. People trusted the banks whose boards and senior executives were packed with globally recruited talent and their non-executive directors included those with proven records in public life. Nobody wanted to believe that their judgment could be faulty or that they were unable competently to scrutinise the risks in the organisations that they managed. A generation of bankers and financiers deceived themselves and those who thought that they were the pace-making engineers of advanced economies.

Some would take issue with aspects of that analysis, but it was undoubtedly true that most economists did not spend time considering bank balance sheets or, perhaps more importantly, the banks' off-balance-sheet activity. The best regulation was considered to be of the 'light touch' variety and, indeed, this was an area in which Britain, thanks to its single financial regulator, the Financial Services Authority, had a comparative advantage over other countries. Economists trusted the bankers to manage their risks properly and they trusted the regulators to make sure they did. International rules such as the Basel capital ratios were considered to be important bulwarks against irresponsible behaviour and not, as it turned out, an inducement to such behaviour.

Does this mean economics was blameless? No. The numbers economists looked at most, and in particular inflation during the inflation-targeting era, suggested a benign economic environment, with few signs of overheating. As long as monetary policy appeared to be doing its job so well, there was no need to ask too many questions, or to demand that economic imbalances be urgently corrected. Economic policymakers stuck to the task they had been set, or set themselves. In the case of the Bank of England, this meant targeting and controlling inflation. In the case of the Treasury and other government departments, it meant trying to improve the economy's long-run growth rate and delivering improvements in public services. Everybody stuck to their task, and did it pretty well within the limits within which they were operating. The problem was that economists advising and conducting policy did not give enough consideration to the systemic risks that were building up.

Not all economists could be tarred with the same brush. Nouriel Roubini of New York University made his name during the crisis, not for spotting the precise way it would unfold but for warning of trouble ahead for the US economy because of its rapidly expanding current account deficit and, when the subprime crisis began, for recognising its seriousness ahead of others. Robert Shiller warned first of the bubble in the stock market and then in America's housing market, even as US policymakers were confident that high prices reflected improved economic fundamentals. Most prescient of all was William 'Bill' White, a quietly spoken Canadian who was economic adviser at the Bank for International Settlements in Basel, the central bankers' bank, from 1995 to the summer of 2008. White's papers, written as the imbalances in the global economy were building, look with hindsight almost eerily accurate in warning of the problems ahead. In one he warned that excessive reliance by policymakers on targeting inflation meant that potentially dangerous rises in asset prices such as housing, the product of excessive growth, were being ignored. In another paper,[3] published in January 2006, he called on countries to consider adopting 'a macroprudential regulatory framework, one that puts more emphasis on the health of the financial system as a whole, rather than the state of individual institutions as is currently the case'. After the crisis, this was precisely what governments, central banks and regulators set about trying to do. One broader group of economists which insisted it should be exempt from criticism were modern followers – many in America – of the Austrian School, a branch of economics dating back to nineteenth-century Vienna. While some aspects of the global banking boom followed the pattern of the Austrian credit cycle, however, predictions of the crisis were harder to find from such economists. Moreover, when the crisis broke, many Austrian School economists, alarmed at the scale of government intervention, said it was exaggerated.

The British Academy promised that, for the majority of experts, next time it would be different. 'In summary, Your Majesty, the failure to foresee the timing, extent and severity of the crisis, and to head it off, while it had many causes, was principally a failure of the collective imagination of many bright people, both in this country and internationally, to understand the risks to the system as a whole,' Besley and Hennessy concluded.[4] The crisis was not a demonstration of the short-comings of economics but, rather, mainly the failure of most economists to use the tools at their disposal to sound the warning. Many would argue that the warnings were there, in reports from the Bank for International Settlements and in regular financial stability assessments from the Bank of England and other central banks. The difficulty was in gauging the scale of any such threats and when they might come to pass. Not only that, but, fearful of being caught out again, experts would inevitably be tempted to warn more frequently and more loudly in the future, even at the risk of being accused of crying wolf. Underprepared last time, the world could find itself over-prepared for the next crisis, unless, of course, the next crisis is completely different in its causes and consequences.

Under attack from within

Plenty of people outside economics found much to criticise in the failure of most economists to warn of the worst economic crisis since the 1930s. To outsiders, economic forecasters had proved the old joke, that they were put on earth to make weather forecasters look good. What was also interesting, however, was how the failure of forecasters provided an opportunity for a settling of some very old scores within economics itself, and how some of the harshest criticisms of economists came from other economists. Paul Krugman, having been awarded the Nobel Prize for economics in 2008, had even more of a platform for his views than usual. He had issued a warning of sorts, in a book called *The Return of Depression Economics*, published in 1999, in which he said that the Asian financial contagion of the late 1990s was ushering in a new global depression (though it was a very different crisis to the one that eventually evolved). Even so, delivering his Lionel Robbins lectures, also at the

LSE, in June 2009, in memory of the distinguished British economist, Krugman pulled no punches in castigating fellow economists and their efforts. Most of the macroeconomic thinking of the past three decades had been 'spectacularly useless at best, and positively harmful at worst', he said.[5] We had, he also said during 2009, been living through a 'Dark Age of macroeconomics', in which essential truths had been forgotten. 'Remember, what defined the Dark Ages wasn't the fact that they were primitive – the Bronze Age was primitive, too,' he said.

> What made the Dark Ages dark was the fact that so much knowledge had been lost, that so much known to the Greeks and Romans had been forgotten by the barbarian kingdoms that followed. And that's what seems to have happened to macroeconomics in much of the economics profession. The ... general understanding that macroeconomics is more than supply and demand plus the quantity equation ... somehow got lost in much of the profession. I'm tempted to go on and say something about being overrun by barbarians in the grip of an obscurantist faith, but I guess I won't. Oh wait, I guess I just did.

Krugman did not have a monopoly on attacking modern economics, or on the use of colourful language. Willem Buiter, a founder member of the Bank of England's monetary policy committee (MPC), on which he served from 1997 to 2000, posted a long and spirited critique on his 'Maverecon' blog in March 2009, under the headline 'The unfortunate uselessness of most "state of the art" academic monetary economics'. Buiter noted that the MPC had a strong representation of academics and other professional economists with serious technical training and backgrounds in the subject. 'This turned out to be a severe handicap when the central bank had to switch gears and change from being an inflation-targeting central bank under conditions of orderly financial markets to a financial stability-oriented central bank under conditions of widespread market illiquidity and funding illiquidity,' he wrote.[6]

Buiter's detailed argument was complex and, it should be said, contentious, but boiled down to a fundamental and fairly straightforward point, which was that the theoretical models developed since the 1970s assumed that a crisis of illiquidity, which is how the crisis of 2007–09 began, could not happen. Just like the old joke about how an economist marooned on a desert island would assume a raft, so the constraining assumptions of modern macroeconomics were that crises of illiquidity and insolvency did not happen. Not only were such questions not answered by the post-1970s macroeconomic theoreticians but they were not allowed to be asked. There were two main responses to Buiter's critique. One is that the version of modern macroeconomics he set out to attack was something of a straw man, which deliberately presented a much cruder version than its proponents would recognise. The other is that it would be a poor policymaker who assumed that their role was simply to put into practice everything they had learned at university. Monetary policy is, or should be, about 'feel' as much as it is about the strict application of theoretical principles. The jibe attributed to Ronald Reagan, that an economist is somebody who sees something working in practice and wonders whether it will work in theory, takes it too far. Professional economists spend most of their time discovering where and how theory does not work and responding to it. Members of the Bank of England's MPC were taken by surprise by the sudden liquidity crisis in 2007 not because the economics they were taught did not allow for it but, rather, because it was such a rare event. Nor were economists ever going to be best placed to decide on whether to supply liquidity to the markets, how best to do it and by how much. Such matters had always been part of central banking lore, and always would be.

For economists such as Krugman, Buiter and others, the crisis provided an opportunity to launch an attack on some of the economics that they had long had doubts about, though had also taught to their students. Even with the global economy in crisis there were scores to settle. In some cases, too, the battles went deeper than that.

The end of consensus

Krugman's attacks were not entirely unprovoked. As a powerful advocate of a large-scale fiscal stimulus to prevent the crisis turning into a second Great Depression, part of his anger with fiscally conservative, mainly neoclassical economists was based on their opposition to such measures. Not only had the neoclassical economists' faith in the markets helped drive the world into a terrifying financial emergency, but many of them, in Krugman's view, were seeking to close off the exit route from the crisis. This, for him, was like a red rag to a bull. The remedy was so obvious as to be staring policymakers in the face. After a period of excess borrowing, consumers and businesses were scrambling to cut back, to shore up their finances by boosting saving. This brought into play Keynes's famous paradox of thrift, which was that while it might be logical for individuals to save in these circumstances, the effect of everybody doing so would be to deepen the recession and threaten a prolonged slump. The normal response to this situation, an aggressive easing of monetary policy, was unlikely to be enough. If even zero-interest rates did not do the trick, the argument for activist fiscal policy was, in Krugman's view, incontrovertible.

Many of the economists responsible for advancing the subject from the 1970s onwards saw the simple remedies favoured by Krugman and his followers as themselves tantamount to a return to the Dark Ages, and a rejection of so much that had been learned in the modern era. Robert Barro (another Nobel Prize winner), professor of economics at Harvard and a fellow of Stanford University's Hoover Institute, graced by the likes of Milton Friedman, led the charge, in an attack on President Barack Obama's fiscal stimulus plan, about the same time that the new president took up residence in the White House early in 2009. 'As we all know, we are in the middle of what will likely be the worst U.S. economic contraction since the 1930s,' he wrote.[7]

> In this context and from the history of the Great Depression, I can understand various attempts to prop up the financial system. But, in terms of fiscal-stimulus proposals, it would be unfortunate if the best Team Obama can offer is an unvarnished version of Keynes's 1936 'General Theory of Employment, Interest and Money'. The financial crisis and possible depression do not invalidate everything we have learned about macroeconomics since 1936. The main point is that we should not be considering massive public-works programs that do not pass muster from the perspective of cost–benefit analysis. Just as in the 1980s, when

extreme supply-side views on tax cuts were unjustified, it is wrong now to think that added government spending is free.

Barro was not alone. When President Obama suggested that his actions reflected the economic consensus, some 250 conservative economists signed a letter,[8] published in leading newspapers, which said: 'With all due respect Mr President, that is not true.' It was reminiscent of the 1981 letter from 364 UK economists disagreeing with Margaret Thatcher's economic policies but from the opposite political direction. There were plenty more such battles over policy. To non-economists, this compounded the shortcomings of those who claimed to be experts. They had failed to spot the crisis coming and now they disagreed profoundly on how to get out of it. To economists it confirmed that the fragile truce that had descended on the subject after the great disputes between Keynesians and monetarists in the 1970s and 1980s had been broken. The macroeconomic consensus was no more.

Fooled by mathematics

For some of the critics of the failure of economics, the rot had set in when the subject tried to turn itself into a science, with a heavy emphasis on mathematics. In the years leading up to the crisis a backlash had been building against the excessive use of mathematics and econometric 'proofs' in the subject, though mainstream economics remained largely unresponsive in the face of such attacks. In April 2009 *Business Week* published a cover article[9] under the headline 'What good are economists anyway?' It quoted Nassim Nicholas Taleb, the best-selling author of *Fooled by Randomness* and *The Black Swan*. Taleb's criticism was fundamental. It was not that economists had got their forecasts wrong, it was that they had deluded themselves, and in so doing deluded many others, into believing that they could forecast at all. The future, in his view, was inherently unpredictable and to pretend otherwise was dishonest. Paul Wilmott, an expert on quantitative finance quoted in the same article, said: 'Economists' models are just awful. They completely forget how important the human element is.' Such criticisms were not new, and most model-builders had long acknowledged weaknesses in their models and the need to apply judgemental adjustments to their projections. The crisis gave the criticisms additional force.

Economics, it appeared, was a pseudo-science after all, and its inability to spot the crisis had exposed its shortcomings. Even when the crisis broke, economists initially floundered, groping for the right response to a series of events their models had failed to predict. Some had been waiting for the moment when economics would show itself up in this way. Though Keynes was a noted mathematician before he turned to economics, Lord Skidelsky, one of his biographers, argued that economics was paying the price for more than two centuries of scientific pretensions. 'Ever since modern economics started in the eighteenth century it has presented itself as a predictive science, akin to a natural science,' he wrote.[10] 'Since the future a year ago included the present slump, it is natural that the failure of the economics profession – with a few exceptions – to foresee the coming collapse should have discredited its scientific pretensions. Economics is revealed to have no more clothes than any other social science.'

Taken to its logical conclusion, this line of argument would appear to suggest that economists should not have anything to say about the future, merely theorise about what has happened in the past in a non-mathematical way. Even then, the more pernickety would be cautious of drawing any useful conclusions. The fear would be that economists would follow the example of Zhou Enlai, the first premier of the People's Republic of China, who, when asked in the 1960s about the economic effects of the French Revolution of 1789, reportedly replied that it was too early to say. Skidelsky was part of a chorus of criticism of the way economics had been taught and researched, not all of it based on the excessive use of mathematical models but all of it critical of the way such models had been used.

Freaks and geeks

For economics, the sad thing about the crisis was that until it happened it all seemed to be going so well. This was not just because the macroeconomic environment appeared so benign. Suddenly, economics appeared to have the answer to everything. In 2005 the American publisher William Morrow launched *Freakonomics: A Rogue Economist Explores the Hidden Side of Everything* on to an unsuspecting world. It became an instant best-seller, initially by word of mouth, later as a result of good reviews. Written by one of America's brightest young economists, Steven Levitt of the University of Chicago, along with Stephen Dubner, a *New York Times* journalist, it was hugely popular, particular among non-economists, who found the authors had brought a famously stuffy subject to life. In its first three years it sold more than three million copies worldwide. The book applied microeconomic principles, and in particular the role of incentives, to a range of subjects running from sumo wrestling, through why drug dealers live with their mothers, to the effect of legalising abortion on crime. Many loved it. Others hated it, but it was hard to ignore. It appeared to confirm that microeconomics was where all the action was. At the end of 2005, thanks largely to *Freakonomics*, *Newsweek* declared that economics was 'the sexiest trade alive'.[11] 'Economics, perhaps the geekiest of geek subjects, got a serious makeover this year,' it said. It was the 'hottest undergrad subject' at Harvard and New York University.

Not everybody joined in the adulation, railing against the trivialisation of economics in *Freakonomics* even before the global financial crisis broke. In a detailed critique published in *New Republic* in the spring of 2007, Noam Scheiber argued that young, technically gifted economists such as Levitt were deliberately eschewing the hard questions that society looks to them to try to answer, such as poverty, inequality and the effects of education, in favour of the minor, even the irrelevant. 'With the 2005 publication of *Freakonomics*, the breezy exposition of Chicago economist Steven D. Levitt's oeuvre, the rest of the world has come to see that economists are capable of spectacular feats of cleverness ...' he wrote.[12]

> Levitt has turned to such offbeat contexts as Japanese sumo-wrestling and the seedy world of Chicago real estate. He has studied racial discrimination on 'Weakest Link,' a once-popular game show, and reflected on the scourge of white-collar bagel-filching. This has, in turn, inspired a flurry of imitators, including papers on such topics as point-shaving

in college basketball, underused gym memberships, and the parking tickets of U.N. diplomats. Within the frequently tedious body of economics scholarship, these papers stand out as fantastically entertaining ... But it does make you worry: What if, somewhere along the road ... all the cleverness has crowded out some of the truly deep questions we rely on economists to answer?

Levitt and Dubner were undeterred. Levitt, in particular, joined in with the criticism of macroeconomics on the *Freakonomics* blog, run in collaboration with the *New York Times*. It had gone wrong, he suggested, because it had forgotten its microeconomic foundations. A follow-up book, *SuperFreakonomics: Global Cooling, Patriotic Prostitutes, and Why Suicide Bombers Should Buy Life Insurance*, was published in October 2009 to strong interest and advance orders. It was hard, though, not to feel a little uneasy. At a time when economics was struggling to come up with answers to some of the hardest questions posed for generations, it was still apparently a fun subject, an entertainment, suitable mainly for delving into life's little curiosities. That was fine if it was what people wanted. Perhaps, however, they were entitled to something better.

When models fail

Some of the criticism of the failure of most economists to predict the crisis, or initially on how best to respond to it, was directed at individuals. Much of it, however, was firmly aimed at their models, and in particular so-called DSGE models, widely used by central banks, governments and private sector forecasters and consultancies. DSGE models, dynamic stochastic general equilibrium models, embodied much of the progress in macroeconomic thinking since the 1970s. Unlike the earlier generations of economic models, built around simple, unchanging relationships between, for example, consumption and income, this new generation of models was much more sophisticated. The European Central Bank built a DSGE model to cover the whole of the euro zone economy. The Federal Reserve and Bank of England's DSGE models (the latter known as the Bank of England quarterly model, the BEQM, or, after the footballer, the 'Beckham') were at the heart of their forecasting processes. These models appeared to include everything policymakers could possibly want. They were 'dynamic', incorporating change, unlike the old static models. They demonstrated the impact of shocks, whether random or deliberate (such as a policy 'shock' from a dramatic lowering or raising of interest rates), which was the stochastic element. They were an essential part of the policymaker's toolkit. No central banker or government would want to be without one.

Unfortunately, these models failed when they were most needed, in spotting the crisis coming and in helping formulate the response to it. This was not just a problem of specification; it was in the nature of the models themselves. 'Generalised problems with liquidity almost always go hand in hand with concerns about solvency, as in 2007,' said Professor Charles Goodhart,[13] a former chief monetary adviser at the Bank of England and member of its monetary policy committee (MPC). 'If you could assume that I can certainly repay you, you would always lend to me unsecured at a risk free rate, an invalid assumption that alas is incorporated into most macro-economic DSGE models.' Worse, the models, by either excluding the financial sector or by assuming that finance, or bank lending, was always on tap, could not have foreseen the crisis. That and the inbuilt tendency of models to return to equilibrium meant that they were singularly inappropriate for addressing the situation that emerged in the run-up to the crisis and subsequently.

The users of these economic models, and in particular the policymakers who based their judgements on them (as well as other factors), appear to have felt particularly let down. Certainly in the case of the Bank of England there was a degree of precision about the timing and nature of its interest-rate decisions that implied the model was hugely influential. Important decisions were significantly more likely to be taken in months when the Bank published a new quarterly inflation report (February, May, August and November), having cranked its model fully into action. The model-based forecast was always a key factor: an interest-rate cut that was accompanied by a new forecast showing inflation rising above the official 2 per cent target would be hard to justify, and vice versa. Other central banks were slightly less structured in their approach, which was probably a good thing, but were also heavily influenced by what their models were telling them. David Blanchflower, another former Bank MPC member, sensed something was going badly wrong in 2008 even when the model was painting a benign picture of the outlook. 'Our macroeconomic models have little to tell us when the tipping point may come …' he said later.[14] 'With no financial sector within macro models, there was little room to assess the macroeconomic implications of financial instability. This may be one reason central bankers were slow to realise the severity of the credit crunch until a full blown crisis had emerged.'

Economic modellers are the equivalent in economics of the IT experts in companies, more concerned about the nuts and bolts of their models, and whether they are internally consistent, than engaging in the rough and tumble of debate. Most left it to others to battle it out on the question of whether they had been responsible for misleading policymakers and dressing up the Great Moderation into something that was no more than a great delusion. Most would argue that a model is a bit like a fast car, dangerous only when driven badly. Others who did speak out emphasised the unusual circumstances in which the models were seen to have failed, when economic variables went off the scale. Models should not be abandoned just because they failed when 'once in a century' events occurred. Certainly there was no evidence that the economic crisis was leading to a widespread abandonment of models but, instead, efforts to improve them. Meanwhile the models had their defenders. 'Much of the criticism seems to result from a failure to understand the use of the DSGE model,' said Josh Hendrickson,[15] who writes a blog under the name Everyday Economist.

> These models come in all different forms. There are rather simple models that seek to explain the response of the economy to a specific exogenous shock. There are others that attempt to evaluate alternative monetary or fiscal policy regimes. Still more are aimed at explaining historical downturns. What's more, there are models that include financial market frictions (although, admittedly, they are less appreciated than they should be). There are also larger models that are used for forecasting within central banks. Ultimately, there are a wide variety of DSGE

models because they are used for a wide variety of purposes. Thus the criticisms of these models must take into account their explicit purpose (which they often do not).

Inefficient markets

If economic models failed during the crisis, so, according to some of the most vocal critics, did something else central to the macroeconomic and regulatory framework in the period leading up to the crisis. This was the efficient market hypothesis, versions of which had been around for most of the twentieth century but which was best defined by Professor Eugene Fama of Chicago University, in a seminal 1970 article, 'Efficient capital markets: a review of theory and empirical work', published in the *Journal of Finance*. Fama's central concept was very simple – that financial markets are efficient in the sense that the price of a company's stock reflects all the known information at the time. There were, according to Fama, various degrees of 'strength' with which the proposition could be stated. In the weakest version, the current price reflected only past information on prices. In the 'semi-strong' version – which is what most people have chosen to use – it reflects all publicly available information affecting the company, while in the strongest version the price reflects all publicly and privately available information. This simple idea was, in its time, revolutionary and drew enormous praise. 'There is no other proposition in economics which has more solid empirical evidence supporting it than the efficient market hypothesis,' said the Harvard financial economist Michael Jensen in 1978.[16] It implied, most obviously, that it was hard for investors to claim to consistently beat the market. Today's price reflected all known information today. Tomorrow's price would reflect the state of information tomorrow, which might be different but which nobody not in possession of that information in advance could hope to anticipate. Prices followed what Fama described as a 'random walk'.

It may have been simple but, as the crisis of 2007–09 unwound, it also appeared that the efficient market hypothesis did enormous damage. Lord Turner, chairman of Britain's Financial Services Authority, carried out a review of the circumstances leading up to the crisis, which was published in March 2009. It poured a large dollop of scepticism on the efficient market hypothesis, effectively blaming it for some of the problems. 'The predominant assumption behind financial market regulation – in the US, the UK and increasingly across the world – has been that financial markets are capable of being both efficient and rational and that a key goal of financial market regulation is to remove the impediments which might produce inefficient and illiquid markets,' Turner wrote.[17]

> In the face of the worst financial crisis for a century, however, the assumptions of efficient market theory have been subject to increasingly effective criticism, drawing on both theoretical and empirical arguments … Given this theory and evidence, a reasonable judgment is that policymakers have to recognise that all liquid traded markets are capable of acting irrationally, and can be susceptible to self-reinforcing herd and momentum effects.

On the face of it, Fama's theory was responsible, nearly forty years on, for untold economic and financial damage. The implications of this failure were profound. Instead of assuming the markets were always right, it would be safer to assume they were usually wrong. This is turn would open the floodgates to opponents of markets in other areas. The 'market solution', whether it be to providing a better deal for consumers, delivering public services in a more efficient way, or any number of other areas in which markets could be extended, could now be called into serious question. It had failed in the financial markets and was probably failing everywhere else.

Or not. The efficient market hypothesis suffered from excessive interpretation by some of those who seized upon it but its most important element appears to have survived intact. This is that the price of a stock or security on a given day is the best distillation of all the available information relevant to it. That does not exclude what critics of the hypothesis describe as 'momentum', or 'herd' effects. The knowledge that other investors are buying the stock or security and intend to buy more is part of the available information that helps set the price. The hypothesis does not say anything about what the price will be tomorrow, or even in a few minutes' time. The information affecting the price can change quickly and drastically. The most important implication of the efficient market hypothesis, moreover, was that professionals could not legitimately claim to consistently beat the markets. There really is no such thing as a free lunch. Long-Term Capital Management (LTCM) came unstuck in 1998 for believing that it could profitably trade market inefficiencies on the assumption that there would always be a return to equilibrium.

Those claiming consistently above-normal returns, whether they were fraudsters such as Bernie Madoff or investment banks asserting that they had uncovered new ways of generating high-yielding returns in a low-yield world, were saying they could beat the market consistently. The efficient market hypothesis should have told regulators there was something suspicious about this. If they were hung up on an extreme, unrealistic and wrong version of the hypothesis – the markets are always right, both now and in what they imply for the future – then it was more fool them. If Wall Street's rocket scientists fell into a similar trap, then they were a lot less intelligent than they thought they were.

The efficient market hypothesis deserved better and so did much of the rest of economics. Though most economists accepted that the crisis had revealed serious shortcomings, particularly when it came to forecasting, some responded robustly to the criticisms. One of the most memorable quotes from Keynes, after all, was: 'If the facts change, I change my mind. What do you do, Sir?' The facts had changed, and very dramatically, over the course of 2008, and in particular in September of that year with the collapse of Lehman Brothers. So, on this view, forecasters were right to predict only a mild, 'technical' recession looking ahead from the summer of 2008, with output slipping by a small amount for a couple of quarters. Only after the banking system had come close to meltdown, and forced an unprecedented rescue effort by governments, was it clear that the global economy was buckling under the weight of its biggest financial crisis since the 1930s. 'Until the Lehman failure the recession was pretty typical of the modest downturns of the post-war period,' wrote Robert Lucas of the University of Chicago.[18]

There was a recession under way, led by the decline in housing construction. [The Federal Reserve] forecast was a reasonable estimate of what would have followed if the housing decline had continued to be the only or main factor involved in the economic downturn. After the Lehman bankruptcy, models ... combined with new information, gave what turned out to be very accurate estimates of the private-spending reductions that ensued over the next two quarters. When Ben Bernanke, the chairman of the Fed, warned Hank Paulson, the then Treasury secretary, of the economic danger facing America immediately after Lehman's failure, he knew what he was talking about.

Who did it?

Economics had its defenders, both inside and outside the subject. It is worth remembering that the vast majority of economists do not engage in the kind of high-level macroeconomic modelling that helped leave policymakers underprepared for the crisis. That said, there were clear shortcomings on the part of some economists. If forecasting and analysis have any purpose, it is to warn when dangerous situations are developing, with a view to preventing them. Charlie Bean, deputy governor of the Bank of England, offered a way forward for those parts of the profession that were caught out in a speech in August 2009. The crisis had a wide variety of causes and it would be a mistake to look for 'a single guilty culprit', he said.[19]

Underestimation of risk born of the Great Moderation, loose monetary policy in the United States and a perverse pattern of international capital flows together provided fertile territory for the emergence of a credit/asset-price bubble. The creation of an array of complex new assets that were supposed to spread risk more widely ended up destroying information about the scale and location of losses, which proved to be crucial when the market turned. And an array of distorted incentives led the financial system to build up excessive leverage, increasing the vulnerabilities when asset prices began to fall. As in Agatha Christie's *Murder on the Orient Express*, everyone had a hand in it.

Everyone in Bean's description included the banks themselves; the regulators; international capital rules (the Basel rules) that unintentionally encouraged risky and off-balance-sheet activity; the rating agencies; individuals and companies who borrowed too much; brokers and lenders who encouraged them to do so; central banks, which failed to spot systemic risks building up beneath an apparently calm surface; and politicians, who were happy to bask in the glory of economic growth and rising prosperity without bothering to ask whether it was on a sound footing, or work harder to try to fix the global imbalances that lay behind the crisis. People will have different views on where to attach most of the blame. It would be hard, however, not to pin the lion's share on bankers, regulators and the rating agencies. Some, however, were willing to accept their share. 'It was our fault; we messed up,' a senior central banker said to me about a year after the Lehman collapse.[20] 'It was our job to set the rules for global capitalism and we did not set them properly.'

Nevertheless, one of the hands on the murder weapon belonged to economists, and Bean had three suggestions for making sure they were not complicit in such a crime again. The first was to be more questioning of the assumption that free financial markets were always and everywhere a good thing. The economics profession had oversold the virtues of unfettered financial markets. 'By the same token, even though not strictly the case in theory, we usually start from a presumption that expanding the range of available securities is beneficial,' he said.[21] 'Yet that has resulted in a deeply unsatisfactory outcome.' Bean's second suggestion was that economists had to be more aware of history and, in particular, that booms, busts, manias, panics and crashes have occurred in the past. They should be thought of as a central feature of capitalist economies and, as such, integral to the economic models that seek to simulate how such economies work. Though he did not put it this way, economists and policymakers too often fall into the 'this time it is different' trap. Finally, said Bean, 'we need to put credit back into macroeconomics in a meaningful way'. While some economists had tried to incorporate financial frictions into their models, nobody had a proper role for financial intermediaries – the banks and other financial institutions. As became clear during the crisis, that role was fundamental in practice.

How much of a crisis for economics was the crisis in the economy? Perhaps less than some critics have suggested. Models that proved inadequate will be improved, respecified or rebuilt from scratch. An industry will evolve around the proper modelling of money, banking and credit, which will become the discipline's new hot area. Behavioural economics, the crossover between psychology and economics, will become even more important, with more attention paid to Keynes's 'animal spirits'. That, however, was happening anyway. The economics that will evolve from the crisis of 2007–09 will be different from the economics that preceded it, but probably not as much as some expect. The crisis did not throw up a new Keynes or, for that matter, any particularly new ways of thinking, though there was plenty of criticism of the old ways. Economists, like bankers, discovered that they were more fallible than they thought and for some that was a humbling experience. Occasionally, that is no bad thing.

13

The New Age of Instability

Initial verdicts on major events are often wrong. Most people who have examined the global financial crisis of 2007–09 have a clear view of its causes, though that will be subject to reinterpretation over time. People will differ on the weight they attach to individual parts of the story. One source of debate is whether the role of the collapse of Lehman Brothers in September 2008 has been exaggerated. Some argue that if it had not been Lehman, it would have been another institution's failure which led to the cathartic bout of extreme turbulence; others that the Lehman shock was essential to spark governments into action, without which there would have been a drift into depression. The arguments over who should be blamed for the crisis, similarly, will go on and will influence future attempts by the G20, the International Monetary Fund and others to shape the global economy. Those countries that ran low saving ratios and current account deficits, notably America but also Britain and some other economies, are seen to have acted irresponsibly over years, if not decades. It takes two to tango, however, and the deficit and low-saving economies could not have maintained their behaviour unless there were plenty of countries on the other side, notably China and other Asian economies, but also those such as Germany, willing to run persistent large surpluses and, in effect, export their high savings. Correcting global imbalances requires an acceptance of the need for change on both sides.

If conclusions on the past necessarily have to be provisional, that is even more the case for predictions about the future. A good candidate for the best book ever written about a financial crisis is J. K. Galbraith's

The Great Crash, because, racy and exciting as it is, it reads like a contemporary account of events. The book, however, was not written until the 1950s – it was first published in 1954 – and relied mainly on newspaper reports, other accounts and congressional hearings. That does not make it any less of a book, and the quarter-century passage of time allowed Galbraith the luxury of knowing what happened in the years after the crash. Even 25 years was not enough, however, to embrace all the thinking about the Depression years. Milton Friedman and Anna Schwartz's *A Monetary History of the United States*, which explained the period in terms of the failure of the US authorities to prevent a collapse in the money supply, an explanation favoured by most modern scholars of the period, including Ben Bernanke (Galbraith may or may not have agreed with it), was not published until 1963.

The recent crisis has already produced a number of books, some of whose initial conclusions appear to be premature. John Gray, the philosopher, wrote in an introduction to a new edition of his book *False Dawn* in the summer of 2009 that the crisis signalled the end of just about everything, including the global free market and America as a great power. Efforts to revive the world economy would fail, he suggested, instead resulting in a great inflation, though he also expected the planet-damaging process of industrialisation to continue. For Gray, the suggestion that America would experience a 'lost decade' of stagnation and deflation, like Japan in the 1990s and beyond, was too optimistic; it would be much worse than that, as it would be for the world as a whole. 'The collapse that is under way is larger than any in history, and is the first to be truly global,' he wrote.[1] 'It is bound to shake every economy, with results that will include regime change or state failure in a number of countries.'

One feature of the crisis was that extreme things happened and that even extreme views and predictions were not extreme enough. Thinking the unthinkable became the thing to do, so views like those of John Gray cannot be dismissed out of hand. To the extent that there was a global free market before the crisis, it was clearly a market made possible only by government support after it. It could be that signs in late 2009 that the global economy was stabilising, even recovering, and that the worst of the banking crisis was over, were themselves a false dawn, and that another shuddering downturn was about to happen. Nevertheless, it looked as though a rerun of the Great Depression had been avoided, largely thanks to the efforts of governments and central banks, and it also looked as though the world had changed rather less than some expected. The crisis did not, for example, signal the end of capitalism, or even the complete demise of the Anglo-Saxon model, though there may have been an element of wishful thinking among those who declared that it would. It did not necessarily mean a permanent increase in the role of government, let alone full-scale nationalisation of the banking system, predicted and urged by many of the world's leading economists at the height of the crisis.

Governments stepped in when they were needed, to prevent a collapse in their banking systems and to prop up other sectors. Most, however, declared their intention to step out again as soon as circumstances allowed. Even the banks, at one stage apparently condemned to a future under state ownership, showed more independent spirit than they were given credit for. Though most were helped through the crisis at least to some degree (and in some cases entirely) by government support, their determination to stand on their own two feet again was strong. Even stand-alone investment banks, which had appeared to be consigned to the dustbin of history, bounced back, making substantial profits and causing controversy by awarding their employees big bonuses. In the second quarter of 2009, Goldman Sachs made $3.44 billion of net profits, having set aside $6.65 billion for bonuses.[2] The following three months it made $3.19 billion, enough to allow it to set aside a cumulative $16.7 billion for bonuses, only fractionally below the record of $16.9 billion in the first three quarters of 2007. Bonuses were back, and perhaps had never really been away, though their return was to provoke the imposition of a one-off windfall tax by the UK government in December 2009 and a $117 billion bank levy by the Obama administration in January 2010. The cull of some competitors left those still standing in a strong position. Things change, and they can change very quickly, but some things change less than might be expected. How might things change in the coming years?

The paradox of stability

In the cold war, the 'stability–instability paradox' became popular among theorists. The idea was simple enough. The apparent instability of a big build-up of nuclear weaponry, proliferation, created its own stability. Mutually assured destruction meant that the nuclear powers, and in particular America and the Soviet Union, would never use the weapons they had acquired. There could be small wars but never a big one. There is a parallel, though not a perfect one, in the paradox of economic and financial stability. The search for stability has been the driver of economic policy in the modern era. After the turbulence of the 1970s and 1980s, policymakers sought to create macroeconomic stability. Nobody was prouder of the record of his ten years as chancellor than Gordon Brown because, above all, it had been a time when the main economic indicators, growth and inflation, were not only more stable than at any time in recent history but were also better than in other countries. The search for stability was and is all-embracing. Central banks have financial stability arms, not divisions to foster instability. Actions coordinated by the G20 during the crisis were aimed at the restoration of economic stability. Macroeconomic stability, however, does not necessarily mean stability at the level of the individual firm. In a speech[3] in 2005, Kate Barker, a member of the Bank of England's monetary policy committee, pointed to research showing that in both Britain and America, firms were subject to much greater volatility in business conditions than might be expected from the macroeconomic numbers. This, she suggested, was because of the impact of greater competition and because, in a stable environment, they undertake more risky investment projects than would be the case if they were worried about an imminent downturn in the economy.

This, in essence, is the problem of stability. You can, it seems, have too much of a good thing if, in the apparent absence of any downside danger, people take too much risk. Stability, or, as the long period of non-inflationary growth came to be called, the 'Great Moderation', contains the seeds of the next disaster. That is true in general, in that policymakers, the financial markets, firms and individuals become complacent. The most obvious symptom of that complacency is the acquisition of too much debt. If the revenues are going to keep coming in, or if there is no risk of unemployment, why not take on debt? Stability also has direct consequences for the behaviour of banks, as Thomas Cooley, dean of the New York University–Stern School of Business, pointed out. 'There is another, deeper possible link between the Great Moderation and the financial crisis that is worth thinking about, because it may help to inform the financial regulation of the future,' he wrote.[4]

> The idea is simply that the decline in volatility led financial institutions to underestimate the amount of risk they faced and overestimate the amount of leverage they could handle, thus essentially (though unintentionally) reintroducing a large measure of volatility into the market. Financial institutions typically manage their risk using what they call value at risk or VaR. Without getting into the technicalities of VaR (and there is a very long story to be told about the misuse of these methods), it is highly likely that the Great Moderation led many risk managers to drastically underestimate the aggregate risk in the economy. A 50 per cent decline in aggregate risk is huge, and after 20 years, people come to count on things being the same. Risk managers are supposed to address these problems with *stress testing* – computing their value at risk assuming extreme events – but they often don't. The result was that firms vastly overestimated the amount of leverage they could assume, and put themselves at great risk. Of course, the desperate search for yield had something to do with it as well, but I have a hard time believing that the managers of Lehman, Bear Stearns and others knowingly bet the firm on a systematic basis. They thought the world was less risky than it is. And so, the Great Moderation became fuel for the fire.

After a crisis, just as after a natural disaster or a big terrorist attack, there is a tendency first to fear that there will be another one straight away and second for people to over-adjust their behaviour. Part of the problem the advanced economies faced after the crisis was that their banking systems were impaired and lending capacity had been lost. Cross-border banking, in particular, shrank sharply. Tied to this, however, was an adjustment in the behaviour of many bankers. Having been addicted to risk, because that was where the rewards lay, some became excessively cautious and risk averse, particularly commercial bankers. The punishment for getting it wrong exceeded the potential rewards for taking risks. This kind of behavioural shift means that, initially at least, policymakers and regulators may not have to worry too much about risky behaviour, notwithstanding the return of bonuses, and probably have to be more concerned about reviving the 'animal spirits', in business but also among consumers, that make economies tick. In the long term, though, the challenge is to find ways of throwing a bit more grit into the machine, of providing regular reminders that things can go down as well as up. Stability will still be the aim, complacency will be the thing to avoid.

The new normal

In May 2009 PIMCO, the California-based fund manager, the world's biggest bond manager, held its annual 'secular' forum at Newport Beach, Orange County. The aim of the forum, as with its predecessors, was to try to determine trends (this is the meaning of the word 'secular' as used by economists) affecting financial markets over the medium term. Key to this was the type of global economy that would emerge from the crisis. Speakers included William 'Bill' White, formerly of the Bank for International Settlements, who was prescient ahead of the crisis; Willem Buiter, the former member of the Bank of England's monetary policy committee; and Peter Costello, the longest-serving Australian Treasurer (finance minister), who was in office from 1996 until 2007. Also in attendance were Alan Greenspan and Michael Spence, the 2001 Nobel Prize winner in economics.

The result of their deliberations was a consensus around what Mohamed El-Erian, PIMCO's chief executive, described as 'the new normal'. Those expecting a return to the conditions prevailing before the summer of 2007 would be disappointed. 'It was clear to us that, despite the very high hurdle that we always apply to such a statement, the world has changed in a manner that is unlikely to be reversed over the next few years,' El-Erian wrote.[5]

Put another way, markets are recovering from a shock that goes way, way beyond a cyclical flesh wound. It is not just about the major realignment of the financial system and the extent to which governments have intervened to offset market failures. And it goes beyond the massive increase in government deficits and government debt in virtually every important country in the world. It's also about the structural change in how savings are mobilized and allocated, nationally and across borders. It is about the shifting balance between the public and private sectors. And we should not forget the potentially long-lasting consequences of the erosion of trust in such basic parameters of a market system as the sanctity of contracts and property rights, the rule of law, and the robustness of the capital structure. Such trust can be lost quickly but takes a long time to restore. The result is a prolonged pause, or in some cases, a violent reversal in certain concepts that markets had taken for granted. We referred to it as the demise of the 'great age' of private leverage, asset- and credit-based entitlements, self-regulation, policy moderation, and shrinking direct government involvement. Not surprisingly given the extent of the gains that were privatized and the losses that are now being socialized, the demise is occurring in the context of popular anger, confusion and what one of our speakers called 'a morality play' in parliaments around the world.

Even in the occasionally dry and technical language of a professional fund manager, this represented a significant shift in the global economic environment. The easy growth of the past, and in particular the 2002–07 period, would have to be paid for in the future. The hangover, in government debts and deficits, in individual and corporate indebtedness, and in a banking system either saddled with toxic debts or forced to pay governments considerable sums to insure them, would be long and painful. In the four years leading up to the crisis the global economy had grown by an average of 5 per cent a year, its strongest performance since the early 1970s. That period of exuberance had been followed by the extreme turbulence of the rest of the 1970s and early 1980s. It had marked the end of the post-war 'golden age' for the world economy, when the resumption of peacetime economic normality and the liberalisation of world trade from the protectionist constraints of the 1930s produced a strong and sustained rise in living standards. It was the era of the easy prosperity of the American dream and the two- or three-car family, and it was also the era when the defeated powers, Germany and Japan, produced their own economic miracles. The golden age ended in economic pain and instability. Was the end of the 'Great Moderation' going to go the same way?

One obvious difference was that, unlike in the 1970s, inflation was not a problem. In many countries, instead, the worry was about deflation. In August 2009 the OECD said that prices on average in its 30 member economies were 0.3 per cent lower than a year earlier, with deflation measured this way in America, the euro zone and nearly half OECD members. Global money supply growth, despite the conventional and unconventional monetary policy efforts of central banks, remained weak. The effect of the world economy's dive into recession, meanwhile, had left a huge surplus of global capacity, particularly in industry, which would take years of growth to reduce. That would not prevent concerns about inflation returning later, however, perhaps two or three years into the recovery. One worry was straightforward: what to do about all that government and private debt. In the past, governments have found it easier to inflate debt away than take the tough tax and spending decisions necessary to reduce it. A second concern was that, in their determination to avoid deflation, central banks might unintentionally let the inflation genie out of the bottle. Calibrating monetary policy is easy when the changes are small. It is harder when interest rates have been cut to unprecedented lows – their lowest since 1694 during the crisis, in the case of the Bank of England – or when unconventional policies such as quantitative easing are being employed. The third fear was that the spare capacity in the global economy would be used up relatively quickly, putting upward pressure on prices relatively soon in the upturn. Factory closures would mean some capacity would be permanently lost while some of that which remained would become quickly obsolete. Investing in new capacity, at a time when bank finance would be constrained and businesses wary of a lurch back into a new crisis, could be much weaker than in normal recoveries.

Even if high inflation does not return, and I would side with those who believe it will not, it will inevitably be more unstable than in the past. Among the many ideas Alan Greenspan gave the world was that policymakers should aim to keep inflation low enough so that it does not interfere with normal economic decision-making by firms and individuals. That was interpreted as implying inflation of around 2 per cent. Even if future inflation is around that average there will still be times in the coming years when it is significantly higher than that, and there may also be times when the fear is of a slide into deflation. The inflation stability of the period leading up to the crisis is unlikely to be repeated. More generally, recovery will be a long haul. The dive into recession is sudden, the way back often slow and tortuous. This appears to be particularly the case for recessions caused by financial crises. Kenneth Rogoff, the former chief economist at the IMF, and his co-author, Carmen Reinhart, studied the economic effects of financial crises going back over centuries. 'What we do know is that after the start of the crisis in 2007, asset prices and other standard crisis indicator variables tumbled in the United States and elsewhere along the tracks laid down by historical precedent,' they wrote.[6] 'It is true that equity markets have recovered some ground, but by and large this is not out of line with the historical experience that V-shaped recoveries in equity prices are far more common than V-shaped recoveries in real housing prices or employment. Overall, our analysis of the post-crisis outcomes for unemployment, output and government debt, provide sobering benchmark numbers for how deep financial crises can unfold.'

Putting banks on the straight and narrow

After the Great Depression, national and world leaders vowed never to let it happen again. Never again would mass unemployment be allowed to arise from a lack of economic vision and understanding. Never again would a flawed international financial system and beggar-my-neighbour protectionism be allowed to sabotage growth and prosperity. Out of this grew the post-war settlement – Bretton Woods, the IMF, the World Bank, the General Agreement on Tariffs and Trade (GATT). Even before that, however, important changes in banking occurred in response to the crisis. The Glass-Steagall Act, introduced in 1933 by Senator Carter Glass and Congressman Henry Steagall, had a simple and logical aim. Commercial banks had been brought to their knees by their exposure to financial markets and in particular by underwriting stock and bond issues. The Glass-Steagall Act, by separating commercial and investment banking, sought to close off that possibility, thus making commercial banking safer. The legislators were not finished there. In 1956 the Bank Holding Company Act specified that bank holding companies owning two or more banks would be prevented from expanding into non-banking activity or buying banks in other US states. Banking across state borders, let alone international borders, was restricted.

The repeal of the Glass-Steagall Act in 1999, towards the end of Bill Clinton's presidency, is pinpointed by some as a key factor in the crisis. Certainly, the timing was terrible. Its repeal was driven by Sandy Weill, the head of Travelers, a financial services conglomerate that owned the Wall Street broker Salomon Smith Barney, who in 1998 wanted to merge with Citicorp, one of America's biggest banks, headed by John Reed. Under the legislation, any merger could have taken place only subject to selling off significant numbers of businesses within the combined operation, which would have defeated the object of creating a new banking and financial services giant. An intensive political lobbying process followed, the merger was given a fair wind by Alan Greenspan and the Clinton White House and, eventually, congressional support for the repeal of Glass-Steagall was achieved. It was the twelfth attempt to repeal the Act in 25 years. Citigroup, the world's biggest financial services company, was born. There were two sequels. One was that, amid considerable controversy, Robert Rubin, Clinton's Treasury secretary, accepted a senior post, effectively second-in-command, at Citigroup. The other was that in the crisis of 2007–09, Citigroup was one of the biggest casualties. Chuck Prince, its chief executive, produced one of the most memorable quotes of the crisis. 'When the music stops, in terms of liquidity, things will be complicated,' he said in July 2007.[7] 'But as long as the music is playing, you've got to get up and dance. We're still dancing.' Four months later he was forced to step down after Citigroup was plunged into huge losses and forced to seek capital from the Middle East and Singapore and eventually, after the collapse of Lehman, concede a 36 per cent US government stake. It goes without saying that without the Travelers–Citicorp merger, and the repeal of Glass-Steagall, things would have turned out differently.

More generally, however, Glass-Steagall had been watered down for years before its repeal. Barely was the ink dry on the Bank Holding Company Act than US banks were successfully lobbying to be allowed to enter the municipal bond market, even as brokers were moving into their traditional territory, particularly from the 1970s onwards, by offering interest-paying money market accounts that had most of the properties of ordinary bank accounts. In the 1980s the lines between commercial and investment banking began to be seriously blurred by a series of decisions by the Federal Reserve; in 1986/87 commercial banks were first allowed up to 5 per cent of their revenues from investment banking, then permitted to underwrite certain securities and commercial paper. So it went on, with the investment banking limit raised to 10 per cent in the late 1980s, and 25 per cent in 1996. In 1997 banks were allowed to own securities firms outright. Glass-Steagall looked like an obsolete relic of the Great Depression, while the Bank Holding Company Act was a product of the overcautious 1950s. As a result of the crisis itself, and the US banking rescue, the lines between commercial and investment banking became further blurred, investment banks being allowed similar access to official funds as their commercial banking counterparts.

Despite this, the question of a new Glass-Steagall has emerged, and not just in the United States. How can banks be prevented from becoming 'too big to fail', threatening their own survival and the stability of the financial system by excessive risk-taking? One answer is to limit the scope, as well as the size, of banks. The economist John Kay, in a paper for the Centre for the Study of Financial Innovation, set out the argument for 'narrow banking' or, as some have argued, separating the banks' 'casino' activities from their roles as monetary utilities. 'The case for narrow banking rests on the coincidence of three arguments,' wrote Kay.[8]

First, the existing structure of financial services regulation (supervision) has failed. Consumers are ill served, the collapse of major financial institutions has created the most serious economic crisis in a generation, and the sector has been stabilised only by the injection of very large amounts of public money and unprecedented guarantees of private sector liabilities. Second, the most effective means of improving customer services and promoting innovation in retail financial services is market-oriented. The growth of financial conglomerates, a consequence of earlier measures of deregulation, has not been in the interests of the public or, in the long run, of the institutions themselves. Third, a specific, but serious, problem arises from the ability of conglomerate financial institutions to use retail deposits which are implicitly or explicitly guaranteed by government as collateral for their other activities and particularly for proprietary trading. The use of the deposit base in this way encourages irresponsible risk taking, creates major distortions of competition, and imposes unacceptable burdens on taxpayers.

There is no doubt that too many people, including regulators, economists and commentators, made the mistake of believing that banks were still mainly risk-averse utilities, rather than excessive risk-takers. Even so, Kay's narrow banking approach, while appealing, is unlikely to be where the banking system ends up. Paul Volcker, former chairman of the Federal Reserve, who was appointed chairman of Barack Obama's Economic Advisory Board in 2009, had his own ideas, which offered a more workable solution. 'As a general matter, I would exclude from commercial banking institutions, which are potential beneficiaries of official (i.e. taxpayer) financial support, certain risky activities entirely suitable for our capital markets,' he told Congress in September 2009.[9]

Ownership or sponsorship of hedge funds and private equity funds should be among those prohibited activities. So should in my view a heavy volume of proprietary trading with its inherent risks. Some trading, it is reasonably argued, is necessary as part of a full service customer relationship. The distinction between 'proprietary' and 'customer-related' may be cloudy at the border. But surely by the active use of capital requirements and the exercise of supervisory authority, appropriate restraint can be maintained.

Broad-based banks argue that much of their wider activity is driven by customer needs. In evidence[10] to the House of Commons Treasury Committee in 2009, Barclays argued the so-called universal banking model gave even its medium-sized business customers access to investment banking products that were previously available only to very large businesses. Late in January 2010, after a surprise electoral defeat in Massachusetts, President Obama shocked the banks and the markets by announcing that he was proceeding with Volcker's proposals. Banks would no longer be allowed to be too big to fail. It was described as the biggest shake-up since Glass-Steagall but it remained to be seen whether it would survive the US political process. Mervyn King, the Bank of England governor, told the same committee[11] that while the idea of separating narrow banking and wider banks was 'very attractive' he did not believe it was a practicable proposition. The wider banks, by offering more attractive returns, would attract the lion's share of depositors, and thus expand more rapidly. Narrow banks would have their own built-in obsolescence.

King, however, was not happy. In a thundering speech in October 2009, he railed against the fact that there had been little progress on meaningful banking reform and that the problem of 'moral hazard', which he identified in 2007, was more serious as a result of the crisis than before. 'Anyone who proposed giving government guarantees to retail depositors and other creditors, and then suggested that such funding could be used to finance highly risky and speculative activities, would be thought rather unworldly,' he said.[12]

But that is where we now are. It is important that banks in receipt of public support are not encouraged to try to earn their way out of that support by resuming the very activities that got them into trouble in the first place. The sheer creative imagination of the financial sector to think up new ways of taking risk will in the end, I believe, force us to confront the 'too important to fail' question. The belief that appropriate regulation can ensure that speculative activities do not result in failures is a delusion.

In November 2009, the government announced a step towards a form of narrower banking, at the same time pledging to increase competition in UK banking. Alistair Darling said that the 'good bank' part of Northern Rock, as well as some of the assets of Royal Bank of Scotland and Lloyds Banking Group, would be sold to new entrants over a three-to-four-year period. The aim would be to encourage firms with simpler banking models to enter the market.

Growing without credit

Even if, as seemed likely, universal banks would survive the crisis, it was clear that their wings would be clipped. Riskier activities would be restricted by more intensive regulation, by bigger and more-targeted capital requirements and by direct intervention in a range of decisions, including policy on pay and bonuses, which banks would have previously said was nobody's business but their own. The shadow banking system, after long years of expansion, would go into reverse. Banks directing assets and lending into Structured Investment Vehicles (SIVs), or other special-purpose and off-balance-sheet entities, would be subject to much tighter scrutiny and control. Regulators would be determined not to get fooled for a second time. The huge increase in leverage in the banking boom years would be followed by a period of deleverage, probably a prolonged one. Banks would be required to be safer, and to hold a higher proportion of low-risk assets. In October 2009 Britain's Financial Services Authority published rules, to be implemented once the economy was recovering, which would require Britain's banks to hold more UK government bonds (gilts) and other safe and liquid assets, warning that the effect would be to limit their lending and reduce profitability.

How reliant had the world economy become on bank lending? Would it be possible for the advanced economies, particularly America and Britain, to grow at all if credit growth was restricted? The International Monetary Fund looked at precisely this question in its April 2009

World Economic Outlook, after examining the experience of countries previously hit by financial crises. Its conclusion was indeed that growth was likely to be weaker, at least in the initial stages of recovery. 'One of the most striking features of recoveries from recessions associated with financial crises is the "creditless" nature of these recoveries,' it said.[13]

> Credit growth typically turns positive only seven quarters after the resumption of output growth. Although the demand for credit is generally lower in the aftermath of a financial crisis as households and firms deleverage, the stress experienced by the banking sector during these episodes suggests that restrictions in the supply of credit are also important. This raises an important question: To what extent do restrictions in the supply of credit constrain the strength of economic recovery? In the absence of financial friction, firms should be able to costlessly compensate for the decrease in bank credit with other forms of credit, such as the issuance of debt, leaving their investment and output decisions unchanged. The presence of market imperfections, however, implies that these different forms of credit are not perfect substitutes, and the result is a slower recovery for firms and industries that are more reliant on credit.

Six months after that assessment, the IMF had some good news, which was that it was revising down the actual and potential write-downs as a result of the crisis by $600 billion. The bad news was that those write-downs would still be a huge $3.4 trillion ($3,400 billion). It was going to take time for credit to come back, and for countries like Britain, with a long tradition of reliance on the banks as the main source of finance for both business and household borrowing, it would be a significant brake on recovery. It would not be bad for everybody and, indeed, a period of 'creditless' growth, as long as it does not slip back into recession, is healthier in the long run. One of the features of the immediate aftermath of the worst of the financial crisis was that many businesses had much better credit ratings than the banks. The question for them was why they needed to use the banks as intermediaries at all, rather than borrow directly from investors. So the nature of credit may well change dramatically. The banks, in increasing their market share and in apparently being cleverer than anybody else, had squeezed out other forms of finance. Excessive reliance on the banks had been a problem for Britain since at least the 1930s. Perhaps this would now change, and policymakers were keen to encourage that change. David Miles, a member of the Bank of England's monetary policy committee, saw the programme of 'quantitative easing', QE, the Bank had implemented as encouraging that change. 'I think the evidence suggests there are some significant effects of QE and they are ones which help us travel on a path towards a more sustainable banking structure – one where reliance upon bank debt by the private sector will likely be lower and where the banks are better capitalised and better able to handle fluctuations in their sources of funding,' he said in September 2009.[14]

Rethinking monetary policy

The era of simple inflation targeting lasted for two decades. Even central banks that did not have formal inflation targets, like the Federal Reserve, behaved more or less like those that did. Those days are gone. Now central banks face a much more complex task. 'The single most important lesson from the financial crisis is the need to expand the range of instruments available to policymakers,' said Spencer Dale, the Bank of England's chief economist, in 2009.[15] 'The inflation targeting framework provides the scope to respond to asset price bubbles and to imbalances that threaten future economic stability. But short-term interest rates are not well suited to managing such risks. The precise design of such new instruments is now the focus of much work and analysis.' A crude instrument for controlling house prices, for example, might be restricting the amount people can borrow, either in relation to their income or to the value of the property they are buying. A more sophisticated approach, though there would be no point implementing it until bank lending has returned to something like normality, would be to set aggregate lending limits; controlling the overall flow of credit into the economy. This was the way monetary policy used to operate, with direct controls on lending. In Britain, for example, the banks were subject to what was known as 'the corset' (its proper name was the

Supplementary Special Deposit Scheme), which imposed penalties on banks whose deposits exceeded preset limits. The corset was dropped in 1980, as a consequence of the abolition of exchange controls the previous year, which permitted overseas banks, or overseas subsidiaries of UK banks, to lend into Britain. Some form of quantitative limits on lending may, however, be the kind of instrument that central banks will need, in addition to interest rates. Just as quantitative easing was necessary when interest rates reached the limits of their power during the crisis, so it is reasonable to expect additional weapons during better times. Interest rates on their own may never be enough.

The second significant change will come from the fact that financial regulators, which in some cases will be located within central banks, will have a bigger macroeconomic impact than in the past. One of the buzz phrases of the new era will be 'macroprudential' regulation, ensuring that the actions of individual institutions do not endanger the system as a whole. Another will be counter-cyclical capital requirements, requiring banks to hoard more capital in the good times, so that they have a capital cushion against losses in the bad times. Spain's system of 'dynamic provisioning' is a version of such capital requirements and helped protect its banks in the downturn, though not, as it turned out, the Spanish economy. It is not hard to see that the setting of these counter-cyclical capital requirements could be as important in their way as changes in interest rates. Making the banks hold more capital, and thus lend less, could diminish the need for interest-rate hikes to slow the economy and keep inflation on target. Easing their capital requirements in a downturn could have the opposite effect. Critics used to say that policymakers relying solely on interest rates were like one-club golfers. Suddenly, policymakers would have several clubs in the bag. An issue would arise, however, if regulators setting counter-cyclical requirements had a different view on the economy's position in the cycle to that of the central bank. Some would say this kind of complication already arises with fiscal policy, which in Britain and America is set separately by their respective Treasury departments. Now there would be three elements of macroeconomic policy, fiscal, monetary and regulatory, making the coordination task harder, though for central banks that are also regulators (the Conservative Party's ambition for the Bank of England) that task would be easier.

Crisis-proofing fiscal policy

Before the financial crisis, Gordon Brown was proud of saying that Britain had one of the strongest fiscal positions in the world. All that was to change. In May 2009, after Alistair Darling's second Budget as chancellor predicted a budget deficit of £175 billion for 2009/10, 12.4 per cent of GDP (figures revised up to £178 billion and 12.6 per cent at the end of the year), Standard & Poor's, the rating agency, put the UK's AAA sovereign debt rating on 'negative' watch. It warned that there was a one-in-three chance of a downgrade that, for Britain, would have been unprecedented.[16] The deterioration in Britain's public finances was dramatic. America was faced with a similar situation. In August 2009 the Congressional Budget Office predicted[17] that the US budget deficit would soar to $1,587 billion in 2009, nearly four times its 2008 level of $459 billion. For the period 2010–14, deficits would total just under $4 trillion – $3,988 billion. As in Britain, a relatively small part of all this borrowing was due to deliberate actions by politicians. Most reflected the impact of the recession on government spending and tax revenues. Internationally, while Britain and America stood out as extreme cases, everybody was suffering. The IMF estimated[18] that for advanced economies as a whole, public sector net debt would rise from an average of 75 per cent of GDP in 2008 to 115 per cent by 2014. The only comfort for Britain was that of starting from a relatively low base.

The global recession was ruthless in its impact on public finances, and even countries without large banking sectors were hit hard. For years New Zealand had run budget surpluses, partly to compensate for the country's chronic balance-of-payments deficit. At the start of the crisis, the government's net debt was comfortably under 10 per cent of gross domestic product. Soon, however, the New Zealand Treasury was looking at projections that would see a decade of big budget deficits and a rise in debt to 60 per cent of GDP and beyond. Action was taken to reduce planned public spending over the medium term. The question for the New Zealand authorities was whether this was enough.

'It is prudent to allow an increase in debt in response to the current economic shock and then ensure that this increase is reversed,' the New Zealand Treasury said in its 2009 *Fiscal Strategy Report*.[19] 'We will keep net debt consistently below 40 per cent of GDP. Over the longer term we consider that it is prudent in terms of future economic shocks and an ageing population to have net debt closer to 20 per cent of GDP.' New Zealand gave the world inflation targeting in the late 1980s and perhaps it was giving governments a new way of looking at managing their public finances. In Britain an apparent debt ceiling of 40 per cent of GDP had been blown away by a collapse in tax revenues. The crisis had exposed just how vulnerable public finances were and how dangerously high previous safe limits were. The lesson for next time was that governments should try to limit their exposure by keeping debt very low during times when the economic weather is favourable.

In the meantime, plenty of pain lay ahead. While the return of growth would help the public finances, as would the winding down of support for the banking industry and the return of government stakes in the banks to the private sector, much more would be needed. In Britain the promised adjustment included a new 50 per cent rate of income tax, higher National Insurance contributions and a three-year squeeze on government departments from 2011 that would result in a cumulative cut of 10 per cent in real-terms spending. Despite this and other proposed measures, Britain's Institute for Fiscal Studies estimated[20] that it would take until the 2030s for government debt to be back below the old 40 per cent ceiling. The hangover would be a long and painful one.

What kind of capitalism?

In their 1993 book *The Seven Cultures of Capitalism*, Charles Hampden-Turner and Fons Trompenaars looked at the different models of capitalism in seven different countries, America, Britain, Japan, France, Germany, Sweden and the Netherlands. Their aim was to warn against the complacent view that what they described as the Anglo-American model of capitalism (which some would call Anglo-Saxon capitalism) was superior to all other forms. Their warning, in the light of subsequent events, looks prescient. 'Something is out of kilter in the

Anglo-American business community, which has for the past forty-five years been the world's chief advocate of capitalist ideology,' they wrote.[21]

American capitalism became the negation of communism, standing for freedom not coercion, individualism not collectivism, private not public ownership, pragmatism not theory. These arguments, a rhetorical defence of capitalism, taken together with the crumbling of communism, have lulled us into a false sense of security. We have believed our own propaganda, and this has prevented us from considering that our wealth creation system could be vulnerable. We have confused our media victories ... with what really works in factories and offices. Above all we have confused the polarized structure of debate – at which we excelled – with the reconciled structures of organisations that create actual products and services.

No list of competing models of capitalism these days would stop with these seven. The Chinese model of controlled (but not necessarily state-owned) capitalism would feature. So would the approaches used elsewhere in the Far East, such as Singapore, a model for some versions of 'stakeholder' capitalism. India has a peculiarly Indian version of capitalism. The two other 'BRIC' economies, Brazil and Russia, are different again. Things will be different – they have to be different – but the question is how? The simplest, most stripped-down approach would simply look at the financial market aspects of Anglo-Saxon capitalism and control and regulate them better in the future, and that will surely happen.

The bigger question is whether the changes need to go deeper. Paul Woolley, the fund manager and academic, founder of the Paul Woolley Centre for the Study of Capital Market Dysfunctionality at the London School of Economics, certainly thinks so. 'It is strange that an industry whose function is the quite utilitarian one of converting savings into real investment should have become so dominant,' he said in a discussion.[22] 'We need to ask how it has come about that this intermediary role is being performed at such a high cost to society, with such complexity and capacity to collapse. There are several explanations. One is the so-called "agency problem" … which confers on banks, fund managers and so on, the power to capture a disproportionate share of the returns from the productive economy.' Instead of individuals making decisions, and influencing how companies behave, the agency problem means such influence is exerted through agents – in the case of firms, their big institutional shareholders – and this creates a culture of both short-termism and what critics describe as 'group-think'. So the question is whether freebooting financial market capitalism has infected and dominated economies to a degree that requires the cleansing process to go much deeper.

Unstable markets

It is easy to think of ways in which infection from the financial sector has infiltrated the wider economy. Though Britain's financial services sector was only 8 per cent of gross domestic product at the onset of the crisis, its influence was felt much more widely than that. The assets of UK banking groups were equivalent to more than four times gross domestic product, more than in most other advanced economies. Only Switzerland, with its banks also reaching out globally, was significantly higher, Swiss banking assets being nine times GDP, similar to Iceland before its collapse. Banks and financial markets were supposed to serve the economy, not dominate it. The financial sector, by offering the highest rewards, claimed a disproportionate share of the country's graduates. It also had a huge influence on wider corporate culture. Roger Bootle, in his book *The Trouble with Markets*, set out the scale of the problem.

'The Great Implosion has laid bare several different sorts of failing,' he wrote.[23]

First, it has revealed just how fragile the financial system is. Second, it has demonstrated the markets' excessive risk taking. Third, it has shown how bloated the financial sector has become. Fourth, it has exhibited a failure of the market with regard to the setting of executive remuneration in general, and pay in the financial sector in particular. Fifth, it has uncovered a deep-seated failure of the corporate system, arising from the separation between owners and managers and the weakness of institutional shareholders in influencing corporate policy. The result has been the revelation of a financial sector hell-bent on pursuing its own profit, while undermining, not promoting, the public good, and a system of corporate governance where managers have been pursuing either their own interests or the short-term performance of the share price – which often came to the same thing. Even Jack Welch, the former CEO of General Electric who is often thought of as one of the originators of the shareholder value movement, has said recently that 'focusing solely on quarterly profit increases is the dumbest idea in the world. Share-holder value is a result, not a strategy.'

To a certain extent, the problem of an excessively powerful financial sector should be self-correcting. Some financial market activities have bounced back very quickly but others will take longer and may not re-emerge at all. For a while, at least, it will be a less aggressive recruiter. It is possible that some of what have been described by the UK Financial Services Authority chairman Lord Turner and others as socially useless activities, particularly certain derivative products which were too complex for their own good, will not see the light of day again. Banks will be forced to hold more capital and will be subject to much tighter restrictions on their ability to engage in risky activity. They may be more highly taxed. At the annual meeting of the IMF and the World Bank in October 2009, held in Istanbul, the IMF proposed a new tax on banks, to be used both to channel finance to poor countries for development and to provide a guarantee fund to be used in future crises. 'Considering that the financial sector is creating a lot of systemic risk for the global economy, and that it is just fair that such a sector would pay some part of its resources to help mitigate the risks that they are creating themselves, having some money coming from the financial sector to create a kind of fund for insurance or funding for low-income countries is something that we are going to consider,' said Dominique Strauss-Kahn, managing director of the IMF, at the meeting.[24] The financial sector will be more tightly regulated and probably more heavily taxed. Achieving the right balance between doing that and having a banking system that supports economic recovery will present a delicate challenge.

Would this kind of approach fundamentally change behaviour, or merely limit the scope of the financial system to do damage? Will it, like so many responses to crises, be effective at fighting the last war but not necessarily the next one? 'The crisis will happen again but it will be different,' said Alan Greenspan in 2009.[25] 'They [financial crises] are all different but they have one fundamental cause. That is the unquenchable capability of human beings when confronted with long periods of prosperity to presume that it will continue.' Ending the culture of short-termism created by the interaction of fund managers interested in immediate performance and executives who know their careers depend on it, similarly, looks like a long shot. Various attempts have been made over the years to bring greater long-termism into corporate decision-making. Gordon Brown reformed Britain's capital gains tax system when chancellor with that aim in mind, though Alistair Darling, his successor, undid most of his reforms. Roger Bootle suggests that shareholders should not receive dividends until they have held a stock for two years. In general, however, the problem is not that investors hold shares only for short periods; it is that fund managers are short-termist in their behaviour, because they are judged on their performance, not over years but over weeks or months. Short-termism is built into the system.

The gloomy message from this is that even a once-in-a-lifetime crisis may not result in the kind of change that many would regard as desirable. 'Finance is, as it were, the stomach of the country, from which all other organs take their tone,' wrote William Gladstone in 1858.[26] More than a century and a half later, that is still true, and it is true even in more controlled and regulated forms of capitalism. Financial markets are prone to bouts of extreme instability and will continue to be, despite the efforts of the authorities. The worry, even more than before the crisis, is that those bouts of instability will be more destabilising for the wider economy than in the past. Every time turbulence hits the markets the fear will be that the nightmare of 2007–09 is happening again. The inclination will be to batten down the hatches. In that respect what happens in the financial sector may be more rather than less important in the future.

It all depends on China

In my book *The Dragon and the Elephant*, published in 2007, a few months before the global financial crisis, I argued strongly that the continued rise of China and India was not only inevitable but should be welcomed by the rest of the world. 'The rise of China and India ... will be the outstanding development of the early decades of the twenty-first century, raising fundamental questions about the structure of the world economy and the balance of global geopolitical power,' I wrote.[27] 'Imagine the world by the middle of the century. The world's three biggest economies will be, in order, China, the United States and India. Beijing, Washington and New Delhi will be where global power lies. Their climb will have been astonishing. Even now China and India combined are only half the size of Japan and barely a fifth of the United States in terms of gross domestic product. Their journey over the next 40–50 years will be a fascinating one, full of huge opportunities and pitfalls.' Their rise was what economists would call a positive economic shock, increasing the global economy's ability to grow. Then came two big negative shocks, first a surge in commodity prices that persisted until the summer of 2008, and then the credit crunch, from the summer of 2007 onwards. What would be the effect of these shocks on the 'shift to the East' and in particular the rise of China and India?

The answer in the short term was that they reinforced the contrast in the economic performance of the two emerging economic giants and the 'old' advanced economies. In 2009 advanced economies as a group experienced a synchronised recession and a drop in gross domestic product of about 3.5 per cent, a post-war record. China, meanwhile, helped by a highly effective official stimulus package and a successful encouragement of its banks to lend that was the envy of Western rivals, grew by around 8 per cent. India was only a little way behind, growing by some 6 per cent. The advanced world would not remain in recession, and the growth gap would close, but the crisis had a profound effect. By leaving China and India relatively unscathed but hobbling most advanced economies with damaged banking systems and a huge public and private debt overhang, it accelerated the shift in the global balance of economic power, in my view, by between five and ten years. The trends that were there before the crisis were accelerated. Some of this shift was palpable. The elevation of the G20 from November 2007 onwards was based on a desire to ensure that the response to the crisis was truly global. Deep down, however, it was all about bringing China on board.

China, meanwhile, became bolder; some of its senior officials openly advocated the replacement of the dollar as the world's reserve currency. 'The outbreak of the current crisis and its spillover in the world have confronted us with a long-existing but still unanswered question, i.e., what kind of international reserve currency do we need to secure global financial stability and facilitate world economic growth, which was one of the purposes for establishing the IMF?' said Zhou Xiaochuan, governor of the People's Bank of China – its central bank – in a speech in March 2009.[28] 'A super-sovereign reserve currency managed by a global institution could be used to both create and control global liquidity,' he went on. 'And when a country's currency is no longer used as the yardstick for global trade and as the benchmark for other currencies, the exchange rate policy of the country would be far more effective in adjusting economic imbalances. This will significantly reduce the risks of a future crisis.' The inference was clear. China saw the dollar's reserve currency status as a significant contributory factor to global financial instability. It had no ambition to see its own currency, the renminbi, step into that role, but something had to change.

Any such change will take decades. In the 1980s and 1990s, France regularly called for a new Bretton Woods conference and reform of the international monetary system, and was generally ignored. China's growing power means that Beijing will be much harder to ignore. Though the central thesis of *The Dragon and the Elephant* was that China and India's rise would continue, there is nothing automatic or preordained about that. For China, the most obvious threats are politics and protectionism. There is also the question, which arose during the crisis, about the extent to which surplus countries such as China are prepared to accept their part of the burden of economic adjustment. For the global economy in the coming years, there is probably no more important question, as Stephen Roach, chairman of Morgan Stanley Asia, put it in his book *The Next Asia*. 'China's Premier, Wen Jiabao, had it right when he worried in early 2007 about a China that was "unbalanced, unstable, uncoordinated and unsustainable",' he wrote.[29]

> The only sustainable answer to the Premier's complaint lies in the rebalancing imperatives of the Chinese economy, namely, shifting away from an export- and investment-led growth model to one that increasingly draws on consumption ... The longer China defers the heavy lifting of its macro rebalancing, the more I remain convinced that it has to happen. The current crisis in the global economy may serve as an important catalyst to this transformation. China elected to respond to this crisis by deploying its standard arsenal – using infrastructure-led investment to buy time until a snapback in external demand prompts a vigorous rebound in export-led Chinese growth. To the extent that external demand remains weak – very much my conclusion for a post-crisis world – China will have no choice other than to accelerate its efforts toward a long-overdue rebalancing.

It is a solid argument. In recovering from the worst financial crisis of the post-war era, the world also has a choice. If it is a question of waiting until advanced economies recover their balance, fix their banking systems and overcome their fiscal hangovers, it will be a very long wait. Much of the burden of pulling along the global economy will have to come from the emerging world, and in particular China. There was evidence that this happened as the world began to emerge from the crisis. A sudden turnaround in export performance in countries as diverse as Japan, Germany and Singapore owed more to China's successful economic stimulus than anything that was happening in America. The International Monetary Fund's October 2009 *World Economic Outlook*, presented at its annual meeting in Istanbul, set out the parameters in projections running through to 2014. On a purchasing power parity basis, in other words adjusted for relative prices, China would make a contribution to global growth roughly twice that of America, right through the period. Together with other emerging countries, China would account for roughly two-thirds of global growth, the remaining third coming from America and the other advanced economies. Not so long before, the proportions had been exactly the opposite way round.

The axis of global growth was shifting and the crisis of 2007–09 would be seen as important in accelerating that shift. In September 2009 HSBC, the British-based global bank, announced that its chief executive, Michael Geoghegan, would be moving from London to Hong Kong. It was a symbolic move but based on what the bank saw as a fundamental economic shift. A few days later, in a piece subtitled 'The rise of the East, the demise of the West', Stephen King, HSBC's chief economist, spelled it out. 'We have reached a tipping point in global economic affairs,' he wrote.[30]

> While there are some encouraging signs of recovery in the developed world, the real economic action is taking place elsewhere. For both cyclical and structural reasons, the emerging nations are set to dominate world economic activity in the years ahead. Although we have revised up our predictions for most countries in the world, the revisions leave the emerging world looking particularly healthy ... Part of the emerging nations' dominance reflects ongoing struggles in the developed world. A combination of low interest rates, quantitative easing and loose fiscal policy has returned stability to financial markets and raised hopes that the worst of the crisis is now safely behind us. Nevertheless, some of the central problems of recent years have yet to go away. Banks no longer enjoy the funding of old. Households and governments are awash with debt. Developed economies remain on life-support systems imposed by policymakers.

It was not quite the apocalyptic vision set out by John Gray at the start of this chapter but it was a fundamental and irreversible shift nonetheless. The advanced economies had grown fat and lazy on easy credit. Their emerging rivals, led by China, were much more virtuous in economic terms and ready to capitalise while much of the West was still struggling to get up from the floor. The 2007–09 financial crisis would be remembered for many things. Handing over the economic baton would be one of them.

14

After the Crisis – Ten Ways the World Will Change

The crisis of 2007–09 gave us something that few who lived through it will forget. This was the first big economic and financial crisis of the twenty-first century and, arguably, the first of the era of globalisation. Its effects were not evenly spread but few escaped some impact. There was a genuine and damaging credit crunch, the first of its kind in living memory. There was a near meltdown in the global banking system, not seen before except in times of world war, the consequences of which could have been economic and social anarchy. In many countries banks clung on to life by their fingertips and we came close to the cash machines running out of money and supermarket shelves not being restocked. Everybody felt the crisis, though few knew at the time quite how bad it could have been. There was a rescue role for government of the kind normally seen only in wartime or at times of extreme civil emergency, but the costs of which were eye-watering. Governments that normally think hard about allocating a few billion pounds, euros or dollars to new projects were suddenly splashing around tens or hundreds of billions in a desperate attempt to avoid collapse. In the absence of a precedent – previous crises had been different in nature and scale – policymakers made it up as they went along.

They succeeded, as they had to, although for several weeks in the autumn of 2008 it was touch and go. Even as this book was being completed at the end of 2009, there were warnings of a relapse into crisis. Tensions remained high. It appeared, however, that the main aim of the authorities, that of avoiding a second Great Depression, had been accomplished. Banks were operating, if not normally, at least on the understanding that they were not about to run out of cash and liquidity. What was also clear, however, was that the cost and the consequences of the crisis would stretch out for decades to come. We will be talking about the financial crisis and the credit crunch and the time the banks nearly failed for many years to come. It will be the modern-day economic episode that every student studies. More than that, people will still be paying for this crisis, if only indirectly through the interest on government debt, and in higher taxes, long after its details have faded in the memory.

What will the world will be like after a crisis as momentous as this? How will it change us? Or will we just breathe a huge sigh of relief and go back to how things were before? There will certainly be changes. The world will be different. Nobody can tell precisely what the long-term consequences of these momentous events will be. They will unfold over a number of years, sometimes in ways that are impossible to predict. Nevertheless, and to conclude, here are some of what I would see as the essential themes for the post-crisis world.

1. A jobs-light recovery

Faced with extreme uncertainty, and a potential collapse in demand, firms cut their workforces. Just as 2009 was the worst year for the global economy in the post-war period, so it was the worst for employment. This was particularly the case in America, where well over seven million jobs were cut between the onset of the recession in December 2007 and the autumn of 2009. The OECD calculated that by the summer of 2009 more than fifteen million jobs had been lost in advanced economics and warned[1] that global unemployment could be on course for 57 million, 10 per cent of the workforce, a post-war record. It takes time after the end of recessions before unemployment turns down, and it takes even longer to get back to what would previously have been regarded as normal. In America it took until 1987 before unemployment got back to its pre-recession low, recorded in 1979, and until 1996 to return to the lows of 1989, even after the relatively mild recession of the early 1990s. In

Britain, partly for demographic reasons, it was more than twenty years, until 2000, before the unemployment rate returned to its level in 1979, two recessions earlier. UK unemployment rose by less than feared in the 2007–09 crisis but nevertheless reached its highest rate for well over a decade. It would take years to fall to its previous lows.

In its December 2009 pre-budget report, the UK Treasury provided projections of the level of unemployment for future years. Though intended to demonstrate that some independent projections were unduly alarmist, it also confirmed that Britain faced years in which the wider unemployment total, based on the Labour Force Survey, would stay high. 'The Treasury has provided a very sober forecast of the medium term outlook for the UK labour market,' concluded John Philpott of the Chartered Institute for Personnel and Development.[2] 'The forecast implies that unemployment will probably remain above 2 million for the first half of the next decade even on what may prove to be an optimistic forecast for economic growth.' The effect on young people entering the workforce was likely to be enduring, raising fears of a 'lost generation'. By late 2009 the average unemployment rate among under-25s in the EU was more than 20 per cent, a total swelled by an astonishing youth unemployment rate of 42.9 per cent in Spain, 28.4 per cent in Ireland and 26.9 per cent in Italy. Getting youth unemployment down to acceptable levels would be a huge task.

2. Reluctantly big government

Before the financial crisis, most governments faced serious long-term problems for their public finances, most notably the effects of ageing populations on health spending and pension provision. Though the crisis diverted attention away from these problems, it did not make them disappear. Governments did not need the effects of the crisis, which raised the average ratio of spending to gross domestic product by more than five percentage points across the advanced countries of the OECD, and by considerably more in the worst-affected countries. Before the crisis, public spending was the equivalent of a fraction over 40 per cent of GDP in the OECD. After it, it was almost 46 per cent. Some of this was the direct cost of implementing banking rescues, the rest the effects of recession. Even politicians with a penchant for bigger government would not have wished for this, though some defended the role of government during and beyond the crisis. 'People rightly talk of the invisible hand of the market, but it goes alongside the enabling hand of government,' said Alistair Darling.[3] The experience of the Scandinavian banking crises of the early 1990s suggested that it takes around a decade for governments to extract themselves from their direct involvement in banking. Reducing the size of government more generally would be an even bigger challenge. After the recession of the earlier 1990s spending-to-GDP ratios took over a decade to drop by 2–3 percentage points, even in favourable economic conditions.

The key question after the banking crisis was how soon governments could safely withdraw emergency support for their economies. Most faced pressure from the bond markets and the rating agencies to reduce budget deficits, and most said that the focus of their fiscal consolidation programmes would be on reducing public spending rather than raising taxes. That is despite the fact that, as Carmen Reinhart and Kenneth Rogoff pointed out in *This Time Is Different*, their study of financial crises, the biggest fiscal impact of such crises is not the cost of bank bailouts but the collapse in tax revenues. One effect of crises, however, is to demonstrate to governments that the stream of revenues on which they were relying would take years to recover. Reducing public spending and government debt poses formidable challenges, particularly in a climate of high unemployment. Bigger government looks to be here to stay.

3. A world of higher taxes

The direct consequences of hard-to-cut public spending and the need to reduce government budget deficits and debt are obvious. Higher taxes are inevitable and in some cases have already been announced. In Britain, the totemic change was Alistair Darling's announcement in April 2009 that the higher rate of income tax would rise to 50 per cent on incomes above £150,000, from April 2010. Not only did this break a specific manifesto pledge by the Labour Party (in 2005 Tony Blair had been re-elected on a pledge not to raise the basic or higher rates of income tax) but it also signalled an end to the political consensus, dating from the time of Margaret Thatcher and Ronald Reagan's supply-side revolution, that high taxes destroyed incentive and enterprise and could result in lower rather than higher revenues. The occasional excesses of the highly paid could be forgiven because they were the wealth genera-tors. Once they had proved themselves to be equally as adept at destroy-ing wealth, this argument was harder to make. The windfall tax on bankers' bonuses introduced by the Labour government in December 2009 was similarly totemic, and the £550 million sum it intended to raise was less important than the signal it sent. The change in attitude it con-veyed was profound. The announcement was just a start and, while it appeared that Britain's competitors for footloose global talent would benefit as the City of London threatened a mass exodus, it was quite likely to be repeated elsewhere.

For years global tax competition had all been about reducing personal and corporate taxes. The crisis marked a change in that, and not just because it was possible to blame some of those footloose individuals and firms in the banking sector for it. The tendency throughout the twen-tieth century had been for the tax burden in economies to increase, to meet the rising cost of publicly provided services and other functions of government. That rising trend had been broken, in some countries, by the Reagan–Thatcher emphasis on smaller government and the sup-ply-side benefits of lower taxes. This was now ancient history. The tax burden had risen consistently under Tony Blair and Gordon Brown, even more rapidly than in most other countries. It seemed certain that it would rise very much farther. The question was how much these higher taxes would stifle enterprise and restrict growth.

4. Slowing globalisation

In 2009, world trade fell at its fastest pace in the post-war era, record-ing perhaps its biggest ever peacetime fall. Fears that the global reces-sion would produce an immediate upsurge in protectionism, equivalent to the Smoot-Hawley Tariff in 1930s America, proved unfounded, but plenty of less significant protectionist measures were introduced and loss of confidence and restrictions on the availability of export credit had a serious impact. It seemed likely, moreover, that world trade would be slower to recover than global GDP, and when it did recover that its growth rate would be much slower than in the past. The IMF, in its October 2009 *World Economic Outlook*, predicted that after a fall of nearly 12 per cent in 2009, world trade would grow by an average of 5.5 per cent a year over the period 2010–14. In the four years leading up to the crisis, 2004–07, the growth in world trade had averaged 8.7 per cent a year.

Jeff Rubin, former chief economist at the Canadian Imperial Bank of Commerce, had already argued that the rationale for the globalisation of trade, separating centres of production from consumer markets by many thousands of miles, was already diminishing, as a result of the rising cost of oil. This, he argued in a book called *Why Your World Is About to Get a Whole Lot Smaller*,[4] would lead to a new emphasis on locally based activity. 'The model of globalisation is not going to be economically viable,' said Rubin.[5] 'What we're going to find is it's not going to make sense to produce things on the other side of the world, no matter how cheap labour costs are there, when it's so expensive to transport things. I think there are a lot of silver linings to this. I think that in many respects, the new smaller world around the corner will be a more enjoyable world to live in.' It could go both ways. The crisis had the effect of pushing oil prices down sharply, thus weakening the effect that Rubin identified. Oil, however, also picked up quickly as evidence of global recovery started to emerge, suggesting that its long-run price would remain higher than in the past. Even more than trade, the process of financial globalisation, cross-border banking and investment flows went into sharp reverse in the crisis. Banks, particularly those bailed out by national governments, tended to retreat within their own borders, and were often under intense political pressure to do so. Global banks would remain, as would financial globalisation. As with trade, however, they would take years to regain their former size and swagger.

5. Constrained consumers

In the ten years from 1997, everything that could go right for Britain's consumers did go right. Employment rose strongly, by more than 3 million; mortgage and other credit was freely available; prices were held down by the combination of global competition (the 'China effect') and a strong pound; real incomes rose; and the saving ratio fell. There was always a risk that at some stage these highly favourable factors would be reversed. In 2004 I wrote in biblical terms about the seven years of feast being followed by seven years of famine, but I was too early. Though income growth weakened, spending did not. Now, however, in Britain and other advanced economies, most of those favourable factors will not be there for some considerable time. Taxes will rise in a way that hurts; rising oil and other commodity prices will stem from the strength of emerging economies, putting upward pressure on other prices; credit will be harder to obtain and households will be under pressure to repay debt. In the case of the UK, sterling fell by 30 per cent during the crisis and the currencies which do well over time will be from countries where most of the economic growth is, such as the Chinese renminbi. The famine years for Western consumers will not mean that they do not spend, but rather that their spending will rise at a much slower rate. This is necessary for the rebalancing of the global economy. After the boom years, and the bust, global house prices will also be subdued.

The biggest issue for the global economy is what happens to the American consumer. Beyond the immediate hangover, the fear is that US consumer spending will remain weak. Even before the crisis some economists were warning that the long boom for consumer spending in America was over. That boom, based on low saving and easy credit, is dated by some back to the early 1980s. The crisis and the debt over-hang will make it harder for US consumers to drive the global economy. According to Edward Harrison of Global Macro Advisers: 'When it comes to US consumers, weak spending growth will last for years. Ultimately, debt levels in the US economy must return to a sustainable level. This can happen over time, which would mean a decade-long low-growth, muddle-through economy – not a terrible outcome either for the economy or for asset prices.'[6] You write off Anglo-Saxon consumers at your peril but this seems very plausible. The question will be whether strong global growth is possible alongside subdued US consumer spending.

6. Risk aversion versus creative destruction

One clear lesson of the crisis for business was that the virtues of risk aversion were rewarded. Companies that had minimised their exposure to risk and debt during the good years were better able to survive the subsequent recession. That applied to banks and it also applied to other firms. So risk aversion, and avoiding excessive debt and leverage, appeared to be clear post-recession strategies. Companies will run on lower levels of debt and higher levels of liquid assets and reserves. Individuals in many countries will also be much more debt averse than in the past. One key challenge for policymakers after the crisis was to ensure that the supply of credit to the economy was restored. Another, however, is to ensure that this process of 'deleveraging' is not too rapid. For individual firms and households, running down debt may be the sensible thing to do. If everybody does it, however, the effect on demand, and therefore economic growth, could be devastating. When central banks cut interest rates to near-zero levels during the crisis, their aim was to prevent economic collapse. They appeared likely to keep the cost of borrowing low for some years to reduce the incentives among borrowers to run down debt too rapidly. The aftermath of the crisis would be a low-interest-rate world, raising fears that central banks would either create new and even more dangerous asset bubbles or usher in a new era of high inflation. In the context of the deleveraging danger, both fears appeared overstated.

Recessions and their immediate aftermath are also, however, fertile periods for what Joseph Schumpeter called 'creative destruction'; new businesses emerging to replace those struggling or failing. One example might be in banking itself, with the entry of new businesses clean of toxic assets, but there could be plenty of others. These two forces, on the face of it, would pull in opposite directions, though could be reconciled; existing firms pursuing risk-averse strategies while new businesses are prepared to be both risk-taking and dynamic. In the case of the latter, finance for innovation would be important, the question being whether it would be forthcoming from risk-averse providers of finance. 'If you take a longer timeframe, such as five to 10 years, I am very optimistic that these problems will be behind us,' wrote Bill Gates, the founder of Microsoft, in his annual 2009 letter.[7] 'A key reason for this is that innovation in every field – from software and materials science to genetics and energy generation – is moving forward at a pace that can bring real progress in solving big problems. These innovations will help improve the world and reinvigorate the world economy.'

7. Staying Green

The recession of 2008/09 had an immediate and beneficial impact on the planet. The sharp plunge in economic activity reduced carbon emissions. The International Energy Agency estimated that global CO_2 emissions fell by 3 per cent in 2009 and would be 5 per cent lower in 2020 than it had previously expected. The nature of the recession, which affected advanced-economy consumer and business spending, particularly on air travel and road transport, was enough to compensate for rising emissions from regions that continued to grow. There were also reasons to believe, however, that the 'green' impetus would be sustained beyond the crisis, in spite of the disappointing outcome for the Copenhagen climate summit. At the end of 2009, after the worst year for the global economy in the post-war period, climate negotiators from 192 countries and more than one hundred national leaders met in Copenhagen for a summit under the auspices of the United Nations Framework Convention on Climate Change. The summit was preceded by new commitments from America, China and India to reduce carbon emissions. After days of wrangling, a non-binding deal was struck, mainly between America and China, with Beijing being blamed for obstructing a wider agreement, and recriminations followed. Despite this, and the fierce rows between advanced and emerging economies over who would bear the costs of adapting to climate change, it demonstrated that the issue would not go away.

Unlike in previous recessions, when environmental concerns were replaced by short-term economic imperatives, even a deep recession and a huge banking crisis had not thrown the political determination to tackle global warming off course. G20 leaders, when they met in Pittsburgh in September 2009, had time to emphasise that 'we are working for a resilient, sustainable, and green recovery. We underscore anew our resolve to take strong action to address the threat of dangerous climate change'.[8] Amid the economic chaos, perhaps this was something to cling on to. The global recessions of the 1970s and early 1990s had seen the environmental agenda take a back seat. This time, despite renewed controversy over the science, climate change looked much more likely to feature prominently on the policy agenda for years to come.

8. Suspicious of markets

For left-of-centre politicians, an important rite of passage during the long pre-crisis economic upturn was to be able to publicly admit that markets were not only good but usually knew best. Tony Blair was probably the first Labour leader to be able to do that hand on heart. The Blair–Clinton Third Way of the 1990s was based on a mutual recognition that while there were market failures, markets were in general a good thing. That was the view of regulators, central bankers and national treasuries. For many that belief will still hold, but the political axis has shifted, and it will stay shifted for some time. Left-of-centre politicians will find it much easier to criticise markets and their right-of-centre opponents will find it tougher to defend them. Gordon Brown, in his 2009 speech to the Labour Party conference, set the new tone. 'What let the world down last autumn was not just bankrupt institutions but a bankrupt ideology,' he said.

> What failed was the Conservative idea that markets always self-correct but never self-destruct. What failed was the right wing fundamentalism that says you just leave everything to the market and says that free markets should not just be free but values free … And these are the values of fairness and responsibility that we teach our children, celebrate in our families, observe in our faiths, and honour in our communities. Call them middle class values, call them traditional working class values, call them family values, call them all of these; these are the values of the mainstream majority; the anchor of Britain's families, the best instincts of the British people, the soul of our party and the mission of our government. And I say this too; these are my values – the values I grew up with in an ordinary family in an ordinary town.[9]

Barack Obama, addressing Wall Street in September 2009, was more measured but also made it clear that markets could not expect to operate in an unfettered way. 'There are those who would suggest that we must choose between markets unfettered by even the most modest of regulations, and markets weighed down by onerous regulations that suppress the spirit of enterprise and innovation,' he said.

> If there is one lesson we can learn from last year, it is that this is a false choice. Common-sense rules of the road don't hinder the market, they make the market stronger. Indeed, they are essential to ensuring that our markets function fairly and freely. One year ago, we saw in stark relief how markets can spin out of control; how a lack of common-sense rules can lead to excess and abuse; how close we can come to the brink. One year later, it is incumbent upon us to put in place those reforms that will prevent this kind of crisis from ever happening again, reflecting painful but important lessons that we've learned, and that will help us move from a period of reckless irresponsibility, a period of crisis, to one of responsibility and prosperity. That's what we must do.[10]

The backlash against the bankers was not surprising. It happened in the 1930s on a larger scale. Something more fundamental had shifted, however. Criticisms of markets went deeper than before. When the Frenchman Michel Barnier was appointed EU internal market commissioner in November 2009, Nicolas Sarkozy, the French president, had little doubt what it implied. 'I want the world to see the victory of the European model, which has nothing to do with the excesses of financial capitalism,' he said.[11] Sarkozy, who took office promising to introduce a version of the Anglo-Saxon capitalism he was now criticising, was reflecting a shift in opinion in his own country and globally. For bankers that would mean a long period of tighter regulation, scrutiny and intervention, combined in some cases with special taxes. Governments would demand their pound of flesh, and they would carry on demanding it. More generally, suspicion of markets would go deeper. Politicians would no longer find it easy to drive through 'market-driven' reforms in public services and elsewhere. Capitalism had had to be bailed out and markets had proved themselves highly fallible, and that would not be easily forgotten.

9. Towards greater equality

As noted earlier, the end of the worst phase of the financial crisis resulted in the return of banking bonuses, in some cases at pre-crisis levels, but it also resulted in the introduction of a windfall tax on those bonuses in Britain, with other countries warning that they could follow suit and America introducing a levy on the banks. There had been so many spectacular corporate failures, inside and outside banking, that questions were raised about the vast rewards enjoyed by business and banking leaders. In banking, the assessment by Lord Turner, chairman of the Financial Services Authority, that some activity within financial services was 'socially useless' and in some cases actually damaging showed that anger over excessive pay and bonuses had intellectual weight behind it.[12] Higher taxes for the better-off would be one response. The 50 per cent tax rate introduced in Britain was one signal that governments, in introducing measures to bring down budget deficits, would seek to ensure that the burden fell most heavily on the higher paid. Such taxes would be much harder for the highly paid to argue against but there would be other responses, driven by governments, regulators and shareholders.

In Britain, the drive against excessive salaries went beyond banking. In December 2009 the government proposed salary freezes and cuts for senior civil servants and said that any public sector employee earning more than £150,000 would have to have their salary directly approved by the Treasury. It would be naive to think that by taking a slice off the pay of those at the very top inequality would suddenly be eradicated. It was, however, possible to see a break in a line of argument stretching back 20 or 30 years. This was that to get the best people it was necessary to pay internationally competitive salaries and, in the case of the public sector, to compete with pay in the private sector. Many of those comparators had been driven by banking and financial services. Those earning high salaries, wherever they were employed, would have to work harder to justify them. Greater income equality is not just about limiting the remuneration of the extremely well rewarded. It is, however, a start, and it could be expected to continue.

10. Tilting faster to the East

This is the second book I have concluded with the prediction that the global economy would tilt to the East. In *The Dragon and the Elephant*, published in 2007, that tilt was based on the rise of China and India, and their effect on neighbouring economies. The crisis of 2007–09, with its disproportionate and enduring impact on Western countries, has had the effect of accelerating the shift, perhaps by five to ten years. The rise of the East was not just evident in long-run trends stretching out over decades but also in the short-term statistics. Though financial markets around the globe remained closely linked during the crisis, and some of the worst stock market falls were in emerging economies, including China, there was a distinct decoupling in economic performance. China and India's ability to grow through the crisis was testimony to that. China's growth exceeded 8 per cent in 2009 and was on course for 9 per cent in 2010, with India growing by some 6 per cent, a far cry from the 4 or 5 per cent GDP falls typical of most advanced economies. In many respects the crisis saw China come of age. Jim O'Neill, chief economist at Goldman Sachs and inventor of the term 'BRIC' economies (Brazil, Russia, India and China), concluded that the crisis had accelerated their relative rise. 'We now conceive of China challenging the U.S. for number one slot by 2027 and the combined GDP of the four BRICs being potentially bigger than that of the G7 within the next 20 years,' he said.[13] 'This is around 10 years earlier than when we first looked at the issue. China has had a good crisis. In terms of China's role in the world the crisis has arguably been very helpful because it has forced China to realize that the next stage of their development cannot be led by export growth.'

Gerard Lyons, chief economist at Standard Chartered, the international bank, characterised the post-crisis world as a new world order, based on 'an Arc of Growth, from China and India and then on to Africa, as the centre of global manufacturing shifts to regions with large and growing labour forces. This longer-term influence is a positive one, although individual countries will be impacted differently'.[14] If that sounds like a depressing conclusion as far as Europe and America are concerned, it need not be. Part of the story of the tilt to the East is based on a process of economic catch-up for countries whose living standards remain well below Western levels. The challenge for Western governments, firms and individuals is to make sure their economies are tapped in to Asia and can take advantage of its rise. After the crisis, there is understandable relief that Western economies are still standing. Standing still, however, will not be enough.

Notes

Chapter 1

1. Richard B. Freeman (2004), 'Doubling the global work force: the challenge of integrating China, India, and the former Soviet bloc into the world economy'. Presentation, Institute for International Economics, 8 November, www.iie.com.
2. Francis Fukuyama (1993), *The End of History and the Last Man*, Penguin, London, p. 46.
3. Alan Greenspan (2008), *The Age of Turbulence*, Penguin, London, p. 12.
4. Greenspan, p. 13.
5. Greenspan, p. 507.
6. Charles Kindleberger (1987), 'The economic historians' view: comparing the collapses', *New York Times*, 1 November.
7. Alan Walters (1990), *Sterling in Danger*, Fontana, p. 108.
8. The World Economic Outlook database is available at www.imf.org.
9. Michael Mandel (1993), 'Jobs, jobs, jobs – it's a recovery without heart: hiring is going to stay agonisingly slow for some time', *Business Week*, 22 February.
10. David Smith (1999), *Will Europe Work?*, Social Market Foundation/Profile Books, London, p. xvi.
11. Will Hutton (1996), *The State We're In*, Vintage, London, p. 106.
12. David Smith (1997), 'Job insecurity versus labour market flexibility', Social Market Foundation, London, p. 37.
13. Quoted in Smith (1997), p. 11.
14. Robert E. Rubin (2003), *In an Uncertain World*, Thomson Texere, London, pp. 194–5.
15. Alan Greenspan (1996), 'The challenge of central banking in a free society', Speech to the American Enterprise Institute, 5 December.
16. Dean Foust (1997), 'Alan Greenspan's brave new world', *Business Week*, 14 July.
17. Joseph Stiglitz (2003), *The Roaring Nineties*, Penguin, London, p. 37.

18. *Sunday Times* (2009), '1989 – the year that changed our world', *Sunday Times Magazine*, London, 3 May.
19. BBC (2001), *Newsnight* interview with Tony Blair, http://news.bbc.co.uk/1/hi/events/newsnight/1372220.stm.

Chapter 2

1. Simon Kennedy (2009), 'Roubini sees global gloom after Davos vindication', Bloomberg, 30 January.
2. Quoted in David Smith (2008), *The Dragon and the Elephant*, Profile Books, London, p. 36.
3. Quoted in Smith (2008), p. 36.
4. Chris Patten (2005), *Not Quite the Diplomat*, Allen Lane, London, pp. 58–9.
5. Patten (2005), p. 58.
6. Peter G. Warr (1999), 'Capital mobility and the Thai crisis', Australian National University, http://econ.tu.ac.th/iccg/papers/peterwar.doc.
7. Quoted in Bhumika Muchhala (ed.) (2007), *Ten Years After: Revisiting the Asian Financial Crisis*, Woodrow Wilson International Center for Scholars, Washington, DC, p. 53.
8. Alan Friedman (1997), 'Soros calls Mahathir a menace to Malaysia', *New York Times*, 22 September.
9. Muchhala (ed.) (2007), pp. 5–6.
10. Paul Krugman (1994), 'The myth of Asia's miracle', *Foreign Affairs*, Washington, DC, November/December 1994.
11. International Monetary Fund (1997), *World Economic Outlook*, Washington, DC, http://www.imf.org/external/pubs/weomay/chapter1.pdf.
12. Muchhala (ed.) (2007), p. 109.
13. *The Economist* (2005), 'Asian squirrels', 17 September.
14. Alan Greenspan (2005), 'Federal Reserve Board's semi-annual Monetary Policy Report to the Congress', 17 February 2005.
15. Ben S. Bernanke (2005), 'The global saving glut and the US current account deficit', Sandridge Lecture, Virginia Association of Economics, Richmond, VA, Federal Reserve, Washington, DC, 10 March.

Chapter 3

1. Robert E. Rubin (2003), *In an Uncertain World*, Thomson Texere, London, pp. 284–5.
2. J. K. Galbraith (1954), *The Great Crash 1929*, Penguin, London, 1992 edn, p. 80.
3. Rubin (2003), pp. 286–7.
4. Roger Lowenstein (2008), 'Long-term capital: it's a short-term memory', *New York Times*, 7 September.

5. Alan Greenspan (2008), *The Age of Turbulence*, Penguin, London, p. 194.
6. Kevin Dowd (1999), 'Too big to fail? Long-Term Capital Management and the Federal Reserve', Cato Institute Briefing Paper, Washington, DC, 23 September.

Chapter 4

1. HM Treasury (2007a), *Chancellor of the Exchequer's Budget Statement*, 21 March, http://www.hm-treasury.gov.uk/bud_budget07_speech.htm.
2. William Keegan (2003), *The Prudence of Mr Gordon Brown*, John Wiley & Sons, Chichester, p. 133.
3. Keegan (2003), p. 133.
4. Keegan (2003), pp. 135–6.
5. Mervyn King (2007), 'The MPC ten years on', Speech delivered to the Society of Business Economists, Bank of England, 2 May.
6. King (2007).
7. James Ashton (2009), 'Eddie George: the governor unafraid to speak his mind', *Sunday Times*, 19 April.
8. Kate Barker (2004), Review of Housing Supply: 'Delivering stability: securing our future housing needs', March, www.hm-treasury.gov.uk.
9. Stephen Adams (2009), 'Maths couple millionaires quit buy-to-let market', *Daily Telegraph*, 3 September.
10. National Housing and Planning Advice Unit (2008), 'Buy-to-let mortgage lending and the impact on UK house prices', NHPAU Research Findings no. 1, http://www.communities.gov.uk/documents/507390/pdf/684941.pdf.
11. Maurice Saatchi (2009), 'The myth of inflation targeting', Centre for Policy Studies, May, www.cps.org.uk.
12. David Smith (2006), 'Bank's credibility gap over "true" measure of inflation', EconomicsUK, 3 September, http://www.economicsuk.com/blog/000369.html.
13. Spencer Dale (2009), 'Inflation targeting: learning the lessons from the financial crisis', Remarks made at the Society of Business Economists' Annual Conference, London. 23 June, www.bankofengland.co.uk.
14. Paul Tucker (2006), 'Macro, asset price and financial system uncertainties', Roy Bridge memorial lecture, 11 December, www.bankofengland.co.uk.
15. John Gieve (2009), 'Back to the drawing board – regulation and economic policy after the crisis', David Hume Institute, 18 June, www.davidhumeinstitute.com.
16. David Cameron (2009), 'Economic priorities of a Conservative government', 20 July, www.conservatives.com.
17. King's Fund (2009), 'How cold will it be? Prospects for NHS funding: 2011–17', July, http://www.kingsfund.org.uk/research/publications/how_cold_will_it_be.html.

18. Institute for Fiscal Studies (2009), 'The 2009 Budget', IFS, London, April, http://www.ifs.org.uk/budgets/budget2009/public_spending.pdf.

19. HMTreasury (2007b), Speech by the Chancellor of the Exchequer to Mansion House, 20 June, http://www.hm-treasury.gov.uk/speech_chex_200607.htm.

20. HMTreasury (2007b).

Chapter 5

1. Ben S. Bernanke (2005), 'The economic outlook', Testimony before the Joint Economic Committee, 20 October, http://georgewbush-whitehouse.archives.gov/cea/econ-outlook20051020.html.

2. Robert Shiller (2008), *The Subprime Solution*, Princeton University Press, Princeton, NJ, pp. 42–3.

3. John Cassidy (2002), 'The next crash', *New Yorker*, 11 November, collected in Michael Lewis (ed.), *Panic! The Story of Modern Financial Insanity*, Penguin, London, 2008, p. 283.

4. Cassidy (2002).

5. Robert Freedman (2005), 'Front lines: Economy', *Realtor* magazine, March, http://www.realtor.org/archives/economymar05.

6. *Time* (2009), '25 people to blame for the financial crisis', February, http://www.time.com/time/specials/packages/completelist/0,29569,1877351,00.html

7. Dominic Rushe (2008), 'Cleveland: ghost town created by America's loan scandal', *Sunday Times*, 24 February.

8. Thomas Sowell (2009), *The Housing Bust*, Perseus Books, London, p. 87.

9. Eamonn Butler (2009), 'The financial crisis: blame governments not bankers', in *Verdict on the Crash*, Institute of Economic Affairs, London, p. 53.

10. George W. Bush (2003), 'President Bush signs American Dream Downpayment Act of 2003', http://www.americandreamdownpaymentassistance.com/whsp12162003.cfm.

11. Harvard University (2008), 'The state of the nation's housing 2008', Joint Center for Housing Studies, Harvard University, pp. 3–4, http://www.jchs.harvard.edu/publications/markets/son2008/son2008.pdf.

12. *Wall Street Journal* (2008), 'Fed's Kroszner: don't blame CRA', 3 December, http://blogs.wsj.com/economics/2008/12/03/feds-kroszner-defends-community-reinvestment-act/.

13. Michael Lewis (2007), 'A Wall Street trader draws some subprime lessons', Bloomberg News, 5 September, collected in Michael Lewis (ed.), *Panic! The Story of Modern Financial Insanity*, Penguin, London, 2008, p. 350.

14. Richard H. Neiman (2007), 'Superintendent Neiman testifies on subprime lending practices', State of New York Banking Department, 29 May, http://www.banking.state.ny.us/sp070529.htm.

15. John Calverley (2009), *When Bubbles Burst: Surviving the Financial Fallout*, Nicholas Brealey, London, pp. 104–5.
16. Rushe (2008).

Chapter 6

1. George Soros (2008), 'Statement before the US House of Representatives Committee on Oversight and Government Reform', 13 November, http://oversight.house.gov.
2. Tobias Adrian and Hyun Song Shin (2009), 'The shadow banking system: implications for financial regulation', Federal Reserve Bank of New York Staff Report no. 382, July.
3. Philip Booth (ed.) (2009), *Verdict on the Crash: Causes and Policy Implications*, Institute of Economics Affairs, London, p. 29.
4. Gary Gorton (2009), 'Slapped in the face by the invisible hand: banking and the panic of 2007', Social Science Research Network, 9 May.
5. Financial Services Authority (2009), 'The Turner Review: a regulatory response to the global banking crisis', March, p. 70, www.fsa.gov.uk.
6. Bank of England (2009), *Financial Stability Report*, June 2009, p. 7, www.bankofengland.co.uk.
7. International Monetary Fund (2009), *Global Financial Stability Report*, April, p. 5, www.imf.org.
8. Philip Augar (2009), *Chasing Alpha: How Reckless Growth and Unchecked Ambition Ruined the City's Golden Decade*, Bodley Head, London, p. 14.
9. Mervyn King (2007), Speech at the Lord Mayor's Banquet for Bankers and Merchants of the City of London at the Mansion House, 20 June, www.bankofengland.co.uk.
10. Berkshire Hathaway Annual Report (2002), 'Chairman's letter', http://www.berkshirehathaway.com/2002ar/2002ar.pdf.
11. Thomas B. Edsall (2009), 'Alan Greenspan: the oracle or the master of disaster?', Huffington Post, 19 February, www.huffingtonpost.com.

Chapter 7

1. William Cohan (2009a), *House of Cards: How Wall Street's Gamblers Broke Capitalism: The Fall of Bear Stearns and the Collapse of the Global Market*, Allen Lane, London.
2. William Cohan (2009b), 'Inside the Bear Stearns boiler room', *Fortune*, 4 March, www.cnnmoney.com.
3. Cohan (2009b).

4. US Attorney's Office, Eastern District of New York (2008), 'Two senior managers of failed Bear Stearns hedge funds indicted on conspiracy and fraud charges', 19 June, http://www.usdoj.gov/usao/nye/pr/2008/2008jun19.html.

5. David Smith (2007), 'Market turbulence gives a sinking feeling', *Sunday Times*, 5 August, http://www.economicsuk.com/blog/000544.html.

6. Bloomberg (2007), 'ECB lends 94.8 billion euros as money rates surge', 9 August, www.bloomberg.com.

7. Larry Elliott (2008), 'Credit crisis – how it all began', *Guardian*, 5 August.

8. Conversation with the author, June 2008.

9. Ashley Seager (2007), 'Profile: Mervyn King', *Guardian*, 19 January.

10. Mervyn King (2007), Speech at the Northern Ireland Chamber of Commerce and Industry, Belfast, 9 October, www.bankofengland.co.uk

11. House of Commons Treasury Committee (2008), 'The run on the Rock', Fifth Report of Session 2007–08, vol. 1, p. 39, www.parliament.uk.

12. House of Commons Treasury Committee (2008), pp. 43–4.

13. House of Commons Treasury Committee (2008), p. 15.

14. Andrew Davidson (2005), 'The MT interview: Adam Applegarth', *Management Today*, 1 March.

15. House of Commons Treasury Committee (2008), pp. 14–15.

16. Catherine Boyle (2009), 'Secret war games identified Northern Rock's weakness', *The Times*, 30 March.

17. Ray Boulger (2007), 'City gets Northern Rock wrong', John Charcol weblog, 27 June, www.charcol.co.uk.

18. House of Commons Treasury Committee (2008), p. 34.

19. BBC (2007), 'Bank chief defends role in crisis', 20 September, http://news.bbc.co.uk/1/hi/business/7004001.stm,

20. Gillian Tett (2009), *Fool's Gold*, Little, Brown, London, p. 221.

21. House of Commons Treasury Committee (2008), p. 53.

22. House of Commons Treasury Committee (2008), p. 53.

23. David Smith (2009), 'Interview: Sir John Gieve discusses his time at the Bank', *Sunday Times*, 1 March.

24. *Hartlepool Mail* (2007), 'Northern Rock customers besiege branch', 17 September.

25. House of Commons Treasury Committee (2008), p. 67.

26. House of Commons Treasury Committee (2008), p. 67.

27. Walter Bagehot (1873), *Lombard Street: A Description of the Money Market*, Republished by Cosimo Books, 2006, pp. 18–19.

28. Richard Lambert (2007), Speech to the CBI North-East Annual Dinner, 26 September, www.cbi.org.uk.

29. International Monetary Fund (2007), *World Economic Outlook*, October, www.imf.org.
30. BBC (2008), 'Darling called "dead man walking"', BBC News, 18 February, http://news.bbc.co.uk/1/hi/uk_politics/7251183.stm.
31. BBC (2008).

Chapter 8

1. International Monetary Fund (2008), *World Economic Outlook: Housing and the Business Cycle*, April, http://www.imf.org/external/pubs/ft/weo/2008/01/.
2. Andrew Sentance (2008), 'The current downturn – a bust without a boom?', Chandos House, London, 9 December, www.bankofengland.co.uk.
3. Sentance (2008).
4. Michael Hume and Andrew Sentance (2009), 'The global credit boom: challenges for macroeconomics and policy', Bank of England External MPC Unit Discussion Paper no. 27, June, www.bankofengland.co.uk.
5. Alan Greenspan (2008), *The Age of Turbulence*, Penguin, p. 3.
6. White House (2001), 'At O'Hare, president says "get on board"', 27 September, http://georgewbush-whitehouse.archives.gov/news/releases/2001/09/20010927–1.html.
7. Andrew J. Bacevich (2008), 'He told us to go shopping. Now the bill is due', *Washington Post*, 5 October.
8. Gillian Tett (2009), *Fool's Gold*, Little, Brown, London, p. 116.
9. Frank Partnoy (2001), 'The paradox of credit ratings', University of San Diego Law and Economics Research Paper no. 20.
10. Committee on Oversight and Government Reform (2008), 'Opening statement of Rep. Henry A. Waxman, Chairman, Committee on Oversight and Government Reform, Credit rating agencies and the financial crisis', 22 October, http://oversight.house.gov/.
11. Alan D. Morrison (2009), 'Ratings agencies, regulation and financial market stability', in *Verdict on the Crash: Causes and Policy Implications*, ed. Philip Booth, Institute of Economic Affairs, London.
12. Committee on Oversight and Government Reform (2008), 'Confidential memo to Moody's board of directors, October 2007', published 22 October 2008, http://oversight.house.gov/documents/20081022111050.pdf.
13. John Lanchester (2008), 'There will be blood', *Guardian*, 22 March.
14. Michael J. Merced (2007), 'Bear Stearns loss presages more turmoil', *New York Times*, 20 December.
15. Kate Kelly (2007), 'Bear CEO's handling of crisis raises issues', *Wall Street Journal*, 1 November, http://online.wsj.com/public/article_print/SB119387369474078336.html.

16. Bryan Burrough (2008), 'Bringing down Bear Stearns', *Vanity Fair*, August.

Chapter 9

1. Decca Aitkenhead (2008), 'Storm warning', *Guardian*, 30 August.
2. HMTreasury (2009), 'Chancellor of the Exchequer's Budget Statement', 22 April, www.hm-treasury.gov.uk.
3. Ben S. Bernanke (2009), 'Current economic conditions and the federal budget', Testimony before the Senate Budget Committee, 3 March, www.federalreserve.gov.
4. Senate Banking Committee (2008), 'Examining the state of the domestic automobile industry: testimony of Mr G. Richard Wagoner, Jr.', 18 November, http://senate.banking.gov.
5. Senate Banking Committee (2008), 'Examining the state of the domestic automobile industry: testimony of Mr Alan Mulally', 18 November, http://senate.banking.gov.
6. Senate Banking Committee (2008), 'Examining the state of the domestic automobile industry: testimony of Mr Robert Nardelli', 18 November, http://senate.banking.gov.
7. World Trade Organisation (2009), 'WTO sees 9 per cent global trade decline in 2009 as recession strikes', 23 March, www.wto.org.
8. Andrew Gowers (2008), 'Exposed: Dick Fuld: the man who brought the world to its knees', *Sunday Times*, 14 December.
9. Gillian Tett (2007), 'Is the storm over? Credit market conditions look changeable', *Financial Times*, 3 October.
10. Marketwatch (2008), 'Wall Street watches Lehman walk on thin ice', 17 March, www.marketwatch.com.
11. Ben White (2008), 'Man in the news: Dick Fuld', *Financial Times*, 12 June.
12. Susanne Craig (2008a), 'Lehman finds itself in centre of a storm', *Wall Street Journal*, 18 March.
13. Craig (2008a).
14. Conversation with the author, September 2009.
15. Jenny Anderson (2008), 'Trying to quell rumours of trouble, Lehman raises $4 billion', *International Herald Tribune*, 2 April.
16. Paritosh Bansal (2008), 'Lehman not in talks for sale – source', Reuters, 18 June.
17. Susanne Craig (2008b), 'Lehman struggles to shore up confidence', *Wall Street Journal*, 11 September.
18. US Department of the Treasury (2008), 'Statement by Secretary Henry M. Paulson, Jr. on Treasury and Federal Housing Finance Agency action to protect financial markets and taxpayers', 7 September, http://www.treas.gov/press/releases/hp1129.htm.

19. *Wall Street Journal* (2008), 'Paulson: "This is not Chrysler"', 15 July, www.wsj. com.
20. Anatole Kaletsky (2008), 'Hank Paulson has turned a drama into a crisis', *The Times*, 16 September.
21. Matthew Benjamin (2008), 'Senator Bunning says Paulson acts like socialist, should resign', Bloomberg, 9 September, www.bloomberg.com.
22. Nouriel Roubini (2008), 'Comrades Bush, Paulson and Bernanke welcome us to the USSRA (the United Socialist State Republic of America)', www.rgemonitor. com, 9 September.
23. *Fortune* (2009a), 'When Wall Street nearly collapsed', 28 September.
24. James B. Stewart (2009), 'Eight days that shook the world', *New Yorker*, 21 September.
25. Stewart (2009).
26. Katherine Griffiths (2009), 'Lehman, Barclays and the countdown to financial crisis', *The Times*, 12 September.
27. Larry Elliott and Jill Treanor (2009), 'Lehman's fall to earth: the last hours of a Wall Street giant', *Guardian*, 3 September.
28. Stewart (2009).
29. Stewart (2009).
30. US Department of the Treasury (2008), 'Paulson statement on SEC and Federal Reserve actions concerning Lehman Brothers', 14 September, http://www. treasury.gov/press/releases/hp1134.htm.
31. Securities and Exchange Commission (2008), 'Statement on Lehman Brothers', 14 September, www.reuters.com.
32. Stewart (2009).
33. *Fortune* (2009b), 'We were looking at the Abyss', 28 September.
34. Conversation with the author, July 2009.
35. Niall Ferguson (2009), 'Why a Lehman deal would not have saved us', *Financial Times*, 14 September.
36. Ferguson (2009).
37. Andrew G. Haldane (2009), 'Rethinking the financial network', Speech delivered at the Financial Student Association, Amsterdam, 28 April, www. bankofengland.co.uk.
38. *Fortune* (2009b).
39. Kabir Chibber (2009), 'Madoff's road to riches ends in court', BBC Online, 12 March, http://news.bbc.co.uk/1/hi/business/7939145.stm.

Chapter 10

1. Gerard Baker (2008), 'Anger, fear and deadlock. President Bush sums it up: "This sucker could go down"', *The Times*, 27 September.

2. Mervyn King (2008), Speech to the CBI, Institute of Directors, Leeds Chamber of Commerce and Yorkshire Forward at the Royal Armouries, Leeds, 21 October, www.bankofengland.co.uk.

3. Brady Dennis (2009), 'Bernanke blasts AIG for "irresponsible bets" that led to bailouts', *Washington Post*, 4 March.

4. Dennis (2009).

5. Dennis (2009).

6. US Department of the Treasury (2008), 'Treasury announces guaranty programme for money market funds', 19 September.

7. Jill Treanor (2008), 'Sir Victor Blank: the City grandee who could soon be leading a bank of Britain', *Guardian*, 26 September.

8. David Wessel (2009), 'Inside Dr Bernanke's ER', *Wall Street Journal*, 18 July.

9. Wessel (2009).

10. *Fortune* (2009), 'The Lehman crisis: one year later', 28 September.

11. *New York Times* (2008), 'Text of draft proposal for bailout plan', 20 September.

12. Bloomberg (2008), 'Ten days that changed Wall Street as Bernanke saw massive failures', 22 September, www.bloomberg.com.

13. *Daily Telegraph* (2008), 'Financial crisis: full statement by Iceland's Prime Minister Geir Haarde', 6 October, www.telegraph.co.uk.

14. BBC (2009), 'The love of money: back from the brink', 24 September.

15. Iain Dey (2009), 'The seven days that saved our banks', *Sunday Times*, 4 October.

16. BBC (2008), 'Rescue plan for UK banks unveiled', BBC News Online, 8 October, http://news.bbc.co.uk/1/hi/business/7658277.stm.

17. Dey (2009).

18. Heather Connon (2008), 'Accounts still to be settled', *Observer*, 19 October.

19. Paul Krugman (2008), 'Gordon does good', *New York Times*, 13 October.

20. Patrick Honohan (2009), 'What went wrong in Ireland?', Prepared for the World Bank, http://www.tcd.ie/Economics/.

21. BBC (2009).

22. BBC (2009).

23. Department of Finance (2009), 'National Asset Management Agency, second stage speech', 16 September, http://www.finance.gov.ie/.

Chapter 11

1. Robert Skidelsky (2009), *Keynes: The Return of the Master*, Allen Lane, London, pp. 18–19.

2. Justin Fox (2008), 'The comeback Keynes', *Time*, 23 October, www.time.com.

3. G20 (2009), 'Communique of the London Summit', 2 April, http://www.londonsummit.gov.uk/en/summit-aims/summit-communique.

4. Ben S. Bernanke (2009), 'The crisis and the policy response', Stamp Lecture, London School of Economics, 13 January, www.federalreserve.gov.
5. David Miles (2009), 'Money, banks and quantitative easing', 14th Annual Northern Ireland Economic Conference, Belfast, 30 September, www. bankofengland.co.uk.
6. Pittsburgh Summit 2009 (2009), 'Leaders' statement: the Pittsburgh Summit', 24/25 September, http://www.pittsburghsummit.gov.

Chapter 12

1. Luis Garicano (2008), 'I did not stammer when the Queen asked me about the meltdown', *Guardian*, 18 November.
2. British Academy (2009), 'The global financial crisis – why didn't anybody notice?', Letter to the Queen, 22 July.
3. William R. White (2006), 'Procyclicality in the financial system: do we need a new macrofinancial stabilisation framework?', BIS Working Paper no. 193, January, www.bis.org.
4. *The Economist* (2009), 'The other-worldly philosophers', 18 July.
5. Paul Krugman (2009), 'A Dark Age of macroeconomics (wonkish)', *New York Times* blogs, 27 January, http://krugman.blogs.nytimes.com/2009/01/27/a-dark-age-of-macroeconomics-wonkish/.
6. Willem Buiter (2009), 'The unfortunate uselessness of most "state of the art" academic monetary economics', www.ft.com/maverecon, 3 March.
7. Robert J. Barro (2009), 'Government spending is no free lunch', *Wall Street Journal*, 22 January, http://online.wsj.com/article/SB123258618204604599.html.
8. Peter Coy (2009), 'What good are economists anyway?', *Business Week*, 27 April.
9. Coy (2009).
10. Robert Skidelsky (2009), 'How to rebuild a shamed subject', *Financial Times*, 6 August.
11. *Newsweek* (2005), 'Economics: sexiest trade alive', 26 December.
12. Noam Scheiber (2007), 'Freaks and geeks: how *Freakonomics* is ruining the dismal science', *New Republic*, 2 April.
13. Charles Goodhart (2009), 'Inflation targeting 20 years on', Sixth Norges Bank Monetary Policy Conference, 11/12 June, www.norges-bank.no.
14. David Blanchflower (2009), 'The future of monetary policy', Open lecture, Cardiff University, 24 March, www.bankofengland.co.uk.
15. Josh Hendrickson (2009), 'Has macroeconomics failed?', The Everyday Economist, 19 July, http://everydayecon.wordpress.com/2009/07/19/has-macroeconomics-failed/.
16. *The Economist* (2009), 'Efficiency and beyond', 16 July.

17. Financial Services Authority (2009), 'The Turner Review: a regulatory response to the global banking crisis', March, pp. 39–40, www.fsa.gov.uk.

18. Robert Lucas (2009), 'In defence of the dismal science', *The Economist*, 8 August.

19. Charles Bean (2009), 'The Great Moderation, the Great Panic and the Great Contraction', Schumpeter Lecture, Annual Congress of the European Economic Association, Barcelona, 25 August, www.bankofengland.co.uk.

20. Conversation with the author.

21. Bean (2009).

Chapter 13

1. John Gray (2009), *False Dawn*, Granta, London, p. xiv.

2. *Daily Telegraph* (2009), 'Goldman Sachs' profits smash Wall Street estimates', 14 July, www.telegraph.co.uk.

3. Kate Barker (2005), 'Economic stability and the business climate', Speech to the Managing Directors' Club, Sheffield University, 24 November, www.bankofengland.co.uk.

4. Thomas F. Cooley (2008), 'How we got here', *Forbes* magazine, 12 November, www.forbes.com.

5. Mohamed El-Erian (2009), 'Secular outlook: the new normal', May, www.pimco.com.

6. Carmen M. Reinhart and Kenneth S. Rogoff (2009), *This Time It's Different: Eight Centuries of Financial Folly*, Princeton University Press, Princeton, NJ, p. 239.

7. John Gapper (2007), 'Wall Street's bruising musical chairs', *Financial Times*, 14 November.

8. John Kay (2009), 'Narrow banking: the reform of banking regulation', Centre for the Study of Financial Innovation, London.

9. Paul A. Volcker (2009), 'Statement before the Committee of Banking and Financial Services of the House of Representatives', 24 September.

10. House of Commons Treasury Committee (2009), 'Banking crisis: dealing with the failure of the UK banks', Seventh Report, Session 2008–9, Part 7, www.parliament.uk.

11. House of Commons Treasury Committee (2009).

12. Mervyn A. King (2009), Speech to Scottish business organisations, Edinburgh, 20 October, www.bankofengland.co.uk.

13. International Monetary Fund (2009), *World Economic Outlook*, April, p. 115, www.imf.org.

14. David Miles (2009), 'Money, banks and quantitative easing', Speech to the 14th Annual Northern Ireland Economic Conference, 30 September, www.bankofengland.co.uk.

15. Spencer Dale (2009), 'Inflation targeting: learning the lessons from the financial crisis', Society of Business Economists' Annual Conference, 23 June, www.bankofengland.co.uk.

16. BBC (2009a), 'Rating agency warning on UK debt', BBC Online, 21 May, http://news.bbc.co.uk/1/hi/business/8061019.stm.

17. Congressional Budget Office (2009), 'The budget and economic outlook: an update', August, http://www.cbo.gov/doc.cfm?index=10521.

18. International Monetary Fund (2009), 'A strategy for renormalizing fiscal and monetary policies in advanced countries', IMF Staff Position Paper, 22 September, www.imf.org.

19. New Zealand Treasury (2009), *Fiscal Strategy Report*, http://www.treasury.govt.nz/budget/2009/fsr/b09-fsr.pdf.

20. Institute for Fiscal Studies (2009), 'Budget 2009 briefing and analysis', April, http://www.ifs.org.uk/projects/304.

21. Charles Hampden-Turner and Fons Trompenaars (1993), *The Seven Cultures of Capitalism*, Piatkus, London, pp. 1–2.

22. Prospect (2009), 'A bad year in the City', *Prospect* magazine, London, September, p. 36.

23. Roger Bootle (2009), *The Trouble with Markets*, Nicholas Brealey, London, pp. 245–6.

24. International Monetary Fund (2009), 'IMF chief puts focus on building stable post-crisis world', IMF Survey Online, 2 October, www.imf.org.

25. BBC (2009b), 'Market crisis will happen again', BBC News Online, 8 September, http://news.bbc.co.uk/1/hi/8244600.stm.

26. Angela Partington (ed.) (1992), *The Oxford Dictionary of Quotations*, Oxford University Press, p. 307.

27. David Smith (2007), *The Dragon and the Elephant*, Profile Books, London, pp. 4–5.

28. Zhou Xiaochuan, Zhou (2009), 'Reform the international monetary system', Speech delivered 23 March, People's Bank of China, www.pbc.gov.cn.

29. Stephen S. Roach (2009), *The Next Asia*, Wiley, pp. 398–9.

30. Stephen King (2009), 'The tipping point', HSBC Global Economics Q4 2009, www.hsbc.com.

Chapter 14

1. OECD (2009), 'Governments must act decisively on jobs crisis, says OECD's Gurria', 16 September, www.oecd.org.

2. CIPD (2009) 'Treasury unemployment forecast points to years of slow jobs growth and continued pay squeeze', Chartered Institute of Personnel and Development, 11 December.

3. Alistair Darling (2009), 'The Callaghan Lecture', 8 September, www. hm-treasury.gov.uk.

4. Jeff Rubin (2009), *Why Your World Is About to Get a Whole Lot Smaller*, Virgin Books, London.

5. National Public Radio (2009), 'Economist: pricier oil means less globalization', 25 May, www.npr.org.

6. Edward Harrison (2009), 'Weak consumer spending will last for years', Roubini Global Economic Monitor, 17 August, www.rgemonitor.com.

7. Bill Gates (2009), '2009 annual letter from Bill Gates; the economic crisis', Bill and Melinda Gates Foundation, www.gatesfoundation.org.

8. G20 (2009), 'Leaders' statement: the Pittsburgh Summit, September 24–25 2009', www.pittsburghsummit.gov.

9. Gordon Brown (2009), Speech to Labour conference, 29 September, http://www. labour.org.uk/gordon-brown-speech-conference.

10. Barack Obama (2009), 'Remarks by the President on financial rescue and reform'. Federal Hall, New York, 14 September, www.whitehouse.gov.

11. George Eaton (2009), 'Can Sarkozy and Brown kiss and make up?', *New Statesman*, 10 December.

12. *Prospect* (2009), 'A bad year in the City', September 2009.

13. Reuters (2009), 'Crisis speeds BRIC rise to power: Goldman's O'Neill', 9 June, www.reuters.com.

14. Standard Chartered (2009), *2010 – The Year Ahead: A New World Order*, Standard Chartered, London.

Index